D0684119

December 1917: **The huge ship loomed before them.**

"Without a word of command, everyone took off his hat, looking reverently toward the Ark."

The entire rear end of the ship was in ice. But the investigating party was able to enter the upper room, a "very narrow one with a high ceiling." There was also "a very large room, separated as if by a great fence of huge trunks of trees," possibly "stables for the huge animals." On the walls of the rooms were cages, "arranged in lines all the way from the floor to the ceiling. . . . There were many various rooms, similar to these, apparently several hundreds of them. It was not possible exactly to count them, because the lower rooms and even part of the upper ones—all of this was filled with hard ice. . . ."

Was it Noah's Ark?

Later explorers would take up the search again!

Noah's Ark: Fable or Fact?

Violet M. Cummings

SPIRE BOOKS

Fleming H. Revell Company   Old Tappan, New Jersey

NOAH'S ARK:
FABLE OR FACT?

A SPIRE BOOK
Published by Pyramid Publications
for Fleming H. Revell Company,
by arrangement with Creation-Science Research Center

Spire edition published March, 1975

Copyright © 1973 by Creation-Science Research Center
All Rights Reserved

Printed in the United States of America

SPIRE BOOKS are published by Fleming H. Revell Company
Old Tappan, New Jersey 07675, U.S.A.

Dedication

This book is dedicated to the memory of Noah, whose faith and adherence to principle amid the prevailing licentiousness of his day make him one of the most outstanding historical figures of all time; and to the proposition that his great ship, the Ark, still exists in a remote fastness of the "mountains of Ararat" on the Eastern Turkish frontier.

Table of Contents

INTRODUCTION

Does Noah's Ark still exist? Can modern man still believe the ancient Biblical story of the Flood? Is there evidence to support the Scriptural claims? Can we accept as truth the ever-increasing rumors that Noah's great ship has been sighted, and even photographed and entered, during the past century of time? Is it possible that the widely publicized and frequently-displayed pieces of hand-tooled timber recovered by Fernand Navarra from a crevasse high on Mount Ararat in 1955, and again in 1969, were once actually a part of the Ark . . .?

These, and many other questions relating to this controversial subject, have stirred the imagination and excited the curiosity of many thoughtful persons today. To provide satisfactory answers to as many of these questions as possible is the purpose of this book. It is the result of 27 years of persistent, painstaking investigation into the subject, and contains authenticated accounts of the various reported modern sightings of the Ark since 1840.

Every effort has been made to be not only factual, but accurate, in reporting each story that has come to light as a result of the long years of research into a subject about which so little has been generally known.

While no effort has been made to coerce the reader into any particular mold or pattern of belief, nevertheless we believe the evidence will speak for itself. For it is the author's conviction that clarification of this subject will figure largely in the eternal destiny of many a bewildered soul in these turbulent and faith-shattering days.

As Lillian Eichler Watson expressed it many years ago: "There has never been a time when the tried and tested philosophies of the past were more desperately needed to give perspective and understanding—to give people something to cling to, something on which to build the strong, firm structure of their own lives."

If this statement was true almost two decades ago, how much more relevant it is today!

As far back as New Testament times the Apostle Peter recognized belief in the Flood as a deterrent to crime, and warned that ". . . God spared not the old world, but saved Noah . . . a preacher, of righteousness, bringing in the flood upon the world of the ungodly" (II Peter 2:5), and then assured his readers "that there shall come in the last days scoffers, walking after their own lusts and saying, 'where is the promise of his coming? for since the fathers fell asleep, all things continue as they were from the beginning of creation.' For this they willingly are ignorant of, that by the word of God the heavens were of old, and the earth standing out of the water and in the water, whereby *the world that then was, being overflowed with water, perished*" (II Peter 3: 3-6; see also I Peter 3: 20).

Likewise Paul, in his masterly dissertation on the great heroes of faith since the beginning of time, spoke of Noah, who "by faith . . . being warned of God of things not seen as yet . . . prepared an ark to the saving of his house" (Hebrews 11:7).

Time and space do not permit the reader more than brief glimpses into the long, long trail of research and adventure that had its initial inspiration many years ago in the heart of a small boy who sat, wide-eyed and enthralled, as he listened to his teacher reading the thrilling story of Noah and the Flood.

". . . and the ark rested in the seventh month, on the seventeenth day of the month, upon the mountains of Ararat."

The teacher finished the story and closed the book. But the usually restless little redheaded boy sat still, a faraway look in his eyes. Some day, he said to himself, some day I'd like to help find that boat . . .!

But it was not until early summer of 1945 that a still youthful appearing, but now almost middle-aged man, laid down the magazine in which he had been absorbed. A story about the discovery of Noah's Ark! "Hmmm . . ." he mused aloud to no one in particular, "I wonder if this story is true, and if Noah's Ark really does still exist? Wonder if I could run this article down . . .?"

10

Thus simply did Eryl Cummings begin the pursuit of the long-forgotten childhood dream.

Although the amateur researcher could not foresee it at the time, the trail upon which he had so blithely set his inexperienced feet was destined to lead into far and unfamiliar fields. "Running down" and authenticating the magazine article that had triggered the research soon became a full-time job, and for a time the signals read "full steam ahead," with smoldering bridges behind.

A tantalizing, will o'the wisp trail it would prove to be, whose length in miles has never been clocked, but whose length in years has spanned a quarter of a century of time; an exotic, hide-and-seek trail, on which the anticipation of imminent success has beckoned provocatively from around every bend in the road!

Circumstances that even the most casual observer must recognize, as the play and counterplay between Truth and Error have ofttimes beset the trail; frustrations have many times checked the eager pursuit of some particularly vital bit of evidence as the research has led head-on into a blank wall of apparent defeat.

As the quest for the truth about the existence of Noah's Ark led to ever-widening vistas and quickening pace, it sometimes almost frighteningly resembled a gigantic jigsaw puzzle spread out over the table of the world!

But, as piece after colorful piece of authenticated data fell slowly into place, the conviction deepened that one day, in God's good time, sufficient facts about this fascinating and controversial subject would be in hand that there could no longer be any doubt that the Deluge of Moses' account had been an actual historical event.

Inevitably, during the course of the investigation concerning the Ark, many other fascinating and related facts have come to light. These we have faithfully endeavored to share with our readers. For those whose memory of the story of Noah and the Flood has dimmed, or for those who may never have read the story for themselves, we have reproduced the most familiar King James version of this cataclysmic event.

And God said unto Noah, The end of all flesh is come before me; for the earth is filled with violence through them; and, behold, I will destroy them with the earth.

Make thee an ark of gopher wood; rooms shalt thou make in the ark, and shalt pitch it within and without with pitch.

And this is the fashion which thou shalt make of it: The length of the ark shall be three hundred cubits, the breadth of it fifty cubits, and the height of it thirty cubits.

A window shalt thou make to the ark, and in a cubit shalt thou finish it above; and the door of the ark shalt thou set in the side thereof; with lower, second, and third stories shalt thou make it.

And, behold, I, even I, do bring a flood of waters upon the earth to destroy all flesh, wherein is the breath of life, from under heaven; and every thing that is in the earth shall die.

But with thee will I establish my covenant; and thou shalt come into the ark, thou, and thy sons, and thy wife, and thy sons' wives with thee.

And of every living thing of all flesh, two of every sort shalt thou bring into the ark, to keep them alive with thee; they shall be male and female.

Of fowls after their kind, and of cattle after their kind, of every creeping thing of the earth after his kind, two of every sort shall come unto thee, to keep them alive.

And take thou unto thee of all food that is eaten, and thou shalt gather it to thee; and it shall be for food for thee, and for them.

Thus did Noah; according to all that God commanded him, so did he.

Join us now for a guided tour of this fabled land. Thrill to the sacred legends, the traditions and beliefs of the indigenous peoples whose forefathers handed down as an unchanging legacy their reverence for "Noah's mountain," and their belief in the existence of the Ark.

Step, for a moment, into Noah's shoes. Hammer in the final peg. Check the blueprint for a thankless task well done. Wearily ascend the gangplank under cloudless skies. Endure the weeks, the months of confinement after the drops begin to fall. Begin life anew in an empty, echoing world. Then, in a quiet, thoughtful mood, let us sit down together and evaluate the persistent stories of a great wooden vessel that can still sometimes be seen as a reminder of those bygone days. . . .

We promise you never a dull moment along the way. We invite you to share with us our own elation as each new facet of discovery comes to light, as each nebulous clue is "run down." We hope you will also share with us the heartaches and disappointments inevitable on a quest of this kind. And, most important of all, we hope that when you have finished your armchair journey to these "faraway places with the (sometimes) strange-sounding names," we will have provided you with sufficiently convincing evidence so that you, too, will share our own conviction that Noah's Ark does, indeed, still exist somewhere on Ararat, that beautiful, mysterious, rugged mountain on the remote Eastern Turkish frontier.

Eryl and Violet Cummings
Farmington, New Mexico

Modern sketch — map showing Greater and Lesser Ararats, in relation to Turkey, Russia, Iran and Iraq.

1

A Catastrophe,
a Challenge
and the Ark

For centuries Mount Ararat (or Aghri Dagh), that great "monarch of the Armenian plains," sat brooding alone in regal isolation while the story of Noah and the Deluge was gradually relegated by the world in general to the obscurity of a bygone age. With the advent of increased skepticism in the authenticity of the Old Testament as an accurate historical account, the tale of an Ark floating on the waters of a universal flood no longer seemed relevant to our times.

During this period there seems to have been no inkling, at least in the distant outside world, that this great fabled ship might still exist on a remote mountain in an ancient land, even though men like Bryce and Lynch, and others with a religious turn of mind, openly avowed their conviction that it had once landed there thousands of years ago.

Until, on the 20th of June, 1840, occurred a catastrophic event destined to begin a new era in relation to the controversy over the Biblical account of Noah, a Deluge, and the Ark. Strangely, it is only since this event that reported modern discoveries of a great ship on Aghri Dagh begin.

On this momentous day, with no warning, the already disfigured northeastern face of the mountain was rocked and torn asunder by a tremendous earthquake and avalanche that uncovered and forever exposed its granitic heart.

According to Major Robert Stuart, who mentions this event in his private Journal in 1856, the eruption seemed to issue from "a large natural chasm" already in existence on that side. This chasm was actually a terrible gorge, said to be nearly 9000 feet deep and surrounded by "monstrous precipices" so rough and rugged that they caused the beholder to shudder at the sight. Tournefort, the adventuresome French botanist, trembled in 1701 "as he overlooked the precipices" and saw that "one of the loftiest mountains in the world (had) opened its bosom to a vertical cleft . . . from the heights above, masses of rocks were continually falling into the abyss with a noise that inspired fear."

Sir Robert Kerr Porter (1831) stated that the two heads of Ararat "are separated by a wide cleft, or glen, in the body of the mountain. The rocky side of the greater head runs almost perpendicularly down to the northeast, and shows to the northwest a broken and abrupt front, opening about half-way down, into a stupendous chasm, deep, rocky, and peculiarly black." It was the noted German geologist, Hermann Abich, who stated that "the chasm itself . . . dates from an epoch beyond the range of history."

Interestingly, echoes of Abich's statement can be found in a Greek version of the story of the "great flood." Sir James G. Fraser recounts it for us in his book, *Folklore in the Old Testament,* published in 1923. According to the Greeks, Deucalion was the hero of the Deluge, which was commemorated by the Greek worshippers of the Syrian goddess Astarte, at Hieropolis on the Euphrates river, not many miles from Aghri Dagh.

It is also interesting to note that of all the various (and varying) Flood legends from around the world, the ones originating closest to the vicinity of Mount Ararat adhere the most closely to the Biblical account. The following story, quoted by Fraser from Lucien, is a remarkable illustration of this point:

"The present race of men . . . are not the first of human kind; there was another race which perished wholly. We are of the second breed, which multiplied after the time of Deucalion. As for the folk before the flood, it is said that they were exceedingly wicked and lawless; for they neither kept their oaths, nor gave hospitality to strangers, nor respected suppliants, wherefore the great calamity befell them. So the fountains of the deep were opened, and the rain descended in torrents, the rivers swelled, and the sea

16

spread far over the land, till there was nothing but water, water everywhere, and all men perished. But Deucalion was the only man who, by reason of his prudence and piety, survived and formed the link between the first and the second race of men; and the way in which he was saved was this. He had a great ark, and into it he entered with his wives and children; and as he was entering there came to him pigs, horses, and lions, and serpents, and all other land animals, all of them in pairs. He received them all, and they did him no harm; nay, by God's help there was a great friendship between them, and they all sailed in one ark so long as the flood prevailed upon the earth. Such, says Lucien, is the Greek story of Deucalion's deluge; but the people of Hieropolis, he goes on, tell a marvellous thing. They say that a great chasm opened in their country, and all the water of the flood ran away down it. And when that happened, Deucalion built altars and founded a holy temple of Hera (the Greek name for Astarte) beside the chasm."

The site of another Greek story is laid at the temple of the Olympian Zeus, at a spot where the guides, as late as "the second century of our era," in "memory of the tremendous cataclysm," still pointed out a "cleft" in the ground where, they assured the curious traveller, "the waters of the deluge ran away."

Whether or not this remarkable story has any connection with Mount Ararat and the statement in Genesis 8:3 that "the waters *returned* from off the earth continually" (it will be recalled that in Moses' account "were all the fountains of the great deep broken up" at the outset of the Deluge, Genesis 7:11), we are not prepared to say. However, it is certain that a great chasm had defaced the northern face of the mountain long before 1840, but for how many centuries we cannot be sure.

Nestled against the side of Ararat, at the mouth of this stupendous chasm and directly in the path of the impending doom, was the ancient Armenian village of Arghuri (Ahora) . . . a place which boasted a remote antiquity. James Bryce tells us that (according to Armenian tradition) it was at Arghuri that Noah built the altar and offered up the burnt sacrifice after the departure from the Ark and safe descent from the mountain with his family

17

and the creatures of every kind. It was at Arghuri, too, according to the same tradition, that the patriarch planted his vineyard and drank to excess of its wine. The inhabitants, he said, treasured an ancient willow, bent by age and the severe action of the elements during the long winter months, that had survived in an isolated spot above the village, "a rare object on a mountain which is almost devoid of trees." It was part of their traditions that the tree had sprung from a plank of the Ark that had taken root, and to them it was a sacred object to be protected from harm, and they would not even permit one of its branches to be broken off.

This settlement owed its existence and prosperity to a stream which issued from the jaws of the chasm, and which was fed by melting ice and snow. The village was situated at the open exit from the gorge, where the trough flattens out into the base.

The church, and most of the village, were on the right side of the stream; on the left, opposite the church, stood a square-shaped fortress built of clay. On a near eminence had been built a spacious palace for the Russian sirdar (a chief or lord) of Erivan. The village boasted considerable vineyards and woods of apricot trees.

The church, which was reputed to have been built on the site of Noah's altar, dated from the 8th or 9th century. Not far beyond was the entrance to the chasm. After two miles of toiling up its rocky hollow the traveller reached the little monastery of St. Jacob, which stood on the edge of a natural terrace several hundred feet above the bottom of the gorge, and facing the right bank of the stream.

The chasm at this point was between 600 to 800 feet deep, and, according to Parrot, the monastery was situated at about 6,394 feet. It was here that he had established his headquarters in 1829. The monastery consisted of a chapel, a walled enclosure, a garden, an orchard, and a small residence for the monk. About 200 feet above the monastery, on the same side and on the edge of the precipice, had been built a tiny shrine of hewn stone. Here, too, was located one of the "rare springs" of Ararat.

As one progressed into the gulf, the sides became increasingly steeper and the abyss deeper and more profound until, about two and a half miles from the cloister, one came face to face with an almost perpendicular wall of rock which towered up to "the snowy cornice of the dome."

Then sudden disaster struck this unsuspecting scene. H. F. B. Lynch describes it for us in his book *Armenia*, published in London in 1902. "On the evening of the 20th of June, 1840, a terrific earthquake shook the mountain, and not only the shrine and the cloister, but the entire village of Akhury (Arghuri or Ahora) were destroyed and swept away. An eye-witness, who was pasturing cattle on the grassy slopes above the chasm on the side opposite to the shrine and the well, tells us that he was thrown onto his knees by a sudden reeling of the ground, and that, even in this position, he was unable to maintain himself, but was overturned by the continuing shocks. Close by his side the earth cracked; a terrific rolling sound filled his ears; when he dared look up, he could see nothing but a mighty cloud of dust, which glimmered with a reddish hue above the ravine. But the quaking and cracking were renewed: he lay outstretched upon the ground, and thus awaited death. At length the sounds became fainter, and he was able to look towards the ravine. Through the dusk he perceived a dark mass in the hollow, but of what it was composed he could not see. The sun went down; the great cloud passed away from the valley; as he descended with his cattle in the failing light, he could see nothing within the abyss except the dark mass.

"Another spectator has left us an account of the various phases of the phenomenon, as they were experienced from a standpoint below the village. He happened to be working in a garden a few versts (a Russian measure equal to slightly more than 3500 feet: hence, about a mile and a half to two miles below the village) from Arkury, on the side of the plain. His wife and daughter were with him; two of his sons appeared towards evening and brought him a report about his cattle. Two riders, returning to the village, exchanged a few words with the party and rode on. The sun was beginning to sink behind the mountains, and he and his people were preparing to go home. In an instant the ground beneath their feet oscillated violently, and all were thrown down. At the same time loud reports and a rolling sound, as of thunder, increased the panic into which they fell. A

19

hurricane of wind swept towards them from the direction of the chasm and overturned every object that was not firm. In the same direction there arose an immense cloud of dust, overtopped towards the upper part of the ravine, by a darker cloud, as of black smoke. After a momentary pause the same phenomena were repeated; only this time a dark mass swept towards them from the direction of the village with a rolling and a rushing sound. It reached the two riders; they were engulfed and disappeared. Immediately afterward the two sons were overtaken by the same fate. The mass rolled on towards the gardens, and broke down the walled enclosures. Large stones came tumbling about the unfortunate peasants; and a large crag swept down upon the prostate witness, and settling by his side, caught his mantle fast. Extricating himself with difficulty, he succeeded in lifting his unconscious wife and daughter from the earth, and in flying with them over the quaking ground. After each shock they could hear the sound of cracking in the chasm, accompanied by sharp reports. They were joined by fugitives, escaping from the neighboring gardens, and they endeavored to make their way to Aralykh. It was morning before they reached their goal; during the night the sounds and shocks continued, always fainter but at periodic intervals. This catastrophe was followed on the 24th day of June by a second and scarcely less momentous collapse. On this occasion a mass of mud and water burst from the chasm, as though some collossal dam had given way. Blocks of rock and huge pieces of ice were precipitated over the base, and the flood extended for a space of about thirteen miles. Not a trace was left of the gardens and fields which it devastated, and the Kara Su was temporarily dammed by the viscous stream."

"One stands in wonder," observes Lynch, as he chronicles this tragic event, "at the force which could have rent that massive pedestal and opened the yawning chasm which confronts the plain."

When Abich visited the site of this great cataclysm four years later (1844) he discovered that the huge piles of boulders, still strewn over the basal slopes, had originated at the upper end of the chasm that overhung the abyss. Amazingly, he was able to locate approximately the position from which the largest of the crags was catapulted into the chasm from the left wall just beneath the ice-cap of the summit, a crag which measured at the base 285 feet in circumference, and 45 feet high. To Lynch and his party, who visited the mountain in 1893, "the position of these crags was a source of amazement."

"As a result of this earthquake," explains Lynch, "the ridge enclosing the uppermost end of the chasm was found to have acquired about double its former extent. The height of the precipice had also increased considerably, especially on the eastern side. The summit remained intact, but the fabric of Ararat lay henceforth exposed to its innermost core. . . ."

Bryce speaks of the "terrific blast of wind" accompanying the earthquake that destroyed the village, the monastery, and also a "Kurdish encampment on the pastures above . . ." and also mentions the "profound chasm" on the northeastern side of the mountain which runs "right into its heart." According to Parrot, the effects of the 1840 earthquake and the avalanche that followed were felt as far away as the Caspian Sea, Persia, and Erivan.

When it was all over, and the earth had ceased to rock, not a trace of the Old Arghuri could be found. Later examination revealed that the walls of the houses had fallen in and the flat roofs collapsed as if some tremendous weight had struck them from above. Gone, too, were the ancient monastery and the tiny cloister of hewn stone, which, according to Col. Alexander A. Koor (Archaeological Sites and Data on Mt. Ararat and the Surrounding Region), contained many ancient relics "of the epoch of Noah, together with ancient manuscripts and books."

But what of the Ark, during the tremendous upheaval of that dreadful day? Had this gigantic reminder of Noah and the Flood also been destroyed in the diabolical explosion that had buried the priceless manuscripts and books . . . ?

The answer is an emphatic No, for it is only since that calamitous event that reports of an ancient ship embedded in an icy grave high on the tortured sides of Mount Ararat have filtered through from time to time to the outside world.

Which once more irresistibly reminds us of the lovely old Armenian tradition that Mount Ararat is guarded by angels who watch over the Ark, which is preserved, so they devoutly believe, in perfect repair in one of the highest recesses, secluded from mortal eyes, and that some day, in the end of Time, it will be revealed again to prove that the Bible and its story of the Flood are true.

Aptly, in this connection it might be mentioned that a modern scientific writer has observed (Sullivan, *Assault of the Unknown;* McGraw-Hill, 1961) that "even great cataclysms are filed away in ice for future reference." Since for more than three quarters of a century before the 1840 catastrophe there had been a marked retreat of glaciers all over the world; and since the great structure so remarkably resembling the Biblical description of the Ark has been sighted in a slowly melting glacier, who can deny that the old Armenian tradition might be true?

Perhaps, though no scientific proof has yet been established, the agonizing paroxysms of the mountain on that day might also have loosed some natural barrier that for centuries had hidden the great ship from view.

This, in turn, may have made it possible for the incontrovertible evidence of the greatest "cataclysm" of all time to be revealed as the gigantic "deep freeze," the glacier where it had been "filed away," gradually melted back.

Perhaps, too, this tragic occurrence may also have been the signal in the great schedule of Divine events, that the "time" of the Armenian tradition had come; that at last the stage was set; that the centuries-old veil of obscurity regarding the Ark was about to be drawn back before the wondering eyes of the whole world; and that Ararat, in all its "amplitude of grandeur," would at last come into its rightful focus as the true "mountain of the Ark."

Such, we believe, was the Divine warning and merciful intent!

So far as is known, the 1840 tragedy on remote Mt. Ararat had not been widely publicized in the Western world at the time it had occurred, since there were few survivors who could have given an eye-witness account. Tidings of tragedies of still greater magnitude in areas more familiar to the average man sometimes failed to reach the outside world for many months in those days of slow and often uncertain communication. It was no doubt only in such carefully-researched but fascinating works as Lynch's *Travels in Armenia,* published more than sixty years later that eye witness accounts finally appeared. Also, since no reports of the discoveries of the ark had yet appeared, even scholars with the leisure to read such ponderous works would have attached no particular significance to the sad but comparatively minor occurrence that wiped out a tiny Armenian village and a cloister with its precious ancient records in the remote Ahora Gorge on equally remote Ararat. It is only in the light of modern research that these facts assume a significance of value to the world today.

Not long after the 1840 disaster (1859) Charles Darwin had published his revolutionary theories on the long-range development of plant life, animals, and man. This, of course, was diametrically opposed to the time honored Scriptural teaching that the world and all it contained had been created and completed by an omnipotent, omniscient God, in the period of one short creation week—a Creator who had not only spoken, and "it was done," and Who had "commanded, and it stood fast" (Psalms 33:9)—but a God who had also brought a great Deluge upon an ungrateful, unrepentant world when the stench of its pollution had filled the very courts of Heaven with loathing and disgust! (Genesis 6: 5-7).

Darwin's *Origin of Species* is said to "have worked nothing less than a revolution in biological science." As with many new and untried theories not yet subject to the acid test of time, Darwin's new ideas quickly gained acceptance among the younger generation of his day. The older, more conservative groups, which included such intellectuals as Viscount James Bryce, still maintained their unflinching loyalty to the historicity and authenticity of the Biblical account.

From the vantage point of history, it appears strikingly obvious that the rise of this new doctrine just prior to the subsequent reports of a great wooden vessel high on the slopes of Mt. Ararat marked a significant turning point in the age old conflict between Truth and Error that had been increasing in tempo since the day in Eden when the serpent sneeringly challenged Eve, "Yea, hath *God* said . . . ?" (Genesis 3:1).

Also, during this period of time, another significant movement had burgeoned into prominence in many parts of the world with the revival of the long neglected and almost forgotten Scriptural teaching of eschatology—the study of last day events. Eschatology was not a new doctrine of the modern church, since it had flourished in Apostolic times. But with the passing of centuries of unfulfilled hope, its bright luster had gradually dimmed, until at last it had almost disappeared from the thinking of the common man.

Here and there, however, in widely-separated areas of the world, interest in the promised return of Christ (John 14:1-3, Acts 1:9-11) never entirely died out, and occupied an important place in the thinking of serious minded Biblical scholars who recorded their opinions and the results of their research in books reflecting remarkably similar reactions to the coming of Christ and the end of the world.

As early as the 15th century, Bengel and Luther, in Germany, were promulgating this long neglected doctrine to the people of their day. Martin Luther believed that the end of the world would take place within 300 years. In England, Sir Isaac Newton had turned his brilliant scientific mind to a study of the Scriptures and produced a book on *Last Day Events* based on his studies of Daniel, the Old Testament Hebrew prophet and statesman; and of John, the Apostle and author of the book of Revelation, the Apocalypse of the New Testament. This was published several years after his death in London in 1727, under the title *Prophecies of Daniel and the Apocalypse of St. John.* Both of these books, of course, deal extensively with prophecies outlining "last day events."

Cotton Mather, a prominent New England clergyman in colonial days; LaCunza, a Spanish Jesuit priest in South America writing under the pen name of Rabbi Ben Ezra, also produced a book on the same subject translated and published in London in 1825.

During this same century the greatest resurgence of interest in the Scriptures, and especially the study of last day events, occupied the minds and affected the personal lives of countless individuals in many parts of the world. This was not confined to any one denomination or group. Participating in this rapidly growing resurgence could be found prominent clergymen of many otherwise divergent faiths, as well as dedicated laymen and Bible students from many walks of life. This unprecedented interest of the com-

24

mon man in the study of the Scriptures can no doubt be traced to the foundation of Bible Societies, the most notable of that time being the British Bible Society (1802), which, about this time, quickly spread over Europe and to the New World, with their widespread dissemination of the Scriptures in a language common man could read and understand. During this same period of time, Joseph Wolff, widely travelled Jew and converted missionary of the Christian faith, went forth from England to proclaim this same message in many of both civilized and pagan lands.

Was this revival of interest in spiritual things also preparing the minds of men for a significant series of announcements, soon to break upon the world at ever accelerating intervals, that have reached even to the present day the reports that a great structure remarkably resembling the descriptions of Noah's Ark as recorded in Genesis 6 had been discovered on Mt. Ararat . . . ?

Against this background and in this atmosphere of religious awakening, and yet with no recognized significance at the time, Charles Darwin began his work. The challenge is startlingly apparent, for by acceptance of the Darwinian theories, faith in the Bible as an actual and historically accurate account of the early history of this world is automatically cancelled out, and the Creator of heaven and earth is relegated to the endless roster of the gods that have been worshipped by untold millions of misguided devotees almost since time began. The foundations of centuries of both patriarchal and Christian faith would be irreparably weakened, and eventually crumble to be swept away in a relentless tide of skepticism and lawlessness that would finally engulf the world.

Multitudes in Darwin's day would soon find themselves in the "valley of decision." Did this challenge to the modern world have any significance in relation to an ancient Armenian tradition that was one of the strongest and most sacred tenets of their Christian faith: that in the "end of time" the Ark would once again be revealed to prove that one of the most controversial and fantastic stories of the Bible—the story of the Deluge and the handful of individuals who had survived because of their unswerving confidence in God's Word—was indeed true?

And, as the controversy raged, a great ship lay quietly

25

awaiting its rediscovery in the security of a glacier where it had long ago been "filed away for future reference," in one of the "highest recesses" of a distant mountain peak . . . !

The first discovery of this era, that might conceivably have ended the burgeoning controversy between Creationism and Evolution once and for all, sad to relate, was made by a group of atheistic scientists who stubbornly refused to acknowledge the evidence of their own eyes. Still sadder to relate, the delayed acknowledgment did not come until some 60 years later, after the insidious poison of the new theories had permeated the minds of multitudes in the Western world. But this astounding story deserves a chapter of its own.

Since 1840, at least a "baker's dozen" of reports of discoveries of an Ark-like structure or of hand-tooled timber on treeless Mount Ararat have been made. These include:

1. The atheists' discovery around 1856.
2. James Bryce's handtooled timber: 1876.
3. The Turkish Commissioners report: 1883.
4. Prince Nouri: 1887.
5. The Russian aviator and the Czar's expeditions: 1915-1916.
6. The Turkish soldiers: 1915.
7. Carveth Wells' hand-tooled timber: 1932.
8. Hardwicke Knight: hand-tooled timbers: around 1936.
9. Aerial sightings during World War II.
10. Reshit, the Kurdish farmer: 1948.
11. Fernand Navarra: hand-tooled timbers: 1955, 1969.
12. George Greene's photos from helicopter: 1953.
13. An eye-witness account of an old Armenian who saw the Ark in 1905.

Since these stories were not discovered in sequence of the dates just given, and since this book is also a history of the research that made it possible, they will be related in the order in which they came to light. We believe that both common sense and reason will dictate the conclusion that the 1840 eruption did, indeed, usher in the modern era in relation to the Ark; and that its ringing challenge to the modern world is strikingly akin to that of Elijah to apostate Israel of old:

How long halt ye between two opinions? If the

Lord be God, follow him; but if Baal, then follow him" (I Kings 18:20).

This ancient challenge also has a modern counterpart: the angel of the Apocalyptic writer who is pictured as flying "in the midst of heaven" with a message for "every nation, kindred, and tongue, and people . . ."

"Fear God, and give glory to him . . . and worship him that made heaven, and earth, and the sea, and the fountains of water" (Revelation 14:6, 7).

And to the archaeologist and the student of sacred history yet another challenge arises: that of the still-buried treasures of the "epoch of Noah's day," believed by Col. Koor to lie deep under the mud and debris that swept down the great chasm to destroy the monastery and cloister and village on that fateful 20th of June so many years ago.

2

A Long,
Long, Trail
Starts Winding

Of course, none of the fascinating information that has formed the vitally important background for this book was even dreamed of by Eryl Cummings and those associated with the budding research away back in 1945. At that time their immediate and most pressing objective was in running down the exciting magazine article that had also intrigued the imaginations of those who shared his interest in the quest.

No one, even in his wildest imagination, could have foreseen at this early date the scope and length of the long, long trail in search of facts that had just begun. But it was amazing how many kindred spirits fell into step along the way. It was nothing less than astonishing, too—the way the leads piled up once the search was under way. One bit of information led to another, and for the first few months the task of running them all down became a full-time job.

Friends and associates came and went as the trail led on. Some have faithfully remained. Others, unfortunately, did not live to see the accumulation of evidence that now augurs well for the successful culmination of the search for the Ark. But all contributed generously, each in his particular field, weaving into the tapestried background of the years the warmth and friendship of their own personal interest in the quest.

There was that distinguished Dean of American Archaeologists, Dr. J. O. Kinnaman, lecturer and writer, the aging champion of Bible science, who urged the importance of scientific investigation in the Mount Ararat area, hitherto largely untouched; there was the already gray-haired Naval Academy model shipbuilder, Fred Avery, who longed with all his heart to see and build a replica of the first boat ever to sail the seven seas; there was a brilliant, award-winning Christian artist in Hollywood, whose lively imagination pictured an animated reproduction of the Flood. There were geologists, college presidents, a well known radio evangelist whose eyes sparkled at the thought that he might some day be able to announce the discovery of Noah's Ark to the world!

There was also Carveth Wells, noted world traveller, and at that time a popular radio commentator over KFI in Los Angeles. Wells had authored the book *Kapoot*, the story of his own trip through Russia in 1932 in an abortive attempt to reach Mount Ararat, where he had hoped to discover and gaze upon Noah's old ship for himself.

It was this same gracious gentleman who suggested a visit with George Mardekian, the famed Armenian humanitarian and philanthropist, owner of the well-known chain of Omar Khayyam restaurants in California; who had sponsored so many of his own people to a new life in his adopted land. The Mardekians would be most interested in this project, said Mr. Wells.

Mr. Wells was right. It was not far from Los Angeles to San Francisco, where Mr. and Mrs. Mardekian did indeed give the researchers a cordial welcome. As they entered the foyer of the Mardekian's beautiful Bay City home, they were entranced by a magnificent painting of the Mountains of Ararat, done for them by the noted Armenian artist, Sardis Kachadorian, who was also a guest in their home that evening.

The Mardekians gave warm approval to the project, and suggested the names of several other prominent American Armenian Christians, whose spiritual roots were still deeply entwined in the faraway land of Mount Ararat, the home of their ancestors for so many thousands of years.

In Los Angeles an Armenian clergyman, the Rev. K. Bedrosian, pastor of the Armenian Gethsemane Congregation Church, added his blessing to the search for facts about the modern-day existence of Noah's Ark, in a cordial letter of introduction to his fellow-countrymen all over the world:

"I am deeply interested in the Noah's Ark expedition," he wrote, "which is full of possibilities and light to be shed upon the present mental chaos concerning the authenticity of the Deluge story. I do pray for the success of such an ambitious enterprise . . . may the Lord crown the daring program and anticipations of all concerned with His manifold blessings and victorious ending.

"I have lived under the shadow of the beautiful Mount Ararat," the Rev. Bedrosian concluded, "with its snow covered dome which challenges centuries. We have looked to it as the everlasting monument of the Christian faith for which my own race has sacrificed millions of precious lives."

(The "Noah's Ark expedition" to which the Rev. Bedrosian referred was the *Sacred History Research Expedition,* organized in November of 1945 for the purpose of further verifying the magazine article that had touched off the investigation earlier in the year. Eryl Cummings was the first president of this organization.)

The trail now veered suddenly eastward. There had been rumors of a somewhat mystical Oriental personage reputed to have claimed the discovery of the Ark in the latter part of the 19th century. It seemed important to verify these rumors, if possible, since certain highly placed and respected individuals denied that such a person had ever existed at all!

It was in Chicago that still another gracious and distinguished personage, the Nestorian, Rev. Sadook de Mar Shimun (B.A., B.D., of St. John's, the Old Apostolic Church of the East) also gave his full approval and warmest wishes for the success of the proposed expedition. The Rev. Mar Shimun also supplied the vital information so necessary to prove the identity of the Oriental discoverer in question—a fellow-Nestorian, the Chaldean Archbishop Nouri, of Babylon and Malabar. But, since we are getting ahead of our story, and because Prince Nouri also deserves a chapter of his own, we will return to the beginning of the trail and share the story that started Eryl Cummings on the long years of research on Noah's Ark.

Had it proven to be fiction—or fact . . . ?

This controversial and widely-circulated story of a Russian discovery of the Ark had appeared in *Life Digest*, an Australian publication, as a reprint from *Answers*, an English weekly. The original copy has long since disappeared. But it contained the account of a Russian aviator who claimed to have sighted the remains of a great ship on the sides of Mount Ararat as he was making a routine flight. For those readers not already familiar with this story, we reproduce it here as it appeared in a special edition of *New Eden*, in an article entitled "Noah's Ark Found." It had been written, ostensibly, by one Vladimir Roskovitsky, and goes as follows:

"It was in the days just before the Russian Revolution. Aviators were stationed at a lonely temporary air outpost about twenty-five miles northwest of Mount Ararat. The day was dry and terribly hot, as August days so often are in this semi-desert land. Even the lizards were flattened out under the shady sides of rocks or twigs, their mouths open and tongues lashing out as if each panting breath would be their last. Only occasionally would a tiny wisp of air rattle the parched vegetation and stir up a choking cloudlet of dust.

"Far up on the side of the mountain we could see a thunder shower, while still farther up we could see the white snowcap of Mount Ararat, which has snow all the year round because of its great height. How we longed for some of that snow!

"Then the miracle happened. The captain walked in and announced the plane #7 had its new supercharger installed and was ready for high altitude tests, and ordered my buddy and I to make the test. At last we could escape the heat!

"We wasted no time getting on our parachutes, strapping on our oxygen tanks, and doing all the half dozen things that have to be done before 'going up.' Then into the cockpits, safety belts fastened, a mechanic gives the prop a flip and yells 'Contact,' and in less time than it takes to tell it, we were in the air. No use wasting time warming up the engine when the sun already had it almost red hot. We circled the field several times until we hit the fourteen thousand foot mark and then stopped climbing for a few minutes to get used to the altitude.

"I looked over to the right at that beautiful snowcapped peak, now just a little above us, and for some reason I can't explain, turned and headed the plane straight toward it.

"My buddy turned around and looked at me with question marks in his eyes, but there was too much noise for him to ask questions. After all, twenty-five miles does not mean much at a hundred miles an hour.

"As I looked down at the great stone battlements surrounding the lower part of the mountain I remembered having heard that it had never been climbed since the year 700 B.C., when some pilgrims were supposed to have gone up there to scrape some tar off an old shipwreck to make good luck emblems to wear around their necks to prevent their crops being destroyed by excessive rainfall. The legend said they had left in haste after a bolt of lightning struck near them and they had never returned. Silly ancients, who ever heard of looking for a shipwreck on a mountaintop!

"A couple of circles around the snowcapped dome and then a long swift glide down the south side, and we suddenly came upon a perfect little gem of a lake, blue as an emerald, but still frozen on the shady side. Suddenly my companion whirled around and excitedly pointed down at the overflow end of the lake. I looked and nearly fainted!

"A submarine! No, it wasn't, for it had stubby masts, but the top was rounded over with only flat catwalks about five feet across down the length of it. What a strange craft, built as though the designer had expected the waves to roll over the top most of the time and had engineered it to wallow in the sea like a log, with those stubby masts carrying only enough sail to keep it facing the waves.

"We flew down as close as safety permitted, and took several circles around it. We were surprised, when we got close to it, at the immense size of the thing, for it was as long as a city block and would compare favorably in size to the modern battleships of today. It was grounded on the shore of the lake with about one-fourth of the rear end still running out into the water, and on one side near the front, and on the other side, there was a great door nearly twenty feet square, but with the door gone. This seemed quite out of proportion, as even today ships seldom have doors even half that large.

"After seeing all we could from the air, we broke all speed records back down to the airport. When we related our find, the laughter was loud and long. Some accused us of getting drunk on too much oxygen, and there were many other remarks too numerous to relate.

"The captain, however, was serious. He asked several questions and ended by saying, 'Take me up there, I want to look at it.' We made the trip without incident and returned to the airport. 'What do you make of it?' I asked as we climbed out of the plane. 'Astounding,' he replied. 'Do you know what ship I believe it is?' 'Of course not, sir.' 'Ever hear of Noah's Ark?' 'Yes, sir, but I don't understand what the legend of Noah's Ark has to do with our finding this strange thing 14,000 feet up on a mountaintop.

" 'This strange craft,' explained the captain, 'is Noah's Ark. It has been sitting up there for nearly 5000 years. Being frozen up for nine or ten months of the year, it couldn't rot, and has been in cold storage, as it were, all this time. You have made the most amazing discovery of the age.'

"When the captain sent his report to the Russian government, it aroused considerable interest, and the Czar sent two special companies of soldiers to climb the mountain. One group of fifty men attacked one side and the other group of 100 men attacked the mountain from the other side.

"Two weeks of hard work were required to chop out a trail along the cliffs of the lower part of the mountain, and it was nearly a month before the Ark was reached. Complete measurements were taken and plans drawn of it as well as many photographs taken, all of which were sent to the Czar of Russia.

"The Ark was found to contain hundreds of small rooms and some rooms very large with high ceilings. The large rooms usually had a fence of great timbers across them, some of which were two feet thick as though designed to hold beasts ten times as large as an elephant. Other rooms were lined with rows of cages somewhat like what one sees today at poultry shows, only instead of chicken wires, they had rows of tiny wrought-iron bars along the fronts.

"Everything was heavily painted with a wax-like paint resembling shellac, and the workmanship of the craft showed all the signs of a high type of civilization. The wood used throughout was oleander, which belongs to the cypress family and never rots, which, coupled with the facts of its being painted and frozen most of the time, accounted for its perfect preservation.

"The expedition found, on the peak of the mountain above the ship, the burned remains of the timbers which were missing out of one side of the ship. It seems that these timbers had been hauled up to the top of the peak and used to build a tiny one-room shrine, inside of which was a rough stone hearth like the altars the Hebrews used for sacrifices, and it had either been caught on fire from the altar, or had been struck with lightning, as the timbers were considerably burned over and charred, and the roof completely burned off.

"A few days after this expedition sent its report to the Czar, the government was overthrown and godless Bolshevism took over, so that the records were never made public and probably were destroyed in the zeal of the Bolsheviks to discredit all religion and belief in the truth of the Bible.

"We White Russians of the air fleet escaped through Armenia, and four of us came to America where we could be free to live according to the 'Good Book,' which we had seen for ourselves to be true, even to as fantastic sounding a thing as a world flood."

This was the story that motivated the beginning of the search.

However, in spite of its sincere and convincing tone, it was soon learned that the Roskovitsky story had been branded a "most exaggerated account" by Benjamin Franklin Allen, a retired Army officer and creation geologist, to whom the writer of the article admitted he had received only the "basic facts" (this story, incidentally, has perhaps been the most widely-publicized and distributed of any story ever printed about the discovery of the Ark. It has appeared in many magazines and papers both in North America and abroad, and has been preserved in countless scrapbooks across the land).

But the incensed geologist insisted that he had been both deluged and embarrassed by inquiries since its publication, and on October 17, 1945, the much-castigated editor who had been responsible offered a public apology and the acknowledgment that he had, indeed (unfortunately, but perhaps understandably!), written up the basic facts "in story form with the intent of making it more interesting to read."

As if the "basic facts" in themselves were not sufficiently exciting to warrant a full-fledged investigation into the actual truth of the reports without resorting to pure and unadulterated imagination!

According to Mr. Allen, these "basic facts" included "the few details originating from two soldiers in the Czarist Russian Army during the First World War, deceased many years ago. The story of these soldiers came to me from their relatives of how a Russian aviator had sighted a suspicious looking structure in one of Ararat's obscure canyons. Infantrymen were sent on foot to investigate and their officers and they decided it must be Noah's Ark, with one end sunk in a small swamp. *These were the only details they gave.* Being a geological worker, I had investigated and speculated on how the Ark could have been saved by glaciation till recent times in view of the sudden origin and subsequent history of glaciation. To (the editor) I gave some of these ideas, very briefly . . . I told him plainly that the story from the soldiers was by no means worthy of publication till it be corroborated from other sources. But, *without my knowledge and consent,* he concocted a masterpiece of fiction and invention and published it as though it was true in every detail. About 95% is pure fiction, but the meager details from the former soldiers *could* be true. . . ."

But what of the possible factual 5%? Could further verification be found?

To winnow the chaff from the wheat, fact from fiction, the literary "embroidery" from the solid material underneath, required considerable effort and time, but emerging facts proved worthy of all the time and effort required.

It is believed that the Roskovitsky story appeared as early as 1935. It is not known at what date Mr. Allen had received his information from the deceased soldier's family —possibly in verbal form—but on April 4, 1940, a Mr. James Frazier, of Malotte, Washington, verified the story in a letter to the Los Angeles geologist:

"Your letter, dated March 30, is at hand, in regard to the Ark of Noah. Yes, my father-in-law, John Schilleroff, told me at different times about the Ark of Noah, but he did not mention any landmarks, though he did mention the town he started from. I could not pronounce the same and have forgotten it. He was German and I do not speak German.

"Mr. John Georgeson, a Dane, formerly my neighbor here, now also deceased, told me the same story, he also having served in the Russian Army in the Ararat region. They had never met, though their accounts fully agree. They belonged to different expeditions and went at different times. They were both sober and reliable men, and therefore I believe their story. The following is the story as they both told it to me.

"While in the Russian Army, they were ordered to pack for a long tramp up into the Mountains of Ararat. A Russian aviator had sighted what looked to him like a huge wooden structure in a small lake. About two-thirds of the way up, probably a little farther, they stopped on a high cliff, and in a small valley below them was a dense swamp in which the object could be seen. It appeared as a huge ship or barge with one end under water, and only one corner could be clearly seen from where these men stood. Some went closer, and especially the Captain. They could not get out to it because of the water and the many poisonous snakes and insects. The captain told them of the details."

Another letter, from an A. H. Booth, reads as follows:

"John Schilleroff, a father-in-law of Mr. Jim Frazier, made a trip in company with 100 soldiers of the Russian Army and found the Ark of Noah. He heard him tell the story of his adventures there, but I cannot recall the details. Mr. Frazier, who wrote you, is my brother-in-law. John Georgesen, formerly a neighbor of Mr. Frazier, was in another military party at the same time. They said the Ark stands high in the mountains in a wooded valley swamp. They could see a part of the Ark, but the swamp was so infested with snakes and insects that they did not get to go out to it."

Through a Mr. F. L. Chitwood, of Klamath Falls, Oregon, came still further information and corroboration regarding the stories of the two men. In a letter to Eryl Cummings on July 27, 1945, he wrote:

"Dear Mr. Cummings: My attention was first called to

37

the Ararat region by an account of a traveller having ascended to the summit and his description of the wonderful view from there. That was about fifty years ago.

"A little later two Armenian packpeddlers and I stayed all night at the home of a Great Uncle and he asked them about where their home country was, and they replied 'At the foot of Mt. Ararat in Armenia.' Uncle Jim then said: 'Mt. Ararat. Why that is where the Ark rested, is it not?' 'Yes,' they replied. 'Tell me,' he further questioned, 'do you know if there are any remains of the Ark there or not?' They replied, 'We cannot say of a certainty, but we do know that high up on the mountains there are timbers of a wood that does not exist in that country today, that appear to have been used as a temporary shelter.'"

It appeared that Mr. Chitwood had received his personal information about John Schilleroff through an elderly lady, a Mrs. Ray, whose brother, Mr. Booth, had told him the following story:

"I have often talked with old man Schilleroff about his experiences in climbing the mountain, but at that time did not see the importance of getting all the information I could and making a record of it."

"I believe the Booths to be reliable . . . people," wrote Mr. Chitwood. "I have known them for nearly forty years." He mentioned, also, that "these men had to contend with poisonous snakes in making the ascent."

Twenty years later great efforts were made to relocate Mr. James Frazier in the hope that he might be able to recall still more detail to the story he had told to Mr. Allen so many years before. On August 8, 1965, Mr. Frazier reiterated the original facts in a letter to Eryl Cummings from Toppenish, Washington:

"Kind sir: In regards to the information you ask, I am afraid I can't give you all the details you ask for. It has been a long time since I have been told . . . However, both men did tell me, almost word for word, and neither man never did see each other. My neighbor was a Dane, and my father-in-law a German . . . I'll try to tell it the best I can remember.

"While in training with the army they were marching up the trail of Mt. Ararat, and on the way up, looking down the side of the mountain, in a heavy swamp one could see

38

the front end of the Ark, pointed toward shore, with part of the back end emerged, down in the swamp. They didn't say how far up the mountain they was, but did say the swamp was quite large and that the banks were quite steep, and brush was quite thick all along the banks. Mosquitoes was so thick that they was kept busy fighting them off their trail, as they said was quite steep and hard going. And of course they wasn't allowed to stop and gander down, but was told, there is Noah's Ark. I don't think that they said which side of the mountain they was on, or how far up it was, but I got the impression it must have been quite high up. . . ."

At the time this letter was written, Mr. Frazier was a man perhaps 75 years of age; still, his memories of the circumstance of the sighting of the Ark were as vivid as when he had written Mr. Allen in 1940.

Thus, through Mr. Frazier and Mr. Chitwood, two of the "basic facts" of the story had been established: that there had, indeed, been an aerial Russian discovery of the Ark, and that there had also been a 2-pronged ground expedition to verify this fact.

But there were other details of the Roskovitsky story too similar to the Biblical description of the Ark to be lightly discarded as false: the great door on one side, the rooms with cages inside, the design which appeared to make provision for wallowing in heavy seas. Were these descriptions to be classed as "pure fiction" too . . . ? Or had the writer of the article had access to other information he had not bothered to disclose to his geologist friend?

Here was a conundrum not easily solved by a tyro in the research field; however, an unexpected turn of events would soon shed much additional light and verification on this very controversial tale.

Meanwhile, another important lead had turned up—a lead that involved that mystical—and mythical—personage, the Chaldean Archbishop known as Prince Nouri of Malabar. Since it involved another claimed discovery of the Ark as far back as 1887, verification of his existence suddenly assumed major importance in relation to the meager but already exciting file of information thus far compiled.

3

Vindication
of a Prince

One of the most outstanding personalities ever to claim the discovery of the Ark was John Joseph, Prince of Nouri, Archbishop of Babylon, and head of the Christian Nestorian Church. His long shadow is easily the most colorful, the most controversial, and the most exotic ever to fall across the trail.

Born in Baghdad in 1864, the youthful but venturesome prince claimed to have climbed Ararat three times in search of the Ark and on April 25, 1887, to have succeeded in the attempt when he was only 22 years of age. His momentous discovery, it was said, had been announced at the World Parliament of Religions at the World's Fair in Chicago in 1893.

Nevertheless, by 1945 his name had already become a legend. Certain highly placed individuals in the religio-scientific world even claimed that the fabulous prince had never existed; that he was merely the figment of someone's overly active imagination. As for his discovery of the Ark —the scoffing was loud and long!

Descriptions of this controversial prince read like something out of an Arabian Night's Tale:

His Pontifical Eminence, the Most Venerable Prelate, Monseignior, the ZAMORRIN NOURI, John Joseph, Prince of Nouri, D.D., LL.D. (by Divine Providence), Chaldean Patriarchal Archdeacon of Babylon and Jerusalem, Grand Apostolic Ambassador of Malabar, India, and Persia. The Discoverer of Noah's Ark, and the GOLDEN MOUNTAINS OF THE MOON.

The article went on to state, in flowery Oriental phraseology, that John Joseph was the "Sacred Crown's Supreme Representative-General of the Holy Orthodox Patriarchal Imperiality," as well as "The First Universal Exploring Traveller" of a million miles. His biography followed:

"His Chaldean Excellency, the Venerable Monseignior, the ZAMORIN, Earl of the Great House of Nouri, was born at Baghdad, on the 7th, and baptized on the 14th of February, A.D. 1865. Graduated, at Mesopotamia, April 5, 1883, and solemnly ordained at Bajirmapolis, Jan. 8, 1884. Consecrated, GRAND-ARCHDEACON OF BABYLON, ON PENTECOST SUNDAY, May 24, 1885."

Could an individual with such fantastic offices and titles ever actually have existed? Or, as the critics insisted, had he really been merely the creation of someone's outsized imagination . . . ?

One of the first and most incontrovertible figures to rally to Nouri's defense was the well-known archaeologist, Dr. J. O. Kinnaman: "Regarding the famous Dr. Nouri, one of the greatest scholars and world-wide travellers the last quarter of the 1880's ever saw," he wrote on August 16, 1946, "allow me to state that at the World Parliament of Religions, World's Fair, Chicago, Ill., in 1893, I had the honor and pleasure of meeting Dr. Nouri personally, and conversing with him several times. There is no mistake that he actually lived, walked and talked upon the earth, for I am sure I was not talking with a ghost. Some maintain that no such man ever lived. Well, if he did not, then there are hundreds of thousands of liars in India. I spent three years in India at the beginning of the century, and heard them comment on his life and works."

It was soon discovered that no less a personage than the President of the World Parliament of Religions, Dr. John Henry Barrows, had himself personally invited Prince Nouri to attend this important assemblage.

In his most interesting and informative book, *World Pilgrimage*, Dr. Barrows also vindicated Nouri's existence and presence at the meet. "The other attendant at the Parliament, unexpectedly met in Cairo," he wrote, "is the traveller and Chaldean Archbishop, Prince Nouri, who has kindly acted as my interpreter in many interesting interviews. He is equally ready in English, French, Turkish, Arabic,

42

Persian and eight other languages. He has traveled almost everywhere, and I doubt if there is any man now living who has made the acquaintance, in their homes, of so large a number of distinguished people."

Dr. Barrows was accompanied from Cairo to India by the Nestorian prince, who continued as translator to his American friend. Dr. Barrows describes their last Sunday in India: "In the morning the Prince Nouri accompanied us in a drive to the hospital, English residency, and the Maharajah's palace. Tichur is a native state, and appears very well governed. It was a great relief to get away from the painted foreheads daubed with the marks of various deities, to this Christian community, where such sights are rare. At half-past nine we attended high mass in the cathedral, conducted by the bishop, who offered special prayer for America and for us. My name and that of my country were the only words I recognized in the entire service. The Gospels were read both in Malayalam and in the old Syriac version. We sat with Prince Nouri in chairs directly in the front of the altar. . . .

"Everything was done for our comfort in the Patriarch's residence . . . and in the evening he read a second address of welcome from himself and the bishops, which was Oriental in its warmth and coloring. . . . In the evening I had a call from a learned, fine-looking priest from Travencore, with whom I and the Bishop Prince Nouri carried on a fraternal triangular conversation. I spoke to Prince Nouri in English, he reported in Arabic to the bishop, who transmitted the message in Chaldean to the priest. Thus the ages and the continent were linked together. The shores of Lake Michigan, the sands of Arabia, and the banks of the Euphrates drew near to each other on the coasts of India; while hundreds of the Christians of Trichur looked up from the courtyard to the balcony where this strange conjunction occurred!"

On the afternoon of that same day Dr. Barrows had made a "long address to one thousand people in the courtyard, and later . . . lectured to two thousand Christians and non-Christians in and around Hindu College . . . Prince Nouri made an eloquent address, and our carriage was followed by many hundreds—one of the strangest sights that my eyes ever rested on. The next morning we regretfully bade goodbye to our generous hearted friends. The Prince accompanied us five miles on our way to the little village before referred to. With tears and Oriental embraces separation took place. The Prince returned in the patriarchal carriage to Trichur. We entered our Jutka, and were driven to Shoranur, saying to ourselves that we had passed through an experience strange and new."

On November 7, 1945, Dr. Barrows' daughter, Eleanor Barrows Greg, wrote the following letter, postmarked Scarsdale, New York:

"Dear Mr. Cummings: I am greatly interested in your research project and glad to write you a brief resume of the bits of information about Prince Nouri in my mother's diary. As I told you, my mother accompanied my father on his trip around the world in 1896-1897. He was sent out to deliver lectures on Comparative Religion on the Haskall Foundation in the University of Chicago. While he was in Cairo he met the Prince. On Sept. 25, 1896, my mother writes in her diary that my father had a long visit from Prince Nouri who told him about his discovery of Noah's Ark on Mt. Ararat, and of his approaching coronation as Patriarch of the Chaldean (Nestorian) Church.

"Prince Nouri accompanied my father on his visits the following week, and I imagine he was acting as interpreter, though I can find no statement to that effect. (Dr. Barrows mentioned something about this in his *Pilgrimage*.)

"Much later, Feb. 27, 1897, the name of the Prince appears in the diary. My parents were then in Trichur, India. Two days later, on March 1, my father and mother left Trichur, and mother wrote, '. . . five miles from Trichur, we left the carriage and the Prince . . . The Prince was the picture of woe when we departed. He shed tears several times over our going.'

"I had hoped to find the Prince mentioned in her diary in connection with the World's Parliament of Religions held in Chicago from Sept. 11 to Sept. 27, 1893, but those were busy days for my mother, and the pages of the diary are blank.

"While my father was on his trip around the world he wrote a number of letters to the 'Interior,' a religious magazine. This afternoon I spent several hours in the New York Public Library and looked up those letters hoping for more information. I found just one reference to the Prince. In the number published July 8, 1894, was the following, 'There in the old city of Trichur, among the Syrian Christians we spent two happy and interesting days as the guests of the young Prince and Patriarch Nouri.'

"Your visit brought to my mind many pleasant memories and I wish you success in your undertaking. . . ."

During the course of the investigation into the authenticity of Prince Nouri, the trail led across the paths of a number of former missionaries, or sons and daughters of missionaries, who had once served at the Presbyterian College located at Lake Urmia in Persia (now Iran). Other diaries, old letters, personal memories, soon played an important and thrilling part in unravelling the mystery of the man who, in comparatively modern times, had claimed the discovery of the Ark.

Vivid memories came flooding back as these individuals recalled their days in the faraway mission outpost so close to the Biblical landing place of the Ark. Perhaps this was one reason why the story of Nouri's discovery had impressed itself so unforgettably on their minds. At any rate, Dr. Clement Cochran, of Buffalo, New York, readily recalled an evening in his parent's home in Iran when Nouri "made a very interesting account of his climb to Mount Ararat, and of his seeing something which appeared to him like a petrified ship."

The late Mrs. F. G. (Mary) Schauffler (formerly the wife of the Rev. B. W. Labree), who in 1946 was living in New Haven, Conn., remembered being invited with her husband to the home of Dr. Joseph P. Cochran and Rev. F. G. Coan, in order to meet an "interesting traveller who was being entertained on the premises."

On November 8, 1945, Mrs. Platt wrote to Eryl Cummings with details of the experience. Although apparently not as enamoured of the visitor's magnetic personality as some of the others who heard him speak, the missionary wife nevertheless faithfully recorded her impressions of the evening:

"My dear Mr. Cummings: Pursuant to our conversation of November 6th, 1945, I am sending at your request the following statement—

"During my years as a missionary of the Presbyterian

Board at Urmia, Persia (now called Resiah, Iran) it was my privilege to be associated with the families of Dr. Joseph P. Cochran and Rev. F. G. Coan, D.D. After the death of Mrs. Cochran, the two families were united at the mission premises called 'The College' four miles outside the walled city of Urmia. The mission hospital was also located in these premises as well as the residences of some of the missionaries and native college teachers.

"By invitation of Dr. Cochran, my husband, Rev. B. W. Labree, and I were invited to spend the night at the Cochran-Coan home in order to meet an interesting traveller who was being entertained on the premises.

"I quote from my diary written at the time:—

'Arch-deacon Nouri was sent for. He is a Chaldean from Baghdad who is now on a mission from the Malabar Christians to Mar Shimun, and claims to have discovered Noah's Ark, also to have found gold in the Mountains of the Moon, and to know fourteen languages. He speaks English very well and is most entertaining. The greatest part of him is his super-natural conceit. He claims to have been put wrongfully into an insane asylum in California, but it is very easy to believe that he may have been insane. His description of his feelings at the time are very vivid.'

"This record was made on May 9th, 1896.

"The memory of this interview is very vivid. With his Oriental features and long, flowing hair, Arch-deacon Nouri reminded us much of some of the conventional pictures of Christ.

"Dr. Cochran, whose medical care had won him many friends among the Kurds and other wild mountain tribes in the mountains of Kurdistan, secured a guide for Nouri who escorted him on the long, hard journey to Kochanis, the home of Mar Shimun, Patriarch of the Nestorians.

"My daughter and I are very deeply interested in the plans you explained to us and your quest for the remains of Noah's Ark in the Mountains of Ararat. Having driven around three sides of those mountains six times, in my journeys to and from Persia, I shall always be especially interested in hearing of any results of that quest. The verification in these modern times of Bible records and incidents is of the deepest significance and importance."

If the former missionary to Persia could have met Mrs.

Elizabeth Verbryke, who had first-hand knowledge of Nouri's unfortunate insane asylum experience, her earlier erroneous impressions of both his sanity and conceit might have been considerably altered. However, apparently the two women had never met.

Mrs. Verbryke, daughter of one Presbyterian clergyman and widow of another, had been interviewed in her home in Berlin, Md., later in the summer of 1945. On August 11 she wrote Eryl Cummings as follows:

"Dear Sir: I am in receipt of your letter of August 8th and hasten to reply. Of course it is many years since I met Dr. Nouri, and like all young people did not realize that if I had asked more questions I would now know more about his travels, etc.

"I was in my twenties in the year 1894, when my father brought him to see us. However, I shall try to give you the facts as best I can after so many years.

"At the time of the Chicago Exhibition in 1893, Dr. Nouri was invited to the Parliament of Religions held in the summer of 1893 in Chicago under the leadership of Dr. J. H. Barrows, pastor of the 1st Presbyterian Church of that city. Dr. Nouri accepted and spoke at the congress of religions and delivered many lectures on Noah's Ark. . . . He then proceeded westward, reaching San Francisco, while there my father and mother met him and were impressed by his looks, manner and deep consecration.

"My father came east as a delegate to a meeting of the General Assembly held in Washington, D.C.

"While he was in the east, my mother received a letter from him (Dr. Nouri) written from the Napa Insane Asylum in California, asking if she could not get him liberated. It seems that while in San Francisco he fell into the hands of thieves who robbed him of all his beautiful jewels, robes, in fact, everything he had. To cover up their crime they cast him into the asylum. He was not insane, but it was almost enough to make him so, all alone in a foreign land. My mother went to Napa, Cal., Insane Asylum and said she would be responsible for him. So as he was destitute he lived in my father's home for weeks, maybe months, as it was the days before registered mail, Post Office Money Order, and telegraph facilities for quick communications, all mails having to go by slow steamers both ways.

"After he received funds he proceeded home and later received more titles and honors in India and the Far East. Dr. Barrows of Chicago, who was deeply interested in Dr. Nouri, later travelled to India and the Near East, made inquiries about Dr. Nouri, and wrote to my father that all the titles, honors, etc. conferred on Dr. Nouri were established facts, and that everything he claimed was absolutely true.

"Dr. Nouri had a very striking face. One could not see him without believing in him. He described his search for the Ark and was rewarded on his 8th Oriental Geographical Expedition. He tried several times to climb the greater Mount Ararat, but was unable to on account of shifting snow. . . .

"Dr. Nouri was born in Baghdad on Feb. 7, 1865, and the Ark was first seen by him on April 25, 1887.

"While east my father, who was Rev. I. Chalmers Easton, D.D., pastor of Calvary Pres. church of San Francisco, received a call to the eastern Pres. church of Washington, D.C., and they moved in the fall of 1893. Dr. Nouri as he was still impoverished came after New Year's and lived in their home in Washington.

"It was at this time that my father brought him over to call. My husband was then pastor of the Gurley Memorial Presbyterian Church of Washington, D.C. I believed every word he (Nouri) said. Many said he looked like the pictures of Jesus Christ. . . ."

Mrs. Verbryke also produced a clipping from a Washington, D.C. newspaper that she had preserved for forty years, in which Nouri was publicly vindicated at last. The article carried the following headlines:

"ARCHDEACON OF BABYLON
John Joseph Nouri's Claim to the
Title Correct. Was Years Ago in
Washington and Thought Insane. Now
Lives in Royal Palace."

The fabulous John Joseph, according to Mrs. Verbryke, died at an early age from pneumonia. It would have been helpful to more modern explorers if he had left a record of the route he had taken to discover the Ark. Perhaps, if he did mention it, his listeners were so fascinated by the discovery itself that they failed to realize the importance of noting the less romantic details of the ascent.

48

In his book, *Yesterdays in Persia and Kurdistan*, Dr. Frederick B. Coan gives a somewhat more detailed story of Nouri's visit to Urmia College: "One is apt to meet with some very interesting characters in the East, one of whom comes to mind, and is worth describing. About 35 years ago . . . one of our Assyrian friends told us of a very interesting guest who had dropped in on him, by the name of Archbishop Nouri. He had come from Malabar, in southern India, where there are today (1939) some 500,000 Nestorian Christians, a remnant of the work of the Nestorian missionaries, who in the very earliest centuries carried the gospel to India and far beyond. Archbishop Nouri said he had been sent by them to be consecrated as Bishop over them, by the Nestorian Patriarch Mar Shimun who, as Patriarch of all the Nestorians in Kurdistan and Persia, lived at Kochanis, Turkey, five days travel from Urmia.

"Now for the story of his wonderful discovery of the Ark. He said he had made three attempts to scale Mount Ararat before he succeeded. At last his toil was rewarded, and he stood overwhelmed and awed as he saw the old Ark there, wedged in between two rocks, and half filled with snow and ice. He got inside, where careful measurements coincided exactly with the account given in the sixth chapter of Genesis.

"We invited him to give a lecture on his marvellous discovery in the College chapel, and missionaries, teachers, and students filled the place, and were deeply interested. He sincerely believed he had seen the Ark, and almost convinced others he had.

"He had gone to Belgium and tried to organize a company to take it to Chicago, to the World's Fair, but they felt the risks of such a long journey were too great, in addition to the heavy costs of transporting it so far. He was much disappointed, for he knew it would be a great attraction, and that people from all over the world would go to see it. So there it lies!"

Perhaps this chapter would not be complete without including the opinion of one of Prince Nouri's own people: the Nestorian, Sadook de Mar Shimun, of the Old Apostolic Church of the East, in Chicago, whose deep interest in the subject of the Ark has been mentioned before. On November 19, 1945, he addressed a letter to Eryl Cummings, then President of the Sacred History Research Expedition:

"I was very glad that you came over to see me about some information you needed concerning the late Dr. Nouri.

"I have heard from my uncle deacon Shlimun de Mar Shimun or Shimunaya, presently residing in Baghdad, Iraq, that he had met Nouri in Kochanis, Turkey." He also stated that "Dr. Nouri was the greatest Assyro-Chaldean traveller of his time," and mentioned that his uncle had told him about Nouri's visit to Urmia, Persia, about that time.

"As far as I can recollect," said the Rev. Mar Shimun, "my uncle told me that Dr. Nouri was a very learned man, handsome in his physical appearance and had a good Christian personality . . . If you happen to pass through Baghdad on your expeditionary journey for discovery of the Ark on the mountain of Ararat, I would suggest that you visit the above mentioned deacon for further information about the Doctor of Divinity in question.

"My uncle is a highly educated man. He reads, writes and speaks Aramaic fluently. He is a graduate of the American Presbyterian College of Urmia, Persia, and he was a professor of Theology in that School. I shall thank you if you will kindly convey my regards to him and give my address so that he may locate and write me.

"Wishing you all success from above and hoping to see you returned with original fragments of the Ark for further propagation of the Word of God and for the approval thereof, I remain in prayers for your happy return."

Thus the existence of the controversial prince and his discovery was verified, his many religious offices confirmed. The true significance of Nouri's vindication and the story of his discovery of the Ark, however, does not lie in his brief visit to a handful of Christian missionaries in far-off Persia, as indispensable to the research as this later proved to be. Neither does it lie in his abortive attempt to transport the old ship across the Atlantic to exhibit to the Western world.

Rather, it lies in the fact that even though announcement of a previous discovery by a Turkish engineering party four years earlier (see Chapter 7) had been received by the British and American public with a mixture of levity and scorn, God had made another merciful appeal. This time He chose, not a Moslem source, but a strikingly impressive personage of the Christian faith to confirm what the Turkish commissioners had found; and to turn the minds of the indifferent modern world back, if possible, to another careless period in the history of mankind when a corrupt, decadent civilization in the days of Noah that no longer loved or acknowledged a Creator has perished in their sins.

For Nouri, like the Apostle Peter on the day of Pentecost so many centuries before, had the opportunity to address "an impressive assemblage of several thousand delegates" from all over the globe at the World Parliament of Religions, September 4, 1893. According to Mrs. Verbryke, Nouri also delivered many lectures on his discovery of Noah's Ark during the time of the Chicago Fair.

It seems astonishing that such a momentous discovery should have made so slight an impression on the minds of the religious leaders and listeners of that day; and that the warning should, at least apparently, have gone unheeded. However, even the most casual perusal of the goals proposed for this historic conference can hardly fail to impress the reader that the minds of the delegates were preoccupied with far different concerns.

According to *The Bibles and Beliefs of Mankind*, a two-volume work containing "the most noteworthy contributions" of the delegates to the solution of the pressing problems of the age, these goals included promotion of "the spirit of human brotherhood among religious men of diverse faiths"; "theism and faith in man's immortality"; and "permanent international peace . . . through bringing the nations of the earth into a more friendly fellowship." It "sought new light on the great problems of the present age, especially temperance, labor, education, wealth, and poverty." In other words, emphasis was placed on a mere social gospel as the solution for the ills of the world.

Even though the delegates had assembled at the bidding of a great Christian nation, and were hosted by the leading Christian clergymen of that time, there seemed "no indication of concern for the doctrinal Christianity which insists on the supernatural character and absolute divine authority of the Bible, on the supreme divinity of Christ, and on a salvation strictly special through faith directed to Christ according to doctrines drawn from the Bible."

Indeed, one eminent but liberal-minded clergyman of the Higher Criticism school so far departed from the historic Christian position that he actually read a paper before all the representatives of all the great systems of religious beliefs around the world, in which he publicly apologized for the Christian view that the Bible is the Word of God; even casting aspersions upon its historicity and trustworthiness as truth! Recognition of Christianity with its world-embracing doctrine of belief in Christ as the only Saviour of mankind, was "conspicuous by its absence." Christ Himself, in large degree, was relegated to the level of the mere human founders of all other religions in the world; and the Bible to a mere piece of literature in the same category with the various other "scriptures" of mankind.

Since it was the influence of these broadly liberal elements which apparently shaped the policies of this great international and "surprising assemblage of wisdom and piety," it is not surprising that Nouri's story created so little stir. Reading and interpreting the Scriptures as they did, "to one end only, that of the spirit of love," this liberal viewpoint had dared to wield the headsman's axe on such portions of Old Testament history that represented, in their particular view, "the vindictiveness of God"; His "jealousy of other gods"; His "cruel disregard of human suffering and life."

Into this atmosphere in which the Creator was made to appear as the indulgent Father of all mankind—in which the Almighty God of the universe had been stripped of all his divine attributes except love—surely Nouri's vindication of the Deluge, wherein an entire civilization had been judged and destroyed for its sins, must have come as a jarring, and no doubt unwelcome note. In a gathering dedicated "to the advance of spiritual enlightenment, to the promotion of peace and good will among the nations and races, to the deepening and widening of universal human brotherhood"—in short a dedication to the Utopian belief that "every day in every way," this old world, through their united and persistent efforts, would get "better and better"; until, in the golden age they so hopefully anticipated, the nations would learn war no more. In this optimistic climate, what need could there possibly be to resurrect a Deity who punishes nations and individuals for their crimes . . . ?

So, Nouri's story went unheeded, and apparently unmentioned in the official reports; which, by candid admission, had deliberately left out "some of the best things in the Parliament," because of pressures from special interest groups; and allowed other outstanding and excellent papers to suffer "prejudiced mutilation." In the face of such frank statements, we may safely assume that Nouri's account of his discovery of the Ark may have suffered a similar fate. Perhaps the majority of his listeners were already so comfortably immersed in the skepticism of the times, that they merely shrugged off the unpleasant reminder that there had once been a historical character named Noah; that he had built an Ark, at the bidding of God "to the saving of his house," and thus escaped the retributive Flood.

It is difficult to comprehend the fact that evidences of the present-day existence of the Ark should have stirred so little response. However, earlier evidences for a Universal Deluge as traced through ancient mythology had also met scant attention and had soon sunk into oblivion. Such scholarly works as Jacob Bryant's "Analysis of Antient (sic) Mythology" (published in London, 1807), while termed "fantastic" by this historian, were at the same time tossed onto the scrap heap as "completely valueless."

Bryant had delved deep into Gentile antiquity to prove the authenticity of the Mosaic account; with the avowed purpose "to divest tradition of fable" by comparison of the mythological systems of the world with the Biblical story. He had succeeded to a remarkable degree in proving "the certainty of an universal Deluge from the evidences of most nations." His purpose in attempting such a colossal and important task is stated in his preface to the Third Volume:

"As the desolation of the world by a deluge, and the renewal of it in one person, are points in these days particularly controverted; many, who are enemies to Revelation, upon seeing these truths ascertained, will be led to a more intimate acquaintance with the Scriptures: and such an insight cannot but be productive of good. For our faith depends upon historical experience, and it is mere ignorance that makes infidels. Hence it is possible, that some may be won over by historical evidence, whom a refined theological argument cannot reach." Surely a much too laudable aim to receive such a chilling reception!

Faber, another able historian and scholar of that generation, had written on a similar theme, and had met with an even less warm response, since his name is not even mentioned in the encyclopedias of our day. In fact, so little interest was shown that so far as is known, only five hundred copies of his three-volume work were published for distribution in Great Britian and America.

Nevertheless, *Faber's Origin of Pagan Idolatry* (published in London in 1816), had also produced convincing historical evidence that the Ararat in Armenia was the resting place of the Ark, through tracing the migration of the nations from that greatly reverenced peak. He had also proved that "a very large part of heathen mythology originated from this history of the deluge: and numerous were the rites of Paganism, which were instituted in commemoration of that awful event." He also states that "pagan accounts of the creation generally contain some strong allusions to the deluge"; also, that "many of the more ancient nations have preserved almost literal accounts of an universal deluge, which corresponds in a very wonderful manner with the history of it as detailed by Moses."

How vastly different might have been the results had the message of these three outstanding men—Bryant, Faber, and Nouri—been recognized and accepted as God's message for these skeptical times! That they were not recognized or heeded, is evident from the chaotic spiritual situation in the world today. For, according to Philip Mauro in *The Creationist* (reprinted by permission in the Bible-Science Newsletter, April 15, 1970), it is the religionists, "not the investigators of nature, the men of the laboratory, but the occupants of the pulpits and the professorial chairs" who are "pushing" and spreading the evolutionary theory of the origin of the world, not as a "matter of science, but of religion . . . the most zealous defenders and propagandists of evolution are the 'liberal Christians' or 'Modernists,' and they make no attempt to disguise the fact."

Thus the echo of the earlier skepticism, unfortunately, can still be heard, even among eminent scholars and churchmen of today. And if it were not for that handful of dedicated men and women in a far-off land, uncontaminated by the blight of the "higher criticism" already rampant in the Western world, and to whom the story of Prince Nouri and his "marvellous discovery" rang true, the facts of this chapter might still lie moldering and forgotten in some dusty, inaccessible archive in the Chaldean Archbishop's native land.

It is to one of these same former missionaries, Mrs. Platt, who ever alert to the glory of God and the vindication of His Word, that we owe a still deeper debt of gratitude; for it was she who opened the door to a sudden, unexpected, and thrilling turn of events in the research so recently begun.

4

The Bolsheviks
and the Ark

It was November, 1945. Mrs. Mary Schauffler Platt, retired missionary from Persia, sat in the living room of her
home in New Haven, Connecticut, casually scanning the
pages of the White Russian publication, *Rosseya,* dated October 6, 1945. Suddenly the title of an article caught her
eye. Could it be possible—another story about Noah's
Ark?

Only a few days ago she had dug deep into her store-
house of memories to recall the story of Prince Nouri who
had come to the Presbyterian College in Urmia to tell of
his wonderful discovery of the Ark. Now what could this
story mean . . . ?

In a glow of excitement, Mrs. Platt reached for paper
and pen. This Russian article might be of paramount importance to Mr. Cummings, the gentleman who had visited
her such a short time ago. She must get in touch with him
at once!

But the trail seemed to have reached a dead end a few
days later when Eryl Cummings, Mrs. Platt's letter in
hand, stood eagerly before the receptionist in the New
York offices of *Rosseya* with his request for a copy of the
coveted issue. Both the editor and his secretary at first
looked askance at the strange caller from California who
seemed so interested in a Russian publication—and a story
about the discovery of Noah's Ark, at that! Why should he
so ardently desire to know the whereabouts of the individual who had written the article? Perhaps there was more to

57

this than met the naked eye . . . ! (And of course there was!)

At last, however, after ten tantalizing days of alternating hope and despair, the name and address of an ex-Russian general, now living in Seattle, were grudgingly divulged. But—no magazine. And, definitely, no further help. The prying American must work out his own problems from there.

Elated and triumphant over even this meager bit of good fortune, the eager researcher hurried at once to the New York Public Library, where the magazine section soon yielded most promising returns. The 4000-word article was found, photostated, and translated into English. And (even at 1¢ a word, according to a notation in the diary) the story it told was well worth the persistent waiting and the price. For it appeared to tie in, excitingly and convincingly, not only with the controversial Roskovitsky discovery, but also with the stories of the two soldiers who had claimed participation in the two pronged expedition of the Czar! Thanks Mrs. Platt, this was, indeed, a most important lead. No time must be lost in running it down.

In addition to coinciding with the main points of the aviator's story, much additional detail was added concerning the more scientific phases of the ground expedition to the Ark. The author of the article hailed its discovery as "one of the most remarkable spiritual events of the century."

Following a lengthy and most interesting discussion of the history and traditions surrounding Mount Ararat and the Flood, the author launched into a detailed account of the appearance of the ship and the reactions of those who saw it.

Here, too, was reiterated the aviator's first impression that the huge structure resembled a submarine from the air, with rounded decks, so as to allow the waves to roll freely over them. Remains of a superstructure in the center, near the nose of the ship, were described, similar to an emergency covering over the hatchway leading to the interior of the ship. The vessel, according to the story, leaned on one side toward the shore of the little lake in which it was partly submerged; and on this side, near the nose of the ship, was an unsymmetrical opening, or hole, perhaps broken by accident or necessity. On the other side was a great doorway with the door itself missing.

It seems it had taken some time for the report of the aviator's discovery to reach the ears of the Czar, who ordered an immediate and scientific ground expedition to ascertain the facts. It was not until the end of December, 1927, according to the article, that the two research divisions of 150 infantrymen, army engineers, and specialists reached the site after a month of the most difficult and arduous work. But at last the hardy, winter-insured Russians did reach the lake and the Ark. They had traversed a "wild and inaccessible locality," braving severe snowstorms and falling ice. It had been necessary to clear a trail and cut steps to the site; they had endured the incredible hardships of sleeping in the snow, hunger, and freezing, as well as shortages of food supplies which were sometimes delayed.

But the rigors of the difficult campaign were all forgotten, said the story, when they finally reached the object of their search. As the huge ship at last loomed before them, an awed silence descended, and "without a word of command everyone took off his hat, looking reverently toward the Ark; everybody knew, feeling it in his heart and soul," that they were in the actual presence of the Ark. Many "crossed themselves and whispered a prayer," said an eyewitness account. It was like being in a church, and the hands of the archaeologist trembled as he snapped the shutter of the camera and took a picture of the old boat as if she were "on parade."

The investigating party found that the ship was, indeed, of a "huge size". Measurements disclosed that it was about 500 feet in length, with a width of about 83 feet in the widest place, and about 50 feet high. These measurements, of course, when compared with a 20-inch cubit, fitted "quite proportionately" with the size of Noah's Ark as described in Genesis 6:15.

The entire rear end of the ship was in ice. But, through the broken hatchway near the front of the boat, the investigating party were able to enter first the upper room, a "very narrow one with a high ceiling." From here, "side by side to it, stretched rooms of various size: small and large ones."

There was also "a very large room, separated as if by a

59

great fence of huge trunks of trees," possibly "stables for the huge animals," such as elephants, hippopotami, and others. On the walls of the rooms were cages, "arranged in lines all the way from the floor to the ceiling, and they had marks of rust from the iron rods which were there before. There were very many various rooms, similar to these, apparently several hundreds of them. It was not possible exactly to count them, because the lower rooms and even a part of the upper ones—all of this was filled with hard ice. In the middle of the ship there was a corridor." The end of this corridor was "overloaded with broken partitions."

"The Ark was covered from inside as well as from outside," the story went on, "with some kind of a dark brown color" resembling "wax and varnish." The wood of which the Ark was built was excellently preserved except 1) at the hole in the front of the ship, and 2) at the door-hole at the side of the ship; there was the wood porous and it broke easily.

The analysis of the wood showed it to be similar to the cedar and the larch tree, which are related to the family of the cypress trees "which cannot decay."

"During the examination of the surroundings around the lake . . . there were found on one of the mountaintops the remains of some burnt wood 'and a structure put together of stones,' resembling an altar. The pieces of wood found around this structure were of the same kind of wood as the Ark." Was this the "altar of Noah," asked the author of the article, or was it built later by some other people . . . ? This question no one can answer.

As in the Roskovitsky story which had first come to hand, this very similar but far more detailed account stated that the description and measurements of the Ark, both inside and out, together with photos, plans, samples of wood, were sent at once by special courier to the office of the chief commandant of the Army—"as the Emperor had ordered."

"But not so had . . . Fate destined," concluded the story. For alas, while the investigating party had been laboriously carving their way through the ice and rock and snow to the Ark and doing their important work, other forces had been at work. By the time the courier, laden with all his precious and documented scientific evidence of the existence of the

Ark, was ready to set out for his distant destination, the Bolshevik revolution had already taken place. Rumor had it, according to the article, that the courier was intercepted and shot, and that the vital information so important to the verification of God's Word fell eventually into the hands of Trotsky himself.

History only gives us tantalizing glimpses of the fate of the other members of the 150-man expedition. Two of the foot soldiers, Schilleroff and Georgesen, apparently escaped unharmed to the northwestern United States. The archaeologist, too, lived to tell the story to his brother, an officer in the White Russian Army. Of the others no record is known. Were all of the results of the investigation entrusted to the ill-fated courier, or did some far-seeing member of the party make duplicates of the important documents they had prepared? Were some of the refugees who succeeded in escaping the turbulent situation in their native land able to deliver copies of the original documents to the proper hands in the course of time . . .?

For there have been persistent rumors that certain documents from this discovery eventually made their way to Geneva, to be deposited for safe deeping in the University Library there.

There is also the conundrum of two faded old photos remarkably resembling the descriptions of the Russian discovery—one showing a barge-like ship, the other an altar built of stone. But we seem to be getting ahead of our story again . . . !

An added touch of pathos from this tragic chapter in the history of the land of the Czars, is reputed to have come from the household of Emperor Nicholas. It concerns the excitement in the royal household when the news of the aviator's discovery reached the palace. The event was freely discussed—about the way the object appeared from the air, about the small lake on the mountainside where it sat, about how the Czar's interest had led him to order the Army to send an immediate expeditionary ground force to the site to investigate what had been found. There was much anticipation in the palace while they awaited the results. However, before the messenger with the pictures and the details could arrive, the threatened revolution had broken loose. Some of the members of the household escaped, but the Czar himself did not live to see the results of the investigation he had ordered.

Strangely, the individual who disclosed this revealing sidelight had never heard of Schilleroff or Georgesen, or even of Col. Alexander A. Koor, whom, Cummings found out later, was the author of the *Rosseya* story. Yet the story agrees uncannily with those of the other sources previously known, even though it did not come to light until twenty-five years later.

With the translation of the *Rosseya* story back in 1945, the trail of research suddenly widened into still more exciting scope. The name of the Russian author so reluctantly imparted by the New York editor bore a Seattle, Washington, address. Would this unknown individual be interested, and willing to help in further pursuit of the quest? Did he have other, as yet undisclosed information that would further authenticate the stories already in the file . . . ?

It was at this point that the fascinating, steadily unwinding trail soared suddenly aloft.

5

The "Karada Inscription" and the Flood

As the silver plane streaked westward across the mountains and plains of the United States, at least one impatient passenger was alternately torn between anxiety and hope. What would Eryl Cummings find in Seattle, that beautiful city a continent away from the Eastern seaboard where he had just made so many astonishing discoveries about Mount Ararat and the Ark? Would he meet with another suspicious reception, as in the *Rosseya* office in New York? Or would the Russian general whose name he so carefully guarded in his breast pocket be friendly, and receptive to the unusual mission that had brought him so far? Was he on the brink of momentous new evidence for the quest . . . ?

But the 80-year-old 4-star Russian general, Alexander Jacob Elshin, proved to be a warmhearted, receptive gentleman. He was also a much-decorated and gallant veteran of two great wars, and considered a "great humanitarian and scholar." He held honorary memberships in both the American International Academy in Washington, D.C., and the Andras Research University in Andras, India. He himself was not the author of the *Rosseya* article in question, he finally revealed after apparently satisfying himself as to the sincerity and good intentions of his new acquaintance; but he would be happy to arrange an introduction to the man who had written it, a Colonel Alexander A. Koor, a close friend as well as a former fellow-officer in the Czar's White Russian Army.

To Col. Koor must go much of the credit for the more technical and carefully authenticated information he so willingly shared concerning the Ararat area and the existence of the Ark. His military background as commander of troops guarding the Araratsky Pass during the closing years of the First World War provided ample evidence of his qualifications as author of the Rosseya story, since he had personally known relatives of some of the members of the land expedition to the Ark. He had also fought against the Bolsheviks, finally escaping with his wife into Manchuria, eventually reaching asylum in the United States.

A warm friendship soon developed with these two charming former Russian Army officers and their delightful families. Since both General Elshin and Col. Koor had been personally acquainted with members of the Czar's expedition, they were overjoyed to learn that further investigation of such an important Biblical research project was under way. Col. Koor immediately offered the invaluable assistance of his own personal knowledge and years of research. During the next few months, as concrete evidence of his deep interest, he supplied much important data for the quest.

On March 1, 1946, the following information was received from Col. Koor:

"Here are some data which should help our research, from the official records of the Russian Caucasian Army, 1914-1917, by General E. B. Mavlovsky.

"The headquarters of the 14th Railroad Battalion was at Bayazit, just southwest of Greater Ararat, with Brigade Headquarters at Maku, southeast of Lesser Ararat, commanded by Col. Sverczkoff. The 14th Battalion came to the front in the summer of 1916, from Russia. I understand that the discovery of Noah's Ark was in the end of 1916, with the scouting parties having to wait until the summer of 1917.

"I know that Sergeant Boris V. Rujansky belonged to the 14th Battalion. I understand, and it is logical, that the first and second parties of the expedition to Mount Ararat were formed from the local force of the 14th Battalion or 3-D Zamorsky Brigade, by order from the local Brigade Headquarters. Sergeant B. V. Rujansky was sent to join the party because he was a specialist. Before the war he worked in the Technological Institute of Peter the Great, and attended the Imperial Institute of Archaeology in St. Petersburg.

In 1916 the 3-D Caucasian Aviation Detachment, under the command of 1st Lt. Zabolotsky, served air duty over the region at Mount Ararat, Lake Van, and Lake Urmia. This aviation detachment served the 4th Caucasian Corps, and the Army Aviation Inspector was Captain Koorbatoff. I hope 1st Lt. Zabolotsky is the man you are looking for, for he, from an airplane, sighted the Ark and started the investigation. Captain Koorbatoff was his supervisor . . .

"I was in the Ararat region in November, 1915, during the war between Turkey and Russia. The general headquarters of the Caucasian Army sent me and other officers in command of emergency forces from Barzem and Pytergorsky for protection of the Araratsky Pass, just northwest of the peak of Greater Ararat and Zorsky Pass a few miles northwest, from the imminent Turkish attack. In June and July, the 3rd Turkish Army had broken through our forces very close to Aghri Dagh, and also the region of Mount Ararat.

"It was during this military service that I learned of the several undeciphered inscriptions, and investigated archaeological sites in that region.

(Signed) Alexander A. Koor"

Col. Koor graciously shared his maps of the archaeological sites, to which he had always dreamed of returning for further investigation some day. He also provided the following certified statement concerning the Russian Expedition in 1916:

"TO WHOM IT MAY CONCERN: This is to certify that I, Alexander A. Koor, former colonel and Chief-in-Command, of the 19th Petropaulovsky regiment, heard the following concerning the discovery of Noah's Ark:

"(1) 1st Lt. Paul Vasilivich Rujansky of the 156th Elisavetpolsky regiment, Caucasian Army. I knew all of Rujansky's family for years. I met them in the city of Kazan, Russia, where I attended the government Military Academy. 1st Lt. Rujansky was wounded in Erzerum when his regiment took Chaban Dede, central fort of the Erzerum fortifications. He was relieved from active duty and sent to work in the Commandant's office, in the city of Irkustsk, Siberia. After the Bolsheviks made an uprising he moved to the city of Harbin, Manchuria, where I found him in 1921.

"(2) Lt. Peter Nicolovich Leslin of the 261st Ahilchins-

65

ky regiment, also of the Caucasian Army. During the Bolshevik uprising he was arrested, but escaped from them, and in December, 1918, he joined my Petropaulovsky regiment.

"(3) About July or August, 1921, I and Lt. Leslin met 1st Lt. Rujansky in Harbin. During one of our conversations, 1st Lt. Rujansky told me about the discovery of Noah's Ark. He (1st Lt. Rujansky) didn't know about the details because he was wounded and sent to Russia, but he knew because his brother, Boris Vasilivich Rujansky, Sergeant of the Military Railroad Battalion, was a member of the investigating party which was sent to Mount Ararat to corroborate the discovery of Noah's Ark.

"Lt. Leslin admitted he had also heard about the discovery of Noah's Ark, not as a rumor, but as news, from the Senior Adjutant of his Division, who had told him that Noah's Ark was found in the saddle of two peaks of Mount Ararat.

"This is all I heard from these two officers, and I am sure both told me the truth.

(Signed) Col. Alexander A. Koor"

Thus the "basic facts" of the Roskovitsky story were fully verified; also the claims of the two former soldiers that there had been a two-phased Russian expedition to verify the discovery of the Ark were also well substantiated.

To Col. Koor—scholar, researcher, author, historian and etymologist of ancient languages; a specialist in the ancient history of Russia and the Far East, as well as a graduate of the Czarist Military Academy of Kazan—belongs the important discovery in 1915 of the ancient Sumerian inscription at Karada near Greater Ararat, on the Araratsky Pass. This inscription tells about the Great Flood of the Bible, and was published by Dr. J. O. Kinnaman, Director of the *Bureau of Bible Research*, in his magazine, *The Bible Archaeological Digest*, in the last quarter of 1946. Although several of the pictorial figures on the cliff had been defaced with the passing of the centuries, the story of the Deluge is clear:

"God sowed the seeds of the word into the waters . . . the waters filled the earth, descending from above . . . his children came to rest on the mountain or peak."

Regarding the authenticity of the translation of this remarkable inscription, Dr. Kinnaman wrote on August 2, 1946: "I have received two letters from Col. Koor . . . and have read and surveyed them critically . . . Col. Koor proves himself a scholar of high degree of attainment. Being familiar with Babylonian cuneiform, Egyptian heiroglyphics, Hebrew, etc., I would say that Col. Koor has made very accurate translations of the inscriptions he has set out to interpret."

On November 2, 1945, John A. Wilson, director of the Oriental Institute of the University of Chicago, impressed with even the meager data compiled to that time, had written a letter to Benjamin Franklin Allen of the *Sacred History Research Expedition* (SHRE) group. Explaining his attitude as being "agnostic but not skeptical or hostile to the specific plan of operation," Dr. Wilson went on to say that, "For many years there have been persistent and circumstantial reports of some remarkable phenomenon on Mount Ararat. As long as these reports come through intermediaries they remain hearsay rather than evidence. The reports refer also to inscriptions in such a way as to suggest that these inscriptions are of a number and length to justify linguistic analysis. I feel that a scientific expedition supplied with personal scientific abilities and with accurate scientific equipment and under the formal control of the Turkish Service of Antiquities should resolve doubts with regard to the existence of these phenomenon. Objective research in a crucial but little known area will make a contribution to scholarly knowledge."

At about this same time also, Dr. Gilbert Grosvenor, of the National Geographic Society in Washington, D.C., showed great interest in the recently organized *Sacred History Research Expedition,* which was formally dedicated to the verification of these "rumors" and "circumstantial reports." Although candidly admitting that his own Society leaned more toward the belief that the story of Noah and the Ark belonged in the realm of "Mesopotamian folklore," he stated that an actual discovery "would create more public interest than any other discovery that has been made to date."

Indeed, added Dr. Grosvenor as he reflected on the impact such an event would make on the scientific world,

"The discovery of the Ark would be the greatest archaeological discovery of all time."

During Col. Koor's tour of duty in the Ararat area he had spent much of his leisure time exploring and mapping out various archaeological sites either investigated by himself or suggested by villagers when they learned of his interest in the ancient history of their land. These maps were carefully preserved; they were brought to America and eventually turned over by Col. Koor to the Sacred History Research Expedition when he learned of their plans to go to Ararat.

In the late summer of 1969, one of these remote areas was finally relocated by Eryl Cummings and Dr. Lawrence B. Hewitt. Ancient ruins answering the descriptions given to Col. Koor by the villagers in 1915 were found. Of their antiquity there can be no doubt. Whether they date from Noah's day remains to be determined. Because of the lateness of the season and the deadline for return to the States, further investigation was necessarily curtailed. However, as Dr. Wilson put it so long ago, "objective research in a crucial but little known area will make a contribution to scholarly knowledge." Perhaps almost as important, in its own way, as a rediscovery of the Ark. . .

6

The Expedition That Went "Kapoot"

In 1933 Carveth Wells, the popular radio commentator over KFI in Los Angeles, had made an abortive attempt to find the Ark. His unhappy experiences during the attempt, graphically recorded in his book *Kapoot*, had in no way dampened his enthusiasm for the plans of the *Sacred History Research Expedition,* which he publicly endorsed over his station in 1945.

It is doubtful whether the Roskovitsky story had reached the public press in 1933: Wells' interest had been sparked by reading James Bryce's account of finding hand-tooled timber on Mount Ararat in 1876. After reading everything available on the subject at that time, Wells secured financing under the sponsorship of the Geographical Society of Chicago, and he and his party set out.

His passport called for passage through Russia and westward across the Araxes River, thence to Ararat. Since 1924 the often-contested mountain had again come under Turkish domain, and the Russians took a dim view of an expedition to find the Ark. Wells and his friends were stopped just short of the border, within tantalizing distance of the majestic mountain they had come so far to explore. In spite of the bitter disappointment, however, the expedition was not a total loss. For Wells and his party secured permission to visit Echmiadzin, reputed to be the oldest Armenian monastery in the world, and situated just across the river in the very shadow of Aghri Dagh. More than a century before, Dr. Friedrich Parrot had visited the same monastery and received a chilling response to his eager announcement that he had come in high hopes of ascending the peak. In contrast, in 1933 the aged Armenian Patriarch, Archbishop Mesrop, welcomed his American visitors with true Oriental graciousness and charm.

"Obviously a great scholar and author," according to Wells, the Archbishop's bookshelves "were lined with valuable books, many on explorations." The library also contained many priceless manuscripts, some of which, believed Wells, had never been translated or published. On the wall hung a magnificent oil painting depicting Noah descending with his family from Ararat, followed by a long line of animals.

The highlight of the occasion, of course, came when Wells finally ventured to ask the Patriarch about the relic of Noah's Ark reputed to be in his possession. The genial Archbishop smiled: "We have the remains of the Ark here in the church. . . . It is the most prized possession of the monastery. We do not class it merely as a relic. This piece of Noah's Ark is in quite a different category and no other church in the world possesses or even claims to possess such a thing."

But to get even a glimpse of the sacred relic required the unraveling of considerable red tape. First, a special meeting of the monks must be called in order to get their opinion and consent. It was a difficult question to decide. Apparently forgetting that Parrot had been shown the piece of wood in 1829, the Archbishop assured Wells that a layman had never before been permitted to gaze upon the sacred artifact.

At last, however, to the accompaniment of Gregorian chanting and the swishing of many brooms, the church was thoroughly cleansed and certain rituals performed in preparation for the special event. A stately procession appeared, led by a bearded, mitered priest bearing the sacred chest in his hands. Carveth Wells was graciously granted permission to open the casket and examine the wood. "You may examine it as much as you like," smiled the Archbishop. "This is the portion of Noah's Ark which was brought down from Ararat by one of our monks named Jacob."

Wells gazed with interest upon a piece of reddish-colored petrified wood, measuring about twelve by nine inches, and about an inch thick. "It was obviously petrified wood," he wrote later. "The grain was plainly visible, but having expected to see a piece of wood that was curved like the side of a boat, I remarked that I was surprised to find it flat."

The Archbishop, with a flash of humor, instantly replied, "You have forgotten the rudder, Mr. Wells!"

This experience with the hospitable Echmiadzin monks had convinced Wells that the Ark was still, "without a doubt," somewhere on the mountain. This is obviously one of the reasons he so enthusiastically encouraged the organization of another expedition that, hopefully, might succeed where he had failed.

Unless there might have been a still more convincing personal reason that has recently come to light. Although Wells had not mentioned it to the budding researchers in 1945, there is reason to believe that he had brought back his own well-guarded secret from his otherwise disappointing trip to Russia. Early in 1970, Dr. John Millish, for two years a research astronomer at Yerkes Observatory, wrote a letter in reply to an inquiry from his long-time friend, Malcolm Randall. In this letter he made the statement that about 30 years ago he had examined a piece of very hard wood, purported to have been brought out of Russia by Wells by dint of bribing a government inspector. "The wood," said Dr. Millish, "was about two feet long and eight inches wide and one and one-half inches thick."

Whether Wells had succeeded in eluding the authorities long enough to cross the river and climb the mountain after all is not clear. But at least, according to John Mellish, some shepherds were involved in the transaction. They had been "up there," (so the story goes) "and found the snow partly melted away from one end of the ship."

And since it is shepherds who have kept alive the tradition that the Ark can be seen occasionally when conditions are just right, who can say that this story is not true . . . ?

7

The Journalists
and the Ark

Another story that came to light in the early days of the search for information concerning the Ark, was the account of a Turkish discovery that had been announced to the world in August of 1883.

This was only seven years after James Bryce had brought back his piece of hand-tooled wood from what he described as a "vast height" on Ararat's rocky slopes, and only four years before Nouri was to claim the personal triumph of finding the great ship itself.

So far as is known, the Turkish announcement was the first publicly reported discovery of the Ark in modern times. It was appropriate that the story should first come out in the Turkish press, since it concerned the great mountain that dominates their own remote Eastern frontier. It was also fortunate, at least for the Western world, that an otherwise unidentified Englishman known only as "Gascoyne" had been with the group of Turkish officials investigating avalanches on the mountain; and that he had been a Britisher on friendly and familiar terms with the Biblical story of the Flood, else he might not have recognized the "find."

The Constantinople release was picked up by the London press, and the following day the story appeared in leading American newspapers across the land:

CHICAGO TRIBUNE: August 10, 1883: "A paper at Constantinople announces the discovery of Noah's Ark. It appears that some Turkish commissioners appointed to investigate the question of avalanches on Mount Ararat suddenly came upon a gigantic structure of very dark wood protruding from a glacier. They made inquiries of the inhabitants. They had seen it for six years, but had been afraid to approach it because a spirit of fierce aspect had been seen looking out the upper window. The Turkish commissioners, however, are brave men, not deterred by such trifles, and they determined to reach it. Situated as it was among the fastnesses of one of the glens of Mount Ararat, it was a work of enormous difficulty, and it was only after incredible hardship that they succeeded. The ark was in a good state of preservation, although the angles—observe, not the bow or stern—had been a good deal broken in its descent. They recognized it at once. There was an Englishman among them who had presumably read his Bible, and he saw that it was made of the ancient gopher wood of Scripture, which as everyone knows, grows only on the plains of the Euphrates. Effecting an entrance into the structure, which was painted brown, they found that the admiralty requirements for the conveyance of horses had been carried out, and the interior was divided into partitions fifteen feet high. Into three of these only could they get, the others being full of ice, and how far the ark extended into the glacier they could not tell. If however, on being uncovered, it turns out to be 300 cubits long, it will go hard with disbelievers."

Already the slightly facetious overtones of the press could be felt, occasioned, understanbly, by the reference to the "spirit of fierce aspect" (reminiscent of the superstitious beliefs of the Kurds, perhaps?), as well as by the journalists' own varying degrees of skepticism or belief. It is interesting to note, also, that the inhabitants of this unidentified area of the mountain had reported seeing the "gigantic structure . . . protruding from a glacier" for a period of six years. This is a point to ponder, although there have been claims that the Ark was dislodged by an earthquake early in this same year. According to a comment in *Watchtower* in September of 1883, tremendous quantities of ice were broken loose, burying entire villages at the base of the mountain under the resulting avalanches. This, of course, explains the presence of the commissioners in this area when they unexpectedly caught a glimpse of this strange anomaly in the ice.

Also, the fact that it had reportedly been seen for six successive years; that Nouri had claimed discovery as early in the year as April; and that the Russian two-phased expedition did not achieve its objective until late in December, gives rise to the conjecture that perhaps explorers for the Ark may be compared to the old Indian who explained: "Indian not lost—teepee lost!" To put it in reverse, the Ark is not "lost"—in fact, it may be visible at almost any season of the year unless temporarily buried by excessive snowfall —but the searchers for it have difficulty finding the exact trail from which it can be seen!

On the same day that the *Chicago TRIBUNE* article appeared, the *New York HERALD* carried the story under the headline:

"Ararat's Antique

"Now let the heathen rage and the free-thinkers call on their respective beer cellars to hide them, for has not Noah's Ark been discovered, and right on the mountain where she discharged her cargo and passengers more than four thousand years ago? Of course, it is the Ark, and not an antiquated craft that some tricky showman has bought for a sou, taken to pieces, dragged up the mountain and reconstructed, for the printed description indicates a model that cannot be found at the present day except in the mudscow fleet of the New York Street Cleaning Department and the navy of the United States, neither of which has yet disposed of any of its antediluvian hulks.

"Well, what are the ungodly going to do about it? There she is, according the Turkish press, which has no possible reason to go so far back into antiquity if searching merely for something to lie about. It will not do for them to make light of the story, for an Englishman has discovered that the ancient cattle boat is of gopher wood, according to specification, and the stalls are in accordance with the plans of the British Admiralty, which body is the modern substitute for inspiration in marine affairs. All that Colonel Ingersoll and Professor Adler can hope for is to persuade the public that the newly discovered antique, although an ark, is not necessarily the handiwork of an amateur ship carpenter named Noah. If arks were the fashion forty-four hundred years ago, why may not dozens of them have drifted from their moorings during the great November freshet of 2616 B.C. and gone ashore on Mount Ararat?

"But whatever they may have to say must be said in a hurry, for an American is reported to have arranged to bring the old tub over here, and argument will stand a poor chance against eyesight. If she is three hundred cubits long, according to contract, it may be quite a job to get her from the top of Mount Ararat to the Mediterranean; but a nation that has seriously thought of a ship railway across Central America cannot doubt that the ark can be brought to deep water. If no American engineers of sufficient ability are on the ground the purchaser need only to send to France for Jules Verne. All but three of her compartments are said to be full of ice, which, at present prices, ought to pay the expense of bringing it over. When she reaches American waters, however, the Navy department ought to purchase her at once, for the world's greatest republic ought to have at least one ship that will not rot as soon as it leaves a navy yard. Her absorption by the government would not prevent the public getting bits of her as relics, even timber enough to make walking canes, pulpit chairs, and poor boxes for all who care to buy; for when our Naval Department does 'improve' a vessel it gets rid of so much of the original matter that, in case of the Ark, Noah would not know his staunch old family scow if he saw it."

One cannot help wondering at this point about the reaction of Ingersoll at being thus publicly included in the tongue-in-cheek baiting over the purported discovery of the Ark. Did the "Great Agnostic" now a middle-aged man at the height of his writing career in Washington, D.C., allow a twinge of conscience to carry him back a half century to the days of his Presbyterian childhood, when his clergyman father must have told him many times about Noah and the Flood?

And what of Bryce, on the other hand, whose Scotch-Presbyterian ancestry had bred in *him* the firm conviction that the stories of the Bible had been true, historical events? It had been only five years since he himself had been ridiculed before the Royal Geographical Society in London because of his belief that the hand-tooled timber he had found might have come originally from the Ark, and because he had so courageously defended his position that

Ararat was, truly, the Biblical peak. Now, with this electrifying announcement from Istanbul, did he experience a vicarious thrill of triumph as a fellow-countryman substantiated his own belief? Did he wish he had lingered a bit longer on that memorable day in 1876 to search for further evidence in those "remote glens" the newspaper story had told about . . . ?

For if Bryce *had* taken time to explore, if he *had* succeeded in finding the Ark, what a story would have burst upon the world! For his word would have carried weight. It is doubtful if even the infidels would have dared to scoff, if a man of Bryce's integrity and international reputation had returned from Ararat with news that the Ark actually did exist and had been seen.

On August 13, *The New York WORLD* published the same story under the headline:

"Great Scientific Find

"Considerable competition has recently been shown by the discoverers of ancient manuscripts and the finders of ancient relics. The latter has suddenly come to the front by the discovery of Noah's Ark in that part of the Armenian plateau still known as Mount Ararat.

"The find was made by a party of Russian (even newspaper journalists have been known to be in error at times!! author's note) engineers who were surveying a glacier. An extraordinary spell of hot weather had melted away a great portion of the Araxes glacier, and they were surprised to see sticking out of the ice what at first appeared to be the rude facade of an ancient dwelling. On closer examination it was found to be composed of longitudinal layers of gopher wood, supported by immense frames, still in a remarkable state of preservation.

"Assistance having been summoned from Nakhchevan, the work of uncovering the find commenced under the most extraordinary difficulties, and in a week's time the indefatigable explorers had uncovered what they claimed to be Noah's Ark, as it bore indisputable evidence of having been used as a boat.

"At this point archaeology could afford to rest at any ordinary period of the world and we should expect the luckiest finders to form a syndicate and open a bazaar for the sale of relics.

"But in our day antiquarian history takes another turn. It isn't looking for merchandise as much as for testimony. We must not forget that the planting of the Cardiff Giant was not so much to make money as to establish the missing link.

"The Noah's Ark syndicate are only following the tactics of the antiquary who recently offered to sell an original manuscript of the Mosaic law signed by Moses to the British Museum.

"They are trying to correct the record with facts.

"With these principles in view, the reader must not be surprised to learn by the latest dispatches from our representative, Mr. Benjamin—who is not going to Persia for nothing—that the engineers have broken through the third compartment of the ark, and in the true spirit of the age have discovered the original log kept by Noah and his sons.

"Startling as this announcement is, it is backed up by the documents, which must stand for what they are worth without any comment of ours. Philology, ethnology, and archaeology must fight it out for themselves. A newspaper can only narrate the occurrence."

However, only the previous day this same metropolitan newspaper had so far departed from its stated policy of narrating "only the occurrence," as to publish a most derisive, derogatory editorial on the entire subject of the Ark as being "a most unnecessary piece of enterprise."

On August 15, the *New York TIMES* carried a reprint of an article clearly designed to put all believers in the Biblical story of the Flood back in their proper places:

"A British newspaper prints a letter from an exceptionally innocent correspondent who, having read the latest yarn about Noah's Ark, goes on to say: 'In these days of skepticism and rank infidelity when men scoff at the truthfulness of the word of God, yes, there are those among us even professing Christianity, who doubt the authenticity of the Pentateuch. Many there are also who disbelieve in the Old Testament altogether and look upon it as an obsolete book. In these days, therefore, it is refreshing to hear from what may be considered a reliable source, that Noah's Ark has been discovered.' This excellent gentleman has been very badly taken in. He should be put into the Ark!"

It is again a temptation to wonder who this "excellent

(British) gentleman" may have been. Bryce, perhaps, whose deeply spiritual nature must have grieved at the tide of atheism sweeping over the land? It is also a temptation to wonder why the Christian world of that day did not rally and send an investigation, posthaste, to bring back further confirmation and pictures of the sensational discovery. Until it is remembered that the land of the Sultan was a far-off country in those days of slow transportation and communication facilities; also, that the year 1883 marked the beginning of a long period of political and religious upheaval in Armenia, and the region about Ararat would not have provided a healthy climate for such a search. Also, as Bryce once pointed out, the public is "extremely fitful . . . and soon ceases to note what does not fill the newspapers. "And so the brief flurry caused by the mostly caustic journalistic comments on the discovery of the Ark died down and was soon forgotten in man's mad pursuit of more mundane things.

8

More Aerial Discoveries

During the Second World War, there was greater air activity over Mount Ararat than during any other period of history, since it was on the direct flight line between the Allied air base in Tunisia and the Russian base in Erivan. Hundreds of flights were made to airlift much needed supplies from the United States to our allies in Russia.

Since this time, rumors and reports of sightings in addition to the 1916 Russian aviator's discovery of Noah's Ark from the air have been circulated far and wide. As early as 1945, a Florida veteran reported seeing motion pictures of Mount Ararat, purportedly taken from a U.S. Air Force plane, in which a large portion of the Ark was visible. But, in spite of a fast trip to Florida to verify the story, the man with the interesting movies had disappeared and has never been heard from since.

A related story appeared in 1961 in a magazine article by Raymond Schuessler titled "Hark, Hark . . . the Ark!" in which he gave a thumbnail sketch of some of the findings in this book. One sketch read like this: "Then came the recent rumors. During the Second World War, two Australian airmen showed, in the bar of an English inn, aerial photographs they said they had taken of Noah's Ark in a cleft of Mount Ararat. If the story is true, it certainly is odd that no more interest was aroused at the time. The Australian airmen vanished, taking their pictures with them."

Was there some connection between these men and the pictures the Florida veteran had seen?

Then there was the story that concerns another Russian flier during that same period of time. Major Jasper Maskelyn, wartime chief of Russian camouflage, reported that one of his men flew over Mount Ararat in a reconnaisance aircraft in an attempt to check out the story of the aviator's sighting in World War I. According to this story, this second flier did discover a partly submerged vessel in an ice lake. Arctic climbers were again dispatched to the scene. They reached the lake, which was partly thawed, and actually found the remains of the Ark, which was reported to be over 400 feet long, and that they said was "very rotted," and "composed of a fossilized wood looking almost like coal."

Which reminds us of the ill-fated courier and his lost documents in 1917, which are believed to have fallen into Bolshevik hands. For this later story seems to provide evidence that this rumor is true, and that documentation of some kind is still in the Russian archives; that the Roskovitsky story is believed; and that there was sufficient curiosity during World War II to send another flier to verify the facts. It is also evident that their information contains detailed instruction as to how to reach the great ship, both to obtain an aerial view, and then to reach it from the ground, which further strengthens the original aviator's story that started the research so long ago!

One of the most widely circulated and tantalizing stories regarding the modern discovery of the Ark concerns the elusive but well-attested article that reportedly appeared late in the summer of 1943 in the U.S. Army publication, *Stars and Stripes,* for the service men stationed in the European Theater of Operations in Tunisia.

That this story is not merely rumor, but fact, has been verified by a number of individuals whose honesty is above reproach. These include two Southern California physicians, a Navy chaplain, as well as several laymen, all of whom recall reading the story of the U.S. fliers who reported seeing a huge ship high on the side of Mount Ararat as they shuttled supplies to Erivan over the peak.

Illustrating the joys of anticipation and the heartbreak of disappointment that have accompanied the research in this field over a long period of years, is the near-brush with discovery of this same *Stars and Stripes* story late in December, 1969. Chance visitors in Eryl Cummings' home one afternoon fell to reminiscing about their experiences during World War Two. One of the men casually mentioned that he had been stationed in Tunisia in 1943.

Tunisia? 1943 . . . ? The hostess gasped and hitched eagerly forward in her chair. Had the gentleman, by some remote chance, ever seen or heard of that long-sought article about the U.S. fliers who had reported seeing or photographing the Ark as they flew back and forth on their regular missions to Erivan? It had been published in *Stars and Stripes,* she explained, and. . . .

The gentleman smiled. Yes, he certainly had. He remembered it very well. In fact, the story had created such a sensation at the base that the French chaplain had been moved to preach a sermon about Noah and the Flood the very next day at church!

The hostess regarded the visitor much as a child might regard a magician about to produce a live rabbit out of his hat! Had he—she almost choked on the fateful words—had he, by any chance, saved that article, and if so, would he be willing . . . .

The gentleman smiled again, but this time his smile was tinged with sadness. Regretfully, he explained how only a couple of weeks before, his wife had transferred all his war-time mementoes from the worn old scrapbook into a brand-new album for a homecoming surprise.

"But the clippings from *Stars and Stripes* . . . ?"

Still more regretfully, the visitor shook his head. "I asked her the same question," he said. But, like all the other tattered, yellowed old clippings in the book, it did not take kindly to a transplant, and not realizing the value of the article on the Ark, she had thrown it away!

So near—and yet so far . . . !

9

"Cold Logic" and
Aghri Dagh

It is perhaps significant that until almost the middle of the twentieth century, probably not more than a half dozen reports of actual sightings and discoveries of the Ark had reached the public press.

These included the brief, either facetious or disparaging flurry over the Turkish commissioner's report in 1883; the largely discounted, little-known story of Nouri's accomplishment in 1887, which is never mentioned in formal, authenticated reports of ascents of Ararat (possibly because of his Oriental background and lack of connection with any of the recognized Western geographical societies of his day); a short and elusive reference to a "death-bed confession" of a London scientist in or near the 1920's (the atheist's story mentioned in an earlier chapter of the book); and, sometime during or after the 1930's, the widely circulated account of the Russian aviator who had spotted the Ark from the air during World War I. Add to these the Major Maskelyn story that had appeared in an Albuquerque newspaper May 22, 1964, about the airman who, in a Russian reconnaisance plane, had sighted a huge ship to corroborate the Roskovitsky story; and the two Australian fliers who had shown pictures of what they claimed to be Noah's Ark in "a cleft of Mount Ararat"—a story remarkably akin to a similar account in the *Stars and Stripes*.

Then suddenly, as if in harmony with the acceleration of modern travel and communication, public interest in Mount Ararat and the Ark began to rise. During the following decade, sightings and rumors of sightings, expeditions and unsuccessful attempts to wrest the secret of Noah's old ship from Mount Ararat multiplied. These sometimes extraordinary stories provided many a controversial column-inch in newspapers around the world, as sympathetic or derisive correspondents penned their lines.

The first event to mark the beginning of this period of quickening interest was another story date-lined Istanbul, on November 13, 1948.

"The petrified remains of an object which peasants insist resembles a ship has been found high up Mt. Ararat, Biblical landing place of Noah's Ark.

"While various persons from time to time have reported objects resembling a 'house' or a 'ship' on the mountain, Turks who have seen this new find profess it to be the only known object which could actually be taken as the remains of a ship.

"Shukru Asena, a 69-year-old farmer who owns large acreage in that faroff Eastern frontier district, told about the discovery in an unheralded visit to the Associated Press bureau here. This is his story: Early in September a Kurdish farmer named Reshit was about two-thirds of the way up the 16,000 foot peak when he came upon an object he had never seen before, although he had been up the mountain many times. He moved around it and then climbed higher to examine it from above.

"There, Reshit said, was the prow of a ship protruding from a canyon down which tons of melting ice and snow had been rushing for more than two months. The prow was almost entirely revealed, but the rest of the object was still covered.

"The contour of the earth, Reshit said, indicated the invisible part of the object was shaped like a ship. The prow, he added, was about the size of a house.

"Reshit climbed down to it and with his dagger tried to break off a piece of the prow. It was so hard it would not break. It was blackened with age. Reshit insisted it was not a simple rock formation.

" 'I know a ship when I see one,' he said. 'This is a ship.'

"He spread the word among little villages at the base of the mountain, and peasants began climbing up its northern slopes to see the weird thing he had found. Each who came back said it was a ship.

86

" 'There is no folklore there about the Ark,' Shukru Bey said, and persons who saw Reshit's find came away in great surprise. There are no cameras out in this wild isolated country where Turkey, Russia, and Iran meet, hence no one came away with a picture. The snows have been falling again and perhaps have covered it by now."

The story of this find of course stimulated much interest in religious circles around the world. Among those determined to investigate this new Turkish story for himself was another Britisher, Egerton Sykes, one-time Army intelligence officer turned archaeologist, who had amassed an impressive amount of evidence that had convinced him that the Ark was indeed on Mount Ararat, and that this was what Reshit had found.

In the United States another fervent researcher, the Rev. Aaron J. Smith, retired missionary to China, and at that time Dean of North Carolina's People's Bible College, ardently hoped to accompany Sykes on a joint venture to find and bring back concrete evidence of the existence of the Ark.

Much journalistic fun had been poked at these two "amateur archaeologists" when their plans were made public. *Time* magazine, on April 25, 1949, referred to the negative reactions of Moscow's *Pravda,* whose "alert editors . . . were not to be taken in by any such fairy tales. Historical materialism does not recognize Genesis," they said, and "no less an authority than the Big Soviet Encyclopedia calls the story of the flood a 'myth' which up until the 19th Century had done great harm to the sciences." Snorted Pravda last week, 'It is quite enough to look at a map to understand the real meaning of the biblical amusements of these Anglo-American imperialists. The true purposes of such an expedition are as far from archaeology as Sykes is from great-grandfather Noah.' " (Whatever happened, we wonder, to the Russian airman who, in one of their own reconnaissance planes, had so recently verified the Roskovitsky find? Had he, too, perhaps met the same fate as the courier in 1971? Or were the well-informed and "alert" editors of *Pravda* merely trying to draw a "red herring" across the trail, with full knowledge that their own secret archives contained documented proof of the existence of the Ark? These, too, are questions for the thoughtful reader to ponder.)

The Reshit story, however, was not the only motivating factor in the plans for a joint expedition. Both Smith and Sykes had spent many years in separate research about the existence of the Ark, and were both fully convinced of its authenticity, and had long dreamed of discovering it and presenting the evidence to the world. Sykes' plans, however, eventually bogged down for lack of financial backing. Smith, undaunted, proceeded to publish a small but popular booklet on his research to help finance an expedition of his own.

Dr. Smith had also worked closely with members of the Sacred History Research Expedition since soon after its inception in 1945. During this period Eryl Cummings had visited him several times in Intercession City, Florida, and the two researchers had become close friends. On July 28, 1948, after Eryl Cummings had disassociated himself from the original organization, he was invited by Dr. Smith to head the party he was planning to send to Ararat to search for the Ark. On August 11, Smith repeated his invitation because, in his own words, "I believe you would search till you find the object." However, Smith's gracious offer of leadership was declined.

Then, in November of 1948, came the electrifying announcement of Reshit's discovery. Excitement mounted and correspondence multiplied. Plans accelerated for the long-dreamed-of expedition to Ararat, and before the end of the year, Dr. Smith had incorporated under the name of the Oriental Archaeological Research Expedition, with the purpose of proceeding as soon as possible to Turkey to further verify Reshit's find.

It was Smith's idea, of course, to relocate the Kurdish farmer and enlist his help. His courage ran high, in those exciting final days of preparation for the trip. A possible failure did not seem to enter his mind. ". . . the discovery will be so tremendous," he wrote on June 18, 1949. "It would only take, perhaps, 10 days or two weeks."

But, in spite of all the eager planning and hopes, the expedition almost met the same fate as that of Egerton Sykes. By departure date sufficient funding had not yet come through, and Smith found himself leaving the shores of

America at the head of a greatly diminished and under-financed group. The determined and dedicated explorer was accompanied to Turkey by Walter Wood, of Sea Cliff, Long Island, as mechanical engineer in charge of transport for the trip; E. J. Newton, of Colfax, North Carolina, photographer; and Weldon Ogg, physicist, from Knoxville, Tennessee. Eryl Cummings, Fred Avery (the model ship-builder from the Naval Academy in Maryland), and the veteran archaeologist, Dr. J. O. Kinnaman, were to follow as soon as news of the discovery could be cabled to the States.

But once on Turkey's unfamiliar soil, Smith's troubles really began. Obstacles undreamed of arose on every side. On July 27, barely a month after such an optimistic begin-ning, the harrassed leader of the expedition wrote from Istanbul that weeks of waiting in a hotel room, plus side trips to Ankara to secure the proper permits, had almost "drained them" of funds. They had succeeded in obtaining "verbal permissions," from the high command, but many of the key officials were apparently vacationing, and the outlook was gloomy for obtaining the necessary written permits. "I would not feel free," wrote Smith, "to invite anyone else to come here now, to go with us on a verbal permission; it might be stalled."

But at last, after a frustrating 2-month delay, Smith and his party were ready to set out for the restricted area in which they wished to work. They were joined by Edwin Greenwald, the Associated Press correspondent who had announced Reshit's purported discovery less than a year before. What an inducement for an imaginative journalist! What a "scoop" to send sizzling out over the wires should the expedition be so fortunate as to repeat the "find"! What an opportunity to participate in the most stupendous, the most exciting, the "greatest archaeological discovery of all time. . . ." And this time, you may be sure, there was a camera and typewriter to record the event.

But Greenwald—and the still optimistic Smith—were doomed to disappointment, for the cagey old mountain was not yet ready to reveal its secret to explorers from the out-side world. The expedition did not succeed. In the first place, because of the many unavoidable delays, from four to six weeks of prime searching time had to be compressed into 15 days, during a period of the year when normally the autumn storms begin to rage. And most disheartening of all, the hoped-for contact with Reshit was never made.

And without a native guide to show the way, the formidable Aghri Dagh can be a "painful mountain," indeed. Perhaps, in an obstreperous mood, it had dropped a fresh mantle of snow over the object for which they searched. Or perhaps it had shrugged its massive shoulders just a bit, and loosed hundreds of thousands of tons of ice and snow to come avalanching down its craggy slopes to bury for a while longer the famous ship. Perhaps it had not been an unusually warm season in 1949, and the ice had not melted back from the glacier in which the great boat was hid. Or perhaps, since the knowledgeable Reshit did not reappear to aid them in their quest, they had merely missed the trail. . . .

Smith himself, at 61, was unable to participate personally in the search. But, as Greenwald later pointed out, "he came with an abiding faith that it would be found; he left with an abiding faith that it will be found one day." The disappointed researcher returned to the States, where he died on November 9, 1960, without ever seeing the fulfillment of his dream.

As for Greenwald, although he had come to Ararat with shining hopes, he did not possess Smith's "abiding faith." Returning to the small Turkish town of Bayazid, he pounded out his melancholy tale:

"Sept. 28, 1949: the ark of Noah, if it ever landed on Mount Ararat, is lost eternally to the ages. It will never be found.

"Some of the Americans who have just completed a grueling search of the great Ararat chain still hope confidently that it will be uncovered some day.

"But use of cold logic makes it certain that it will not. Either it rests forever beneath deep and perpetual ice and snow at the peak of the 17,000-foot mountain, or else it has been destroyed and its fragments buried in this volcanic wilderness.

"The four-man expedition, first formally organized searching party in Turkish record, explored every crevice and every clew. It scouted through the villages for 100 miles around, seeking anyone who might know anything.

"The sum total, as expressed so monotonously by the

Turks in the villages, is simply: 'Hich birsey!' (An emphatic 'Nothing.')

"In the mountains we climbed laboriously across dead volcanoes and burned-out stone. We scrambled over small plateaus lifeless with biting volcanic ash. In the villages the old men and the young had heard the legend that a great boat once rested in the snow way up there.

"But no one had ever seen it, and they knew of no one who had."

It seems that Necati Dolunay, the 36-year-old departmental director of antiquities and museums for Turkey, had also accompanied the expedition. His professional opinion convinced the correspondent that the expedition had not been a total loss after all.

Said Necati Bey: "It is indisputable that this expedition has done a great deal for science and research as regards the ark. It finally has utterly disproved opinions and observations during more than 100 years that the ark is in plain sight. It had disproved the all-too-frequent claims that it is on a mountain plateau that reaches between small Ararat and big Ararat. Many persons, including Russians, have held to this contention."

Necati Bey, according to Greenwald, "was certain from the start that nothing would be found." His explanation for the expedition's lack of success indicated not only skepticism regarding existence of the Ark, but a definite leaning toward the theory that if it existed at all, it must be in the area between the Tigris and Euphrates rivers, and "somewhat west of Ararat." "This is a volcanic area," he said. "During all the thousands of years since the ark was supposed to have sailed atop the deluge, anything that might have been here would either have been covered or destroyed."

The American members of the expedition reacted to their disappointment in various ways. Dr. Smith remained unshaken in his conviction that the Ark was on the mountain and that one day it would again be found. "We have made an attempt but failure of it does not imply the ultimate failure of the Ark's recovery," he said. Newton agreed with Smith, but insisted it would require months of exploration to find it. Walter Wood "sized it up" for both himself and Wendall Ogg "with a curt, 'I've had enough. But at least I am satisfied personally that it is not here.' "

Their discouragement is not difficult to understand. It had been a rough summer. It seemed that nothing had gone right. In 1949, too, so little was known of the great mountain in the Western world, or of the almost insurmountable problems involved in exploring its rugged and forbidding heights. Carried away with enthusiasm and their high hopes of success, the group must surely have been unprepared for the many dangers they would encounter in this wild "triangle where Turkey, Russia, and Iran come together."

Said Greenwald, "From the mountain we looked down on the three countries and a heavy detachment of police and gendarmes kept us under exceptionally heavy guard to prevent any incident. The Russian press had already complained that the expedition was a group of spies rather than searchers after the ark.

"But probably of greater concern to Turkish security forces was the possibility of the group clashing with smugglers and Kurdish bandits who slip into Turkey from Iran in the area under exploration. Lt. Halil Borek, 25-year-old commander of gendarme field forces, came along personally. His men carried machine guns and kept scouts far ahead."

Thus in this armed and hostile atmosphere, neither Reshit nor Shukru Asena had reappeared. It seems incredible that no one in the "100 villages" scouted for information about Reshit's discovery should remember anything at all about such an unusual event! What had happened to all the peasants who reportedly had climbed the mountain the year before to see the "weird" structure he had found? Surely, such a strange anomaly as a "ship" on a mountain as far inland as Aghri Dagh should have provided an endless and unforgettable topic of conversation around their campfires for many months to come! That Smith had counted heavily on this assistance is indicated in a letter dated December, 1948: "If we contact these farmers, and their story is true, we should have no trouble finding the Ark."

It might have been some small comfort to the frustrated explorers to recall that Bryce, too, had encountered the same solid phalanx of uncooperation in 1876. "Nobody at Aralykh knew anything of former ascents," he complained, "nor of how it (the mountain) ought to be attacked."

A partial explanation for these problems may lie in the fact that the native populations of the villages on or near the mountain have an inbred hostility and fear of strangers from a foreign land who wish to climb their sacred peak. The Armenians, of course, believe the Ark too sacred to be lightly exposed to the casual view. And the Moslem Kurds and Turks view with centuries-old suspicion anything that bears the name of Christian.

Occasionally, however, the age-old barriers have been broken down, and even a Moslem villager has been known to offer his cooperation to a Christian when his confidence has been won. In 1961 the mayor of a village close by the base of Aghri Dagh so far forgot his inbred mistrust as to divulge the following information to an American physician who had shared his medical skills with many of the ailing inhabitants of the area. He had once talked with a man, admitted the mayor, who told him he had been to the Ark and examined it. The mayor had been skeptical of the story at the time, he confessed, until an American expedition had appeared to search for the Ark, and he had decided that the man might have been telling the truth. The name of the man. . . ? The mayor, unfortunately, could not recall this most important part of his story. Could this mysterious person have been Reshit. . . ?

Again, in 1966, an aged but flock-wealthy shepherd on the mountain also in gratitude for medical services received, offered to guide an American party to the Ark. However, the old man became too critically ill to carry out his offer, and was never able to go. Could this ancient Kurdish shepherd have been one of the curious villagers who climbed the north side of the mountain so many years before to see Reshit's "weird" find for himself?

Probably the answers to these questions will never be fully known. But it is obvious that kindness still "begets kindness," and that even the simple and superstitious villagers respond in the spirit of Henry Burton, who asked, "Have you had a kindness shown? Pass it on."

10

A Sacred Legacy
Changes Hands

It is almost beyond human comprehension to fathom the scope, the long-range planning, the diabolically-timed machinations of the evil forces that have battled all through the ages to silence the voice of Truth. In this unsavory category can surely be classified the senseless, wholesale slaughter of the Armenian race.

Why . . . ? Why the Armenian persecutions that persisted through seemingly endless, tortured centuries of time. Why, of all the multiplied millions on the face of the earth, should this much harrassed nation have been chosen for utter annihilation. . . ?

One answer to this heartbreaking question may lie in the fact that the Armenian people, who have claimed the land of Ararat as their ancestral home since before the dawn of recorded history have most faithfully preserved the knowledge of the Ark and its "approximate location" through the years; and that through this people have come some of our most authentic accounts.

This race of ancient culture and great capacities was officially declared a Christian nation by King Tiradates around 300 A.D.— a century before the Roman emperor, Constantine, emblazoned his banners with the symbol of the Cross.

Since that time they have succeeded, against terrific odds, in maintaining their religious identity, and still cling tenaciously to their Christian faith, even to our modern times.

The Armenians, according to James Bryce in his address before the Royal Geographical Society of London in 1878, seem to have inhabited the "extremely high country" of their ancestors "since the beginning of things." There is no such thing as a country called Armenia, said Bryce—it is merely a "geographical expression" denoting a nation that has been divided between the three great neighboring empires of that day—Turkey, Persia, and, on the northern boundaries, the vast territories of the Russian Bear.

Armenia, explained Bryce, was "perfectly undefined, with no definite natural boundaries or any distinct political limits," nor with "any single race" which conspicuously prevailed. And yet, in this ancient land, with its ancient peoples, Mount Ararat reared its stately summit to the heavens as if eternally pointing mankind to the Creator of them all.

The Armenians, observed Bryce, are "a people who have had a great past." They are also a people, we might truthfully add, who have had a tempestuous and heartrending past.

In the middle of the fifth century, so history goes, Armenia lost her independence to the fire-worshipping king of Persia. The Armenian princes were ordered by their new monarch to give up Christianity and embrace the religion of their conquerors. Eghiche, an Armenian historian of that era, has preserved for us the text of the remarkable document of refusal, drafted and unanimously adopted by a great council of bishops and laymen of the church:

"After answering at some length the arguments of the Persian king against Christianity, they said in conclusion: 'From this faith no one can move us—neither angels nor men; neither sword, nor water, nor any deadly punishment. If you leave us our faith, we will accept no other lord in place of you; but we will accept no God in place of Jesus Christ; there is no other God beside Him. If, after this great confession, you ask anything more of us, lo, we are before you and our lives are in your power. From you, torments; from us, submission; your swords, our necks. We are not better than those who have gone before us who gave up their goods and their lives for this testimony.' "

For this boldly courageous stand Armenia received swift and deadly retribution in the form of an invasion by 200,000 Persian troops, who defeated the small Armenian forces in the very shadow of the Mountain of the Ark.

But the obstinate resistance offered by the Christians—men, women, and children alike—convinced the king of Persia that he could never make fire worshippers out of them. As the old historian quaintly expressss it: "The swords of the slayers grew dull, but their necks were not weary." Even the high priest of fire saw that the Persians had undertaken an impossibility, and thus advised the king: "These people have put on Christianity, not like a garment, but like their flesh and blood. Men who do not dread fetters nor fear torments, nor care for their property, and, what is worst of all, who choose death rather than life—who can stand against them?"

As "the scroll of centuries unrolled," the Armenian people "lived and suffered and died for their faith during the troubled years." Last of all, the "conquering sword of Mohammedanism" sought to show them the error of their ways; but even this failed to dim the Armenian courage and their Christian faith.

Such were the people to whom God had entrusted the knowledge and the secret of Aghri Dagh. There were periods, fortunately for the survival of the race, when "the fires of persecution burned low." During these periods the "thrifty, hardy, ambitious" Armenian people prospered and progressed. Many of them moved into the land of Turkey, where they became a powerful, even though not a political, influence wherever they settled down. Those who lived in mountainous areas built up large flocks of cattle, sheep, and horses. Others became well-to-do business men. Always firm believers in education, they established schools, "and many of their brightest young people became leaders in the professions—lawyers, doctors, teachers."

However, as in ancient Egypt, a new ruler arose in Turkey—a ruler fearful of the potential power of the industrious and capable people who now constituted the greatest portion of his domain. Accordingly, orders were soon issued for the extermination of the Armenian race whose staunch adherence to their ancient faith was a constant source of annoyance to their neighbors in the predominantly Moslem world in which they lived.

It is a long, sad story—a dark blot on the checkered history of "man's inhumanity to man." But when it was all over the Armenians as a people had been well-nigh wiped out. And around Ararat, their ancestral home, scarcely a trace of the ancient race could be found. The prosperous little Armenian towns and villages had all but disappeared. Last-ditch gun emplacements on the high slopes of Aghri Dagh still witness silently, even today, to the "painful" aspects of the mountain that witnessed the final struggle of a race that fought to the death in an effort to maintain that most basic of all man's freedoms, a conscience "devoid of offense toward God."

But there were some who miraculously survived. One of these was a small lad who, with his sister, succeeded in eluding the soldiers who came to their island home on Lake Van, in the very shadow of Aghri Dagh. They watched, trembling in fear and horror, from a hiding place, as their parents paid the supreme sacrifice in defense of the faith they loved. That night, under cover of darkness, the terrified orphans escaped to the mainland in a small boat. They eventually reached the home of their grandfather, who had also somehow escaped annihilation in the general massacres of the area, and who still lived in the village of Bayazid at the base of Aghri Dagh. Here, one day, occurred a most significant event.

Taking his grandson aside, the old man told the boy a story he was never to forget. In his youth, the grandfather confided, he had tried to climb the white-capped mountain that loomed so majestically over their heads—had tried, and failed. His strength had not been equal to the strenuous ascent. Some day, he solemnly charged the boy, he must accomplish the task that he, himself, had been unable to perform, and bring back a fragment of the Ark.

The Armenian lad grew up and sought his fortune in the outside world. But, to his bitter disappointment, he did not develop into the sturdy mountaineer of his grandfather's dream. And one day, far from his native land, he chanced to meet a young French soldier who had the qualities he himself so ardently desired.

Did we say "chanced" . . . ? For here again, if we only have the spiritual discernment to comprehend, can be witnessed a thrilling preview of the ultimate triumph of right over wrong: of the constant, unfailing watchcare of God over His own. For, even though the Armenian plains had been all but scoured of the race that had preserved the knowledge of the Ark, one special old man and one special young lad had been saved alive as instruments in God's hands to transmit this precious secret to the Western world.

A warm friendship soon developed between the two young men of such differing backgrounds and race. And one day in 1937, on a mountain climbing excursion under sunny southern skies, the Armenian confided to the Frenchman the story of his life. He related his grandfather's attempts to reach the Ark. He confessed his doubts as to his own ability to fulfill the old man's dream. The Frenchman, he suggested, was a much better mountaineer than he—perhaps he was the logical person to take his place!

The Armenian youth could not have told his story to a more receptive ear. For the young French soldier, Fernand Navarra, had been fascinated by the story of Noah and the Ark ever since his mother had told him the tale many years before. The poignant challenge of his friend's sad story appealed irresistibly to the youthful mountaineer. In his heart was born the determination to some day carry out this strange behest.

It took fifteen years of careful training before Navarra felt he was ready for his initial attempt—fifteen years of careful research, accumulation of equipment and means, all sandwiched in between pressing family and business responsibilities—but at last the Frenchman stood on the snowy slopes of Aghri Dagh and gazed down, enchanted, on what appeared to be the shadow of a great hull embedded in the ice below.

The story of Navarra's research and his three expeditions to the "Mountain of the Ark" is one of the most thrilling sagas of our time. And his eventual recovery of hand-tooled timber from a deep crevasse has set off a controversy that still rages in civilized countries around the world: did Fernand Navarra actually discover the remains of the Ark? Did the bequest from the old Armenian grandfather find its fruition on that momentous day in 1955, when the Frenchman felt his fingers close around a piece of blackened wood in the melting ice of a glacial lake . . . ?

Only Time—and continued investigation—will tell the tale.

11

"What Else Could It Be?"

Hard on the heels of Smith's unsuccessful attempt to locate the Ark, Fernand Navarra launched the first of his own three expeditions to Ararat.

In July, 1952, the Frenchman, accompanied by four friends, at last set out for the mountain of which he had dreamed for so many years. It was not until August, however, that the party arrived at its destination, confident that the excessive heat of late summer would be ideal weather to aid their cause.

They too, as so many travellers and explorers before them, were enchanted by their first glimpse of the majestic peak before which, as Navarra later wrote, "All the neighboring mountains seem to bow . . . as if to their suzerain." One feels drawn to it despite oneself, he admits, "by an indefinable, irresistible, and magnetic attraction . . . all our memories, all that we had read, came back in a flash to our minds, all the great efforts men have made to snatch from the mountain of the Flood humanity's greatest secret."

Navarra, too, encountered the same historic and superstitious resistance concerning the mountain as he sought information among the native inhabitants of the area. Friendly and helpful in every other way, when the subject of searching for the Ark arose, the shadow of a strange reticence and fear seemed to settle upon them. One of the party's first objectives was to scale the summit of the peak. When this was noised abroad, even the women muttered dolefully as they passed that the Frenchmen would never accomplish their goal—that no one had ever reached it!

Their second, and most important objective, was to explore the Ahora Valley, to penetrate as far as possible into

The Great Chasm so mutilated by the upheaval of 1840. It was Navarra's opinion that never, since the day of the legendary St. Jacob, had any human being made an investigation in this direction for the remains of the Ark.

From the old men of Bayazid, Navarra had received repeated assurances that the Ark was "indeed on the mountain," but that "it would never be found." They had also received numerous warnings about the snakes, bears, and wolves they might encounter; but at last they set out from the new village of Ahora (which had been rebuilt about a mile from the old village of Arghuri that had been destroyed in the 1840 disaster), in the direction of the peak. As the party progressed they were regaled with tales of former "pious pilgrimages" to the Ark, but were once more assured that they could never negotiate the steep cliffs ahead. "You can't go that way," warned a young shepherd, "because there's magic there." And at an elevation of 10,000 feet their native escort abandoned them with significant glances, and refused to go a step farther into the "magic" zone.

It had been Navarra's hope to discover the concealed lake under the ice cap where, according to some ancient beliefs, the Ark is said to lie "partially submerged." However, when the party reached the great, forbidding canyon wall at the upper end of the Gorge, they were forced to abandon their plans for reaching the vast ice fields from that direction.

A few days later, having completed their investigation of the Ahora Gorge and the mountain from Bayazid to the north face, an aged man approached them as they sat sipping lemonade in an Igdir cafe. Navarra describes the moment in his book, *The Forbidden Mountain:* ". . . there, coming up to us, was a tall old man, very thin, with an emaciated face, and deep and sombre eyes. He was Akki Usta, 'the historian of the village,' we were told, he to whom the ancients had transmitted by word of mouth their legends. 'He knows everything there is to know about Ararat,' they told us. We invited him to our table. He would only accept a cup of tea. Once more Demir acted as interpreter for us. The old man spoke slowly, deliberately, and his grave voice resounded in our ears like the muezzin of the mosque at Urgup in the evening. Prophets should always speak in such tones. Sometimes he seemed to be reciting verses from the Koran. And we listened to him, our chins in our hands, our eyes turned toward the Holy Mountain. Thus on August 11th, 1952, Akki Usta, the historian of Igdir, spoke to us:

" 'Young men of France, you have come to explore Noah's mountain, and you think to find the Ark there. Well, this is what I have to say to you:

" 'You know the legend, the beautiful legend of the vessel which God the Father brought to land on Ararat with its cargo of men and animals. And it was as a result of that loving kindness of God that the Earth was repeopled after the Flood had satisfied His wrath. While Noah, his family and the animals were able to descend from Ararat and to go in the direction of Ahora and Erivan, the Ark stayed on the mountain. You know that.

" 'And now listen to what I am going to say. The Ark is still there! This I was told by the greybeards, and they were told it equally by those who were old during their youth. And all of us here believe it. All the people of Igdir, of Bayazid, of Erivan, to the last shepherd on the twin mountains, all believe it. And we shall hand on that belief to our children, with the bounden duty of passing it on to their descendants.'

"What are your grounds for stating this with so much conviction?" we asked him.

" 'Are there not enough signs? Do you believe that the monasteries of Ahora, of Koran and of Etchmaidzin could have arisen if these historic facts were not true? Know ye that to reach it (the Ark) one must be as pure as a newborn child. . . .'

"We gazed at each other with questioning eyes, and Akki Usta looked back at us enigmatically.

"It must be confessed that at that moment we each emptied our glass of lemonade as if on a word of command.

"He went on straightway: 'Have you noticed that those monasteries were built half way up the mountain? We think that shows wise planning, since that is the zone of pastureland where it is possible to cultivate the soil.

" 'Yes, indeed, because beyond the pastureland which God created so that our people could survive in the deserts of Ararat, none can venture without infringing the Law.

The Ark cannot be submitted to the outrage and sacrilege of the eyes of men.' "

But, in spite of the gloomy prognostications of the village folk, and the solemn warnings of the aged man, a wiry old shepherd finally agreed to lead the way. Up, up the mountain they climbed, not following any of the regular trails. Up, up the grassy slopes of the north side they ascended, zigzagging through ravines, valleys, around escarpments—a "hellish route," as Navarra described it later. Their destination was Kop, a gem of a little mountain lake on the northwest side. Was it here that Roskovitsky had sighted the Ark partially submerged in the melting waters of a frozen lake?

But there was no sign of the Ark at Kop. . . .

Onward, upward they climbed, until at 13,500 feet they were confronted by a formidable glacier wall. Here they were again abandoned by both their Turkish friend and their lightly-clad 75-year-old native guide.

Up, up, they continued, only one ice ax between them, scrambling over a deadly conglomeration of rocks of various colors and types, narrowly escaping death when an especially treacherous rock gave way under their feet just as they got a precarious hold on the cliff above.

But at last they set foot on firmer ground, and came out on a great gravelly platform of moraine they had glimpsed from the Ahora Gorge a few days before. Here they stood gasping for breath, not only from their exertions, but from sheer astonishment over the vista that unfolded below them. There was a deep ravine to their right, the beginning of a glacier to their left. There were bands of scree and ice blocking the valley below, the enormous and dazzling ice cap of Aghri Dagh above. They overlooked the Great Chasm of the Ahora Gorge; but here, in this wilderness of ice and snow, as Navarra was to write later, there was still no sign of the Ark.

As the weary and disappointed explorers turned to retrace their steps, the dull rumbling of an avalanche shook the mountain under their feet. As the reverberations of this terrifying experience died away, four bears emerged from behind a glacier not more than a hundred yards away and started toward the unarmed men. Bears! They had been warned that they might run into bears, and now here they stood, on the edge of the Ahora Gorge, with only an ice ax between them for defense! Navarra whacked on the ice with the ax; his companion tried to frighten the huge creatures by whistling through half-frozen lips. Yet on they came. The Frenchmen were lost! There was no way of escape. But suddenly the bears' attention was diverted in another direction and they ambled off down the slopes.

But now the dream, the hope of finding the Ark, surged over them again. Temporarily submerged in disappointment over not seeing visible signs of the Ark, nor in finding a lake in this icy expanse, they had been almost ready to abandon their quest. They recalled the legendary story of the angel who had guided St. Jacob to the Ark, and wished fervently that they might have his help.

The explorers glanced at the western sky, advancing slowly over the ice. It was only two o'clock in the afternoon. The sun was shining down upon the mountain at a 45-degree angle. They were alone, except for an eagle and the wind, which bore the fearless bird in regular circles against the sky.

They advance a few more steps, over ice that is transparent and deep. Suddenly they glance once more at the sky. Has one of Ararat's sudden storms dropped this dark shadow across their path? But no, the sun still shines, the eagle still floats aimlessly over their heads. They look again, more intently this time, and see an "astonishing patch of blackness within the ice, its outlines sharply defined."

"Fascinated and intrigued," as Navarra was to write later in his book, "we began straightway to trace out its shape, mapping out its limit foot by foot: two progressively incurving lines were revealed which were clearly defined for a distance of three hundred cubits before meeting in the heart of the glacier. The shape was unmistakably that of a ship's hull: on either side the edges of the patch curved like the gunwales of a great boat. As for the central part, it merged into a black mass the details of which were not discernible.

"Conviction burned in our eyes: no more than a few yards separated us from the extraordinary discovery which the world no longer believed possible. We had just found the Ark."

In his second book, *J'ai Trouve l'Arche de Noe* (I

Found Noah's Ark), Navarra gives more detailed descriptions of his emotions as he looked down upon the shadow in the ice: "I have never been subject to visions; I am perfectly clear-headed, and I can call upon a faculty not possessed by crazy people: good sense.

"At this altitude, in this wilderness of ice, what could it be? The ruins of a structure, a church, a refuge, or house . . .? The wreck of a plane? Even in the greatest periods of aviation beams of this size would never be used for an air frame. The evidence must be acknowledged: the remains are those of the Ark, if only because it cannot be anything else."

Unfortunately, Navarra had not realized the possibility of finding the object of his quest in the bottom of a deep crevasse. He had brought no equipment to descend into the spot where constantly falling rocks increased the hazards of further investigation. Marking as carefully as possible in his mind the landmarks by which he could relocate the discovery, Navarra turned reluctantly away, swearing that he would return. "The Ark is really here," he marvelled to himself, "but inaccessible."

A year later Navarra was back. Once again, in the same spot, he saw the outline of what appeared to be a great ship embedded in the ice. This time, a sudden and overpowering illness forced him and his companion to abandon their plans and return to camp. It was two years before he found himself on the mountain again.

On his third trip to Ararat, Navarra brought his 11-year-old son, Raphael, to share in what he hoped would be the culmination of his dream of many years; the great experience that had haunted him ever since his first glimpse of the dark shadow under the ice.

Imagine the excitement of the plucky 11-year-old lad as he stumbled eagerly in his father's footsteps over the grueling route about which he had heard so much before! Perhaps he would hear the avalanche! Perhaps they might even get to see the bears . . . ! But, most thrilling of all, he looked forward to seeing the boat-shaped object under the ice. This time his father had come well-equipped to descend into the crevasse. And this time—what a story they would have to tell when they got back to France . . . !

On this third expedition, however, nothing at first looked

the same. The glacier which had been Navarra's landmark had melted back to some degree, and it took him a few minutes to orient himself and locate the spot where he had been two years before. Painstakingly, with infinite care, father and son wormed and worked their way up and across a tremendous mountain of ice until at last they had reached the crucial spot.

It was Raphael who saw it first. Crawling on the end of a rope over the brittle, fragile ice to the edge of the sheer dropoff, the excited youngster peered over, then announced, very simply, "Yes, the boat is here, Papa. I can see it very well."

This time Navarra was able to reach the bottom of the deep crevasse. But it was Raphael who urged him on in the end. For Navarra, sweeping away the layers of newly fallen snow to reach the dark mass he had seen in the ice, was suddenly seized with an overpowering conviction that all his bright hopes of uncovering the Ark had been a mirage —this close to the dark mass it appeared to be only ice and moraine.

Raphael, boyishly cheering his father on from a safer vantage point at the top of the crevasse, merely shouted for him to "dig." So Navarra, to please the boy, attacked the heavy crust with his ice ax; and at 7:00 a.m., on July 7, 1955, he burst through the ice and was rewarded for his efforts as he felt his fingers closing around a piece of hand-tooled timber under the frigid waters of the slowly melting glacier.

The ruins of a structure? a church? a refuge? a house . . .? The wreck of a plane? Whatever it would prove to be, Navarra sincerely believed he had found the Ark. It was a thrilling and triumphant moment—a monument to the Frenchman's tenacity and faith, coupled with gratitude for the encouragement of his son. For even as personal satisfaction flooded his soul, the words of a wise old story teller echoed through his mind: ". . . to reach the Ark, one must be as pure as a child—!"

Eryl Cummings' first inkling of Navarra's work came on Easter Sunday, 1958, when an article entitled "I Found Noah's Ark" appeared in the *American Weekly*. It was with great surprise and joy that he learned of a fellow-researcher in France who had followed much the same lines of investigation, and, in addition had actually succeeded in climbing the mountain and in claiming discovery of the Ark.

No time was lost in contacting the French explorer, who immediately indicated his deep desire to go on another expedition to Ararat to bring back enough wood, as he put it, "to reconstitute . . . at least a part of the Ark in order to convince the unbelievers." In a short time an autographed copy of Navarra's French book, *J'ai Trouve l' Arche de Noe* (I found Noah's Ark), arrived in the mail, together with a small sample of the timber he had retrieved from the bottom of the 80-foot crevasse.

There are Doubting Thomases, of course, who question the authenticity of Navarra's discovery. But it is difficult to discount the sincerity of a man who has returned to the site again and again with exploratory or scientific parties to assist in a gigantic effort to verify and excavate his find.

Admittedly, there appear to be discrepancies between Navarra's discovery and the descriptions of the structure reported by other discoverers through the years—a structure that boasts several stories, a great door in one side, and cage-like rooms. A giant prow extending from a glacier is also mentioned, and it appears to have been broken "a good deal in its descent"—to quote the Turkish commissioners of 1883. (A "descent" from where . . . ? Unfortunately the news releases of the time did not elaborate on this tantalizing thought!)

However, Navarra does not claim to have found the superstructure of the Ark (which he apparently believed was destroyed many centuries ago). In defense of his position, we quote again from his book, *The Forbidden Mountain:* "The evidence must be acknowledged: the remains are those of the Ark, if only because it cannot be anything else. According to all probability, these are the remains of the flat bottom of the Biblical vessel, whose upper parts have been dispersed. Does not Berosus, the Chaldean historian, tell us that in his time the inhabitants of the region around Ararat tore the Ark apart in order to get pieces of the wood and the bituminous covering? The beams which they spared are still there, intact throughout the ages, protected by nature. . . ."

How to reconcile these varying reports is puzzling, until

one remembers that Josephus, in his *Antiquities of the Jews,* makes the apparently discrepant statement that God instructed Noah to "make an ark of four stories high." The Mosaic account, of course, specifies only three. Might his extra "story" be the "flat bottom of the Biblical vessel" that Navarra believes he found—a barge-like foundation on which the ark itself was built and on which it would float . . . ?

In a letter dated January 29, 1960, from Bordeaux, France, Navarra states that Reshit's discovery in 1948 was close to the same location in which he had found his wood. He also stated that the timber he had brought back to France and later submitted to a Carbon-14 test, places the age of the structure he had found at 4,489 years. "Of that," he wrote, "there is no doubt."

During the years since 1955, this controversial specimen of wood has been the subject of much skeptical discussion in scientific circles across the land. So dark in color as to appear almost black; so deceptively light as to weight; so hard of texture that it dulls and even breaks the blades of any ordinary saw, Navarra's wood is still a conundrum that has never been solved. One analysis identifies it as oak. How can it have come from the Ark, ask the critics, when Noah was commanded to use timber of "gopher wood"?

It may be helpful at this point to ponder the definition for "gopher wood" as given in Strong's *Exhaustive Concordance of the Bible:* that the word "gopher" comes from "an unused root, probably meaning to house in" or "a kind of tree or wood (as used for building) apparently the cypress." Thus it appears that there may legitimately be a choice of a definition as to the original meaning of the word "gopher." Another point to ponder in this connection is the thought that perhaps parts of the interior were made of various other kinds of wood—for storage or partititions, for example—and that what Navarra found were these discarded timbers that had been left on the ground beside the ship.

In spite of the many tantalizing, even baffling questions that arise, the fact remains that Navarra's motivation and information came largely and almost first-hand, from one of a race that had lived for uncounted centuries in the environs of Aghri Dagh, and knew its history the best—a race that still believes implicitly that the great ship-like structure reported to be concealed on Ararat's forbidding heights is truly Noah's Ark.

12

The Atheists
and the Ark

The story about to be related has been bursting at its seams ever since it was first mentioned in Chapter 1. In sequence of time and importance, it should rightfully have headed all the other stories in this book. But then, if the truth had been disclosed at the time this event took place, there doubtless would never have been any stories of expeditions or research to record—for the existence of the Ark would have been verified, and either pious or curious pilgrimages to see the great ship would no doubt have converged on Mount Ararat from all over the world. In fact, one might even go so far as to conjecture that the religious history of the entire civilized world would have been altered, and that the conflict between Creationism and the evolutionary theory would have been over before it had fairly begun! Unfortunately, because this is not the way it happened, the end of the story is not yet . . . even though it had its beginnings long ago in the middle of the 19th century.

This amazing story fell across the trail in a most unusual and unexpected way. A gentleman tapped Eryl Cummings on the shoulder following a church service in Tucson, Arizona, sometime in the early spring of 1952. This gentleman proved to be Roy Kinzer, a favorite professor from high school days. After the usual pleasantries and reminiscences had been exchanged, the former teacher inquired about his erstwhile pupil's present line of work.

"Among other things," replied Cummings, "I've been doing research on Noah's Ark. . . ."

"Noah's Ark!" echoed Kinzer. "Why, you should have been in our church last week. The pastor talked about that very subject! Why don't you come over this afternoon and I'll tell you all about it."

The astonishing story was soon gladly verified by Harold H. Williams, at that time pastor of the Logansport, Indiana, Seventh-day Adventist church. In a letter addressed "To Whom It May Concern," Eryl Cummings first learned of what is probably the earliest known discovery of Noah's Ark in the modern era; and, significantly, as with Fernand Navarra in France, the knowledge was to come through a member of the Armenian race. Subsequent investigation would reveal that this historic event took place sometime close to the year 1856.

"In the year of 1915," so the story began, "Mrs. Williams and I were living at Pacific Union College where I was taking special classes at the College. We were operating a private nursing home. My parents were living on Telegraph Avenue, in Oakland, California.

"One day while visiting my parents, a young man was sent by Elder B. E. Beddoe, pastor of the Oakland Seventh-day Adventist church, with a request that I go at once to see an old man who had not been to church for some time. They were afraid that he might be ill.

"This man's name was Yearam in Armenian, which is Jeremiah in English. When he was a young man he had made a pilgrimage to Jerusalem from Armenia, thus gaining the title of Haji, so was ever afterward known as Haji Yearam, or Jeremiah the Pilgrim.

"I found Haji nearly dead with bloody dysentery in the attic of his house. He was so nearly dead that I could not move him for several days, so had to doctor and nurse him where he was. As soon as he was sufficiently recovered, I removed him to the home of my parents, and thence to my own home, where Mrs. Williams and I cared for him for many months, free of charge, because we supposed him to be a pauper.

"Haji was one of the most earnest and consecrated Seventh-day Adventist Christians I have ever known. He was the first foreign convert of our first foreign missionary, J. N. Andrews. I have forgotten the place and circumstances of their meeting, but after his conversion Haji Yearam

112

came to the States and worked in the old Battle Creek (Michigan) Sanitarium. He had formerly been a merchant in the city of Constantinople. Three different times Haji built up fortunes in business in the United States and planned to return to the Old Country, but each time was robbed of everything he had before reaching his destination. For the fourth time, there in Oakland, California, he was working through a real estate and antique business to build up a fortune for his old age. He was then about seventy-four years old and was growing blind, having cataracts.

"In May, 1916, Mrs. Williams and I moved to South Lancaster, Massachusetts, where I had been hired by Prof. Machlan as a member of the faculty. Haji Yearam was by this time almost totally blind, so we took him to the home of my parents in Oakland where he lived until he died. It was finally discovered that he owned considerable property. He willed one home to my mother in return for his care until he died.

"One day while living with us at Pacific Union College, Haji asked me to get a composition book and write down carefully a story he was very anxious to tell, because he was sure that it would be of use some day after he was dead and gone.

"Here is the story as accurately as I can now give it from memory, checked by the memory of Mrs. Williams who also heard it.

NOAH'S ARK

"Haji Yearam's parents and family lived at the foot of Greater Mount Ararat in Armenia. According to their traditions, they were descended directly from those who had come out of the Ark, but who had never migrated from that country. The descendants of Ham and his sympathizers had migrated over into the land of Shinar and built the tower of Babel, and others had migrated to various countries, but Haji's forebears had always remained near the mount where the ark came to rest in a little valley surrounded by some small peaks about three-quarters or more up on the mountain.

"For several hundreds of years after the flood his forebears had made yearly pilgrimages up to the ark to make sacrifices and to worship there. They had a good trail and

113

steps in the steep places. Finally the enemies of God undertook to go to Ararat and destroy the ark, but as they neared the location there came a terrible storm that washed away the trail, and lightning blasted the rocks. From that time on, even the pilgrimages ceased, because they feared to betray the way to the ungodly, and they feared God's wrath. They took that terrible storm to be a token that God did not want the ark disturbed until near the end of the world, when they believed that its presence would be revealed to the whole world. However, the tribesmen there handed down the legends from generation to generation, and from time to-time lonely shepherds or hunters in very hot summers came back with stories that they had reached the little valley and had actually seen one end of the ark where it had been made visible by the melting snow and ice.

"When Haji was a large boy, but not yet a man fully grown, there came to his home some strangers. If I remember correctly there were three vile men who did not believe the Bible and did not believe in the existence of a personal God. They were scientists and evolutionists. They were on this expedition specifically to prove the legend of Noah's Ark to be a fraud and a fake. They hired the father of young Haji Yearam as their official guide. (Haji at that time had not yet become a Haji, and was just a large boy.) They hired the boy to assist his father as guide.

"It was an unusually hot summer, so the snow and glaciers had melted more than usual. The Armenians were very reticent to undertake any expedition to the Ark because they feared God's displeasure, but the father of Haji thought that possibly the time had come when God wanted the world to know the ark was still there and he wanted to prove to those atheists that the Bible story of the flood and the Ark is true.

"After extreme hardship and peril the party came to the little valley way up on Greater Ararat, not on the very top but a little down from the top. This little valley is surrounded by a number of small peaks. There the ark came to rest in a little lake, and the peaks protected it from the tidal waves that rushed back and forth as the flood subsided. On one side of the valley the water from the melting snows and glacier spills over in a little river that runs down the mountain. As they reached this spot, there they found the prow of a mighty ship protruding out of the ice. They went inside the ark and did considerable exploring. The whole structure was covered with a varnish or lacquer that was very thick and strong, both outside and inside the ship. The ship was built more like a great and mighty house on the hull of a ship, but without any windows. There was a great doorway of immense size, but the door was missing. The scientists were appalled and dumbfounded and went into a Satanic rage at finding what they hoped to prove nonexistent. They were so angry and mad that they said they would destroy the ship, but the wood was more like stone than any wood we have now. They did not have tools or means to wreck so mighty a ship and had to give up. They did tear out some timbers and tried to burn the wood, but it was so hard it was almost impossible to burn it.

"They held a council, and then took a solemn and fearful death oath. Any man present who would ever breathe a word about what they had found would be tortured and murdered.

"They told their guide and his son that they would keep tabs on them and that if they ever told anyone and they found it out they would surely be tortured and murdered. For fear of their lives, Haji and his father had never told what they found except to their best trusted and closest relatives.

"In the year 1918 we moved to Brockton, Massachusetts, where I took the position of Supervisor of Manual Arts in the High School of that city. I was soon put on permanent tenure by the State Board of Education and held that position for nearly eight years until I entered the gospel ministry.

"Now, if some atheistic scientist had found an elephant's knee cap that looked something like a skull bone, they would have proclaimed it a missing link and it would have been printed in large letters across the top of the daily newspapers, but any news that would support the Bible is largely ignored.

"One evening (I am pretty sure it was in 1918) I sat reading the daily paper in our apartment in Brockton. Suddenly I saw in very small print a short story of a dying man's confession. It was a news item one column wide and, as I remembered it, not more than two inches deep. It stated that an elderly scientist on his death bed in London was afraid to die before making a terrible confession. It gave briefly the very date and facts that Haji Yearam had related to us in his story. I got out the composition book containing the story he had me write. It was identical in every detail. Haji Yearam had died in my parent's home in Oakland, California, about the same time that the old scientist had died in London. We had never for one moment doubted Haji's story, but when this scientist on his death bed on the other side of the world confessed the same story in every detail, we knew positively that the story was true in every detail.

"I kept the sheet of that newspaper in the composition book with Haji's story for many years. In 1940 the school and sanitarium that Mrs. Williams and I had worked hard for nine years to build up in Louisiana was destroyed by fire in twenty minutes by a butane explosion. Everything we owned in the world was burned up, and my son Nathan and I were nearly burned to death. The composition book containing Haji's story and the newspaper sheet containing the atheistic scientist's confession on his death bed were burned up in that fire along with all that we owned on earth.

"It is with deep regret that I am unable to submit these two testimonials as they were originally written. All I can offer is the vivid memory of the story as it was told to Mrs. Williams and myself as I wrote it down, and the identical story as printed in the paper. At that time there were two daily papers in Brockton. I do not remember whether it was one of these or a Boston paper in which we found the story, as I used to buy first one and then another. But this I feel sure of—Noah's Ark is still on Mount Ararat, and when it pleases God, some expedition will give the news and facts to the world so that skeptics will have no excuse.

Sincerely and in haste,
(Signed) Harold N. Williams"

This simply written and obviously sincere story gave new impetus to the research that had been slowed almost to a standstill for some time past. It was one of those periods of time when it seemed that the trail had disappeared underground like a desert stream. The A. J. Smith expedition had failed, and Fernand Navarra's work, although in progress, had not yet come to light. Now here was an exciting new clue on which to work. . . .

Harold William's own deep interest and willingness to help is reflected in his reply to a query of July 10, 1958: "Yes, indeed—you are welcome to use the story I sent you regarding Haji Yearam. . . ." And consistently, through the years, Harold Williams continued to reinforce Haji's story with additional details as requested or as they came to mind, never deviating from his original account. On June 18, 1960, he wrote, "I regret so very much that Haji Yearam's story was burned in our fire . . . If we only had that story now we would know where Haji lived as a young man and would know where to start to ascend the mountain to the Ark in the glacier. We would at least have a starting point. Haji's father might have guided them in many devious ways to reach the spot as is often required in mountain climbing, but it would be a starting point. . . . We also know that the Ark rather resembled a house built upon a tremendously strong boat bottom, not like our stream-lined pleasure ships."

During the same year Harold Williams had also written: "He (Haji) knew he was soon to die, and he wanted his story preserved so that when the right time came it might encourage brave men to go and locate the Ark and give to the world such proof as could not be denied.

". . . certain facts stand out so strongly that I have no hesitancy at all in what I have given you previously: Haji was born about 1840 because he was 75 years old when he had me write the story in 1915-16. He was a lad of about 15 years of age or a little less when they made the expedition. My memory and impression says between 13 and 15, so they made the expedition about 1853 or 1854. . . .

"Haji lived with us and with my parents for several years before he died in my parents' home. His word was absolutely reliable. He would have no reason to concoct the story. . . . Evidently Haji's father had previously seen the Ark or knew from others exactly where to find it because he took the scientists directly to it—BUT IT WAS A VERY EXHAUSTING AND PERILOUS EXPEDITION, high up on the mountain.

"The scientists were so enraged . . . they tried to burn it

. . . and 'chop it,' but it was so mammoth in size that they could not have destroyed it anyhow. . . . The great door was removed from the ark and was lying up on rocks forming a sort of roof under which was an ancient altar and smoke from the altar was on the rocks and underside of the great door. . . . It is my strong impression from memory that Haji believed that Ararat is about 16,000 feet high, but I know that he said it (the Ark) rests in a glacier and that only in a very hot summer could its prow be seen protruding from the melting end of the glacier where it feeds a stream that flows down the mountain. . . .

"Of recent years Noah's Ark and Mount Ararat have become live subjects of interest. One expedition went to Ararat last year. I read that a French expedition is about to try it. I have also been informed that an American expedition is now contemplated.

"Keeping my promise to old Haji Yearam, I am now giving and have already given the story to certain men who are trying to organize an American expedition to explore Ararat . . . old Haji was so very concerned over it and so anxious that his information be given when needed to give men courage, I am fulfilling my promise to the grand old man whom I rescued from a lonely death thinking him a pauper when he was not. . . ."

In answer to a query as to the old Armenian's physical appearance, Harold Williams' description of his old friend almost brought him "alive": "Haji was not a large man, perhaps 5 feet seven inches in height, and only weighing about 150 pounds when well. But he was broadshouldered and muscular, with typical Armenian features and gestures, and straight, fine hair. Although grave, earnest and sincere, his brilliantly smiling eyes lent animation to his features. He was deeply religious, but never fanatical, and because of his many excellent qualities, soon became a beloved member of the Williams family."

The search for additional corroborating clues to Haji's mysterious expedition and the deathbed confession was destined to lead far afield and to cover years of time.

Insofar as the expedition is concerned, the disillusioned atheists covered their trail well, and it seems that no official record of the journey was ever made. There is some reason to believe that they may have been men of considerable stature in scientific circles in their native land, and admission of their unexpected discovery to their atheistic colleagues would indeed have caused them embarrassment and distress; at any rate, nothing that can actually be authenticated has been found.

There are nebulous clues, of course. During the period around 1856 there were evidently several expeditions to Ararat about which nothing definite is known. Perhaps the atheists' expedition was one of these. As Bryce put it, in his address before the Royal Geographical Society in 1878, after carefully enumerating all climbers or expeditions known to have made the ascent to that time: "For aught we know, it *may* have been ascended *once or twice besides,* but there does not seem to be any *accurate record* of the different ascents in existence." (Emphasis supplied.)

Hermann Abich, too, the noted geologist and authority on Ararat and Caucasian affairs, seems to be confused about that period of time. "In the beginning of 1853," he says, "I left the Caucasus for five years. On my return I heard of some ascents of Ararat in the interval. Major Stuart's may have been one of these." We know, of course, that the Stuart party does not fit Haji's description of the atheists, since they all believed they were treading on the hallowed ground of the Biblical account.

In a letter dated May 23, 1958, Fernand Navarra mentioned receiving a call "from a Frenchman whose grandfather had participated in an expedition in Ararat under Napoleon III and had brought back a piece of wood given to him as a gift from the natives." This must have been sometime between the years 1852-70.

To a Danby Seymour is attributed another ascent in 1856 with a party of Englishmen. Also, a Henry Danby Seymour is given credit by Abich for an ascent in 1845, although Seymour's obituary places the date in September of 1846, and states that the account of the feat was not published when it took place, and that "his name is seldom or ever included in the list of successful climbers of the mountain."

Regarding the ascent, Abich quotes Seymour's somewhat evasive account: "I cannot lay my hands on my notes now. My companions were two Armenians and a Cossack officer. I remember that we slept in a woody dell before commencing the ascent in charge of a Cossack guard. (It will be remembered that Ararat was in Russian territory in 1856: author.) We could obtain no porters, and one of the Armenians who served as guide refused to come because he had no boots. I had to give him my own boots and wear some Persian slippers. . . ."

This particular Seymour who, according to his obituary, held "advanced Liberal Opinions," and served for many years as a valued member of the "Council Board of the Royal Geographical Society," appears also to be the same individual identified elsewhere as simply "Danby Seymour." He was also a brother-in-law of the noted Assyriologist, Sir Henry Rawlinson, who corroborated the 1846 ascent during the discussion of James Bryce's address before the Royal Geographical Society in 1878. Whether Seymour actually made two ascents, or if there is merely a discrepancy in dates, is not known.

There is also no known connection between Seymour's ascent in 1856 and the atheists' expedition believed to have taken place about the same time. However, it is not difficult to believe that the scientists, in harmony with their "death oath" never to reveal the truth of what they had seen, must have widely disseminated a false account upon their return.

For thirty years later, Rawlinson was still so indoctrinated with the opinion that Ararat could not possibly be the "biblical mountain" that he publicly challenged Bryce before the entire distinguished body of Royal Geographical Society members: "Anyone who had really gone into the question," he scoffed, "could not doubt that the popular notion (of Ararat and the Ark) was a fallacy." The skepticism of the President of the Society is also reflected in his remark before Bryce had even begun his speech, that he was "afraid that Mr. Bryce had not brought back any authentic relic of the Ark."

Was this generally prevalent tendency to skepticism about the Biblical account of the Deluge and the Ark, so rampant in the England of that day, one reason why Bryce pounced so "gleefully" upon the piece of handtooled timber as he climbed the famous peak—because it was at least a "straw in the wind" indicating that the atheistic ex-

120

pedition had falsified or concealed the true facts in its reports?

Was this one reason why the pious Bryce had gone to such pains to research the subject before ever attempting the climb? Was his hope to find some evidence of the Ark what he had in mind when, just before they were ready to begin the ascent, he "sat down to write a few lines home, wondering what the next few lines would have to report"?

A "report" to whom? And about what . . . ?

Similar frustrations arose in trying to run down the elusive "deathbed confession." Twenty years had elapsed between the time the article had appeared and been filed away in the Harold Williams' cherished family documents. There it had lain, undisturbed, until the disastrous day of the fire. And dates, even for the most intimate family affairs, have a maddening way of "fuzzing up" after a few years unless they have been written down and preserved in black and white. And once they have been destroyed it is almost impossible to call them back after the passage of a number of years.

The search for corroborating facts on both the atheists' expedition and the newspaper story ranged far and wide: The American Weekly, The New York Public Library, The Hammond Star, the Central Press Association, The Boston Globe, the Times Picayune Publishing Corporation—all these and many more. The files bulge with fruitless queries for the all-important item. Even the London Alpine Club and the Royal Geographic Society responded with precious original copies of documents published at that far-off date. These, of course, furnished much additional and fascinating information which has added immeasurably to the interest of this book. But nothing—absolutely nothing—of documentary value regarding the identity or date of the atheists or their ungodly expedition; and nothing about the "deathbed confession" of the aged scientist in London!

In an effort to locate Haji's birthplace and thus to learn the place from which they had started up the mountain to show the atheists the Ark, his death certificate was discovered through the Bureau of Vital Statistics in Oakland, California. This interesting document revealed that Haji Yearam, an Armenian born in Turkey, had died of arteriosclerosis on May 3, 1920, that he had never married; that

121

he had been buried in the Sunset View cemetery by the Tufft and Co. undertakers on May 6; and that the individual supplying these facts was Ettie Williams, with whom Haji had made his home for "4 years and 6 months"; also that he had died at the ripe old age of 82 years.

Although Mrs. Williams had not been able to supply the birthplace of her aged charge, the document did establish the fact that Haji had been born in 1838—just two years before the 1840 catastrophe. This, of course, would have made him a couple of years older than Harold Williams remembered him, and a lad in his mid-teens ("a large boy, not yet fully grown") around 1856.

Harold Williams, as always, did everything possible to help. Regarding the "confession," he wrote on January 16, 1961: " 'Noah's Ark' caught my eye, or I would not have read what I did. It was one of those 'fill-in' sketches editors put in to fill up a column. It was only one column wide and my impression is that it was only one or two inches in length and at the bottom of the page. I am also not positive —but I believe it was on the front page. I attached the sheet to Haji's story in the composition book and kept it with many other stories and news items relative to the subject in a package until all we possessed was destroyed by explosion and fire in 1940."

Rachel Cartland, of the Brockton Public Library in Brockton, Massachusetts, was also very helpful. On December 13, 1962, she wrote: "The day before your letter was received someone came to the Library to do research on this same matter and . . . spent two days searching the Brockton Enterprise and the Brockton Times. . . . This person did not locate it but one of our reference librarians is going to continue the search. This librarian seems quite certain that she has seen this item in the Brockton papers at some time and that she will be able to locate it." Alas! it is apparent that she did not succeed. . . .

Adding both zest and frustration to the search, other reports of the same story trickled in from time to time. It appeared that the "confession" had been published in various newspapers and feature magazines across the land. The story had been remembered very well, but the exact date— well, that was what seemed impossible to track down! Since the article was of the "filler" type, the task of tracing it was doubly hard.

Dr. Lawrence B. Hewitt, a physician in Huntsville, Alabama, was one of the individuals who remembered the story well. He had been a teen-age boy, he recalled, and his vivid memory even recalled the location in the newspaper he had read. It had been only a small item, as Harold Williams had said, about two columns wide and two or three inches deep. It was below the center of the page, toward the lower left-hand side on either the second or fourth page. It had appeared in a Thursday edition, he was sure, of either the *New Orleans State-Item*, or the newspaper known as the *Hammond Vindicator* during those years. The boy's attention had been arrested by the boldface headline, "Scientist Makes Deathbed Confession," and it made an indelible impression on his mind.

It was easy to remember the details of the story, but pinpointing the date for research purposes was more difficult to do. It had to be no earlier than 1918—the newspapers were still concerned with the immediate aftermath of World War I. The doctor remembers his boyish wonderment that such an unimportant story as a deathbed confession away off in London should take up space in a newspaper that should have been devoted to more current topics! The article could not have appeared later than the early 1920's, since Harold Williams had discovered it at about the time of, or shortly after, Haji's death, which had occurred on May 3, 1920.

To complicate the matter still more, it was well-nigh impossible to trace the story to its London source, since a filler-type human interest feature may be picked up for reprint many months after its original release, although much time, money, and effort has been spent on this angle of the search. Inquiries to the two southern newspapers also netted no return. The busy doctor, as time permitted, also participated in the search.

It was not until the spring of 1967 that the opportunity finally came for Eryl Cummings to make a personal visit to the south. And in the office of the erstwhile *Hammond Vindicator* where inquiry was made for the long-sought "confession," a more-than-passing-strange tale unfolded. The publisher, a very gracious southern lady, regretfully related how, on a certain Sunday morning some years before, an overly-ambitious janitor had surveyed with distaste the stacks of old newspaper files in the storeroom of the plant.

"Now why do you suppose they've kept all these newspapers so many years," he mused. "I think I'll surprise them and clean this room all out. . . ."

So—armload after armload of irreplaceable old newspapers saved over a period of many years were carried out and consigned to the flames!

"Everything was burned," concluded the woman with a commiserating smile. "But there's one other place I might suggest. . . ."

With soaring hopes and a borrowed car, Eryl Cummings sped down the highway to Baton Rouge. Yes, there were a few old copies of that particular newspaper in the files, the university librarian thought. She would be glad to check it out. But when she returned to her desk, the "few" copies she thought were available had been reduced to only one . . . !

Eagerly (for the date on the ancient masthead appeared to be about right) the newspaper was unfolded and scanned for clues. And suddenly the soaring hopes crashed, head-on, into another of those frustrating walls of temporary disappointment and apparent defeat. For there, on the second page, toward the lower left-hand side, below the center of the page (just as the doctor had described!) appeared a mocking void just two columns wide by two or three inches deep! It was only too evident that some unidentifiable person—at some unknown time in the past—had found this missing item of news so irresistibly intriguing or important that he (or she) had clipped it from the page.

Could this have been the missing "deathbed confession"? Perhaps we shall never know for sure. And yet the hope persists that perhaps—just perhaps—(if this was, indeed, the long-sought sequel to Haji's story) it may still be discovered carefully preserved between the pages of an old Bible, possibly marking the chapters about Noah, the Deluge and the Ark. Or, perchance, someone leafing idly through the tattered, fragile pages of a yellowed old scrapbook may yet come across the story of a last-minute confession that should have taken place many years before!

It was a rule of Hebrew jurisprudence that "at the mouth of two witnesses, or at the mouth of three witnesses, shall the matter be established" (Deuteronomy 19:15).

May we not also apply this ancient rule to the well-attested stories of two old men, who with an ocean and a continent between, and each believing himself to be the sole surviving witness of a dastardly hoax, told identical stories to set the record straight before they died . . . ?

13

The Mystery of
the "Phantom" Ship

For a number of years the subject of Noah and the Ark lay more or less dormant or almost forgotten in the public mind. Even the research had been partially superseded by the hurry and press of more mundane affairs. Then, suddenly, with an exciting Associated Press announcement of a possible new discovery, the entire subject zoomed into prominence again.

On November 10, 1959, the Albuquerque (New Mexico) *Journal* published an aerial photograph taken for the Turkish Geodetic Survey, in which a clearly outlined object remarkably resembling a ship in both dimensions and shape, lay revealed. The picture had been taken by one Sevket Kurtis, a Turkish student then enrolled in the Institute of Geodesy at the Ohio State University in Columbus, so the article said.

The story appeared almost simultaneously in various publications across the land. The following article is a translation from the German as it appeared in the *Staats Zeitung und Herald*, published in Woodside, New Jersey, on November 15, 1959:

"Stereo-Airphotos at Mount Ararat Show
Petrified Boat in a Field of Lava, Possibly
Noah's Ark of the Bible

"Columbus, Ohio, 14. Nov. (AP)—If Noah's ark is really at Mount Ararat in Turkey, then there is a discovery from a young Turk who is living in Columbus, Ohio. Sevket Kurtis has filtered sterographic airphotos in Turkey, from which maps can be produced, and he has made a curious discovery.

"Even if it is not Noah's ark, discovery will be something quite extraordinary.

"The 'discovery' has not yet been verified. However, Kurtis assumes that the curious form of the discovered object could be the Ark of Noah, which is described in the Bible and the Koran.

"Discovered with Stereoplanograph

"The airphotos were taken a year ago on behalf of the Geodetic Institute of Turkey. But the curious object was just recently discovered in one of the photos. The 'ark' was not recognizable with the unaided eye. It was discovered when, in Ankara, Captain Ilhan Durupinar used a stereoplanograph in order to prepare maps. With this instrument this object was discovered, which could not have been created by nature itself but by human hands. Kurtis reports that Captain Durupinar has worked on thousands of square miles in this method for the preparation of maps, but has never seen a similar object in stereographic airphotos. Captain Durupinar is convinced, because of his topographic experience, that this discovery must be an object created by human hands. The size corresponds with the description of the Ark in the Bible and in the Koran. The object has the form of a boat, is 450 feet long, and 160 feet wide.

"Expedition next spring

"Kurtis said that at this time of year it is not possible to send out an expedition for the verification of the discovery, because the whole area around Mount Ararat is covered by snow. So one must wait until spring comes and the snow is melted.

"The place on which, according to the airphoto, the discovery was made is about fifty miles south of Mount Ararat, close to the Russian border. This area is volcanic, mountainous, and uninhabited. It was never before topographically registered.

"Kurtis said that the object, which could be the Ark, is sunk in a field of lava. Through heat the Ark might be preserved like Herculaneum and Pompeii. If it is really Noah's Ark, then it must be 7000 (4500) years old.

"Dr. Arthur Brandenberger of the Geodetic Institute of

Ohio State University said after he had seen the stereophotos he also is convinced that this discovery cannot be a 'product of nature' but possibly a 'petrified boat.' He added that if it were really Noah's Ark it would be a sensatioal discovery.

"In the last years several expeditions searched in vain for Noah's Ark near Mount Ararat. However, every time the mountain peak was scoured but not the fields of lava fifty miles south of the mountain. Nobody thought to search from the air."

Some of the excitement of the occasion was suggested in a feature story in *The Star Weekly* (Toronto, Canada) in a report on July 23, 1960:

"The most recent chapter in the long history of the search for Noah's Ark began in a Turkish military laboratory in September of last year.

"During a routine examination of aerial photos made during a geodetic survey, Capt. Ilhan Durupinar stopped short, stared in stunned disbelief at one negative that was remarkably different from the thousands of others he'd studied.

"Clearly outlined in the photo was something shaped like a large ship, apparently embedded in a stream of lava. And the photo had been taken high over Mount Ararat, said to be the Ark's last resting place!

"Bubbling with excitement, he called other officers. All were convinced that 6,000 feet up in the Ararat range was a ship of gigantic dimensions, and immediate orders were issued to work out its measurements. Experts soon calculated that the object was about 450 feet long, 150 feet wide, about 18 feet deep. These measurements are close to the description of Noah's Ark in Genesis 6:15 and 16.

" 'Make thee an ark of gopherwood: rooms shalt thou make in the ark, and shalt pitch it within and without with pitch.

" 'And this is the fashion which thou shalt make it of: The length of the ark shall be 300 cubits, the breadth of it 50 cubits, and the height of it 30 cubits.'

"Among the experts who studied the photo was Dr. Arthur Brandenberger, a professor at Ohio State University and one of the world's top experts in the field of photogrammetry and geodesy. 'There's a ship on Ararat,' he declared positively, 'and someone had better find out how it got there.'

"Several interested groups immediately applied to the Turkish government for permission to go deep into Eastern Turkey and investigate. Eventually, the government authorized an expedition by the Archaeological Research Foundation of Washington, D.C. The team was headed by George Vandeman and included Dr. Brandenberger and Capt. Durupinar. Because in winter Ararat temperatures go down to 45° below zero, the expedition was held off until early this summer."

This exciting announcement, of course, generated a fresh burst of enthusiasm and an irresistible challenge to those already interested in the discovery of the Ark. One of these intensely interested individuals, of course, was researcher Eryl Cummings. By November 12 two letters were in the air en route to Sevket Kurtis in Ohio, and Captain Durupinar in far-off Turkey, outlining his years of research on the subject, and requesting more detailed information and a picture of the "ship."

There followed weeks of anxious waiting and eager anticipation for replies. At last, on December 29, the first of Captain Durupinar's letters arrived. A copy of the picture which had been published in the Turkish magazine *Hayat* on October 23 was enclosed, together with the assurance that it had not been "retouched."

His delayed reply, he explained, was due to his inability to decide between various offers of assistance to investigate the object from the ground, which had been received from "some other gentlemen from abroad and from my country."

"Your offer seems to be the most interesting one," he wrote. Although eager to participate in planning an expedition to the spot, he was not able to carry out such an expensive project alone. "I hope you are willing to prepare such a party, including authorized personnel, to judge whether the thing proves to be the Noah's Ark. Considering your experience I believe you are capable to prepare such a party which is equipped properly to carry its endeavors to success. Then I would gladly join this party and plan the expedition together with you."

However, on January 12, a letter from Sevket Kurtis, the

Turkish student from Ohio State, stated that on New Year's day "some people from Washington, D.C." had come to Columbus to visit him, and that he believed they already had plans to investigate the site. Surprisingly, the name and address he enclosed for further information were those of George Vandeman, internationally-known evangelist and producer of the popular *It Is Written* television series, some of which had been filmed on location at various Middle Eastern sites. Having been interested in Biblical archaeology from his youth, and convinced that this possible discovery of the Ark was based on the solidly scientific background of map-making, rather than on tradition or lore, Vandeman, too, had taken rapid steps to ascertain the facts. The possibility of filming such a discovery was an alluring prospect indeed. Thus his visit to Columbus to meet the photographer who had taken the photos, and Dr. Arthur Brandenberger, under whose direction the photogrammetric mapping had taken place, and to invite them to join an expedition the following summer.

Immediately, upon confirming the TV evangelist's plans by long distance phone call, Eryl Cummings cancelled his own plans for an expedition in favor of the Vandeman group, and wrote Captain Durupinar to that effect, urging him to join and assist the other already financed expedition, if possible, if contacted when Vandeman came to Turkey to arrange permissions for the probe.

At a meeting in Sioux City, Iowa, the weekend of February 6 and 7, the two men, Vandeman and Cummings, met personally for the first time and discussed the various aspects of the project in which they had both now become so involved. Interested only in helping to prove the existence of the Ark, and hoping to fit into any future plans where his years of research might prove of value to the new organization, Cummings gladly turned over an impressive file of information that had been compiled to that time. This included the Karada inscriptions that told the story of the Flood; the Rosseya translation confirming the Russian aviator's discovery in 1915; and the Harold Williams story of Haji Yearam and the "deathbed confession," as well as the names of the very capable men who had been associated with the project from the beginning of the quest.

Vandeman had already made a preliminary flight to Tur-

131

key to prepare the way for a later group. By January 25 he had a letter of permission in hand. Together with a guarantee of cooperation from the Turkish government, which was also vitally interested in proving whether the object on the lava flow was actually the Ark.

By May 13, 1960, the Archaeological Research Foundation was formally organized as a non-profit corporation in the State of New York, with George Vandeman as its founder and first Director. Its purpose: "to conduct original archaeological studies"; its "first project": "to investigate what appears to be the ruins of a village and a large ship revealed in an aerial survey photograph from the section near Dougabayazit, Turkey."

Meanwhile—after the first flush of excitement over the aerial photos had somewhat calmed—a new evaluation of the facts surrounding the "discovery" began to take place. Although at that time even Eryl Cummings did not "anticipate disappointment from the present trip," still a number of provocative and momentarily forgotten facts began to clamor for review.

For instance: all the other purported discoveries of an object believed to be the Ark had taken place in a remote, inaccessible area high on the sides of the Greater Ararat mountain itself; and while the Tenderick foothills were remote, they were certainly not "inaccessible" nor at a high elevation. Also, the villagers were said to have climbed the "north side of the mountain to see the weird thing Reshit had found." If this boat-shaped object was truly the Ark, as everyone eagerly hoped it would prove to be, how could it possibly have arrived at its present location on the opposite side of the mountain, and some 50 miles away . . . ? Then, too, a number of former reported sightings had mentioned a melting glacier or a lake—and there was no sign of either a glacier or a lake in these pictures of what was believed to be a "lava flow."

However, as the old Chinese proverb reminds us, "One picture is worth a thousand words"; the photos were convincing, and the facts must be ascertained before any final conclusions could be drawn. Plans for the expedition moved on apace, although leaders emphasized that only the scientists in the group would be able to determine if the mysterious object was really Noah's Ark, and that no claims were being made that it was actually the ship it resembled from the air.

In a letter dated May 20, 1960, George Vandeman formally welcomed Eryl Cummings as a member of the expedition as assistant to the purser, Wilbur Bishop. But in the end, he never left American soil. Insufficient funds at the last moment grounded some members of the group.

Once in Turkey, the expedition made its way to the remote area near the Eastern frontier with as much dispatch as possible. A military escort provided protection. They were accompanied by the discoverer of the object, Captain Durupinar, and Captain Sevket Kurtis.

Viewed from the ground, the tear-shaped formation looked more than ever like a streamlined ship. The measurements were reasonably accurate, the contours excitingly resembled the rounded deck of a boat. Could it *really* be the Ark, buried under centuries of mud and debris . . . ?

The eager excavators seized their implements and started in. At first they uncovered nothing but dirt. This, of course, had been expected. The ship itself would be buried deep. Down, down, they dug. Deeper and wider grew the hole. Still—nothing but dirt; disappointing, unpromising dirt.

As the excavation deepened the spirits of the excavators also sagged. Must they bury all their cherished hopes of finding the Ark in this pile of unproductive earth . . . ?

At last it was decided to try that abomination of all careful archaeologists: dynamite. Captain Durupinar had the necessary permits; the soldiers departed in a flurry and soon returned with the materials to do the job. The fuse was set. There was a scramble to safer positions some distance away, and—Bang!—when the dust had settled there was still nothing but earth . . . ! There was no sign whatever of "archaeological remains." But the mission had been accomplished: "to determine whether the object revealed in the photograph was or was not a boat." It was not. Thus, the hoped-for "full-scale investigation to carry on extensive excavation at the site" was not justified, and the project was reluctantly abandoned.

It was a disenchanted group that returned a few days later to Idlewild Field in New York. It was difficult to adjust bewildered minds to the fact that what they had set out to investigate with such high hopes of success had turned out to be nothing more than a "natural phenomenon," a "freak of nature," a mere "phantom" resembling the ship they had hoped to find.

The outcome did not surprise Clifford L. Burdick, a Tucson, Arizona, structural geologist who had predicted that the expedition would discover nothing more than a "clay uppush in a lava flow." "However," wrote Burdick on July 6, after the disappointed party had returned, "even if it did not turn out to be the Ark of Noah, it may well have been in the providence of God to call the attention of the world to God's inspired historical account of the destruction of the antediluvian world by flood."

But the Archaeological Research Foundation was not yet ready to give up the search that, hopefully, would solve the age-old secret of Noah's Ark. To the determination of the Foundation to pursue this endeavor must go much of the credit for the continuing interest in the story of Noah and the Deluge since 1960. The story of their later endeavors will be told in another chapter of this book.

14

The Case of
the Missing Photos

A few weeks after the Frenchman, Navarra, had discovered what appeared to him to be the outlines of a ship deeply embedded under the ice, an American made a discovery of his own.

In the late summer of 1953, George Jefferson Greene, a sandy-haired Scotch-Irish oil and pipeline engineer, on a helicopter reconnoitering mission for his company around the northeastern flanks of Mount Ararat, looked down and saw a strange object protruding from a moraine below.

The day was beginning to wane, but the slanting rays of the westering sun clearly illuminated what appeared to be the prow of a great ship resting on an imbricate fault, or ledge, of the mountain before his startled eyes. "The Ark!" was his first reaction, as childhood memories of Old Testament stories came flooding back. "I must be looking at Noah's Ark . . . !"

With an engineer's mathematical mind, Greene noted that the prow was pointing northward and slightly west. Only one side of the great structure was exposed, as it sat in a morass of brush, mud, stone, and large chunks of ice, but the joints and the parallel horizontal timbers were plainly visible.

Luckily, the finest of company camera equipment was within reach. Directing the pilot to maneuver the craft as closely as possible to the huge wooden object below, the excited engineer clicked the shutter again and again. Closer and closer the whirly-bird edged, while Greene recorded his discovery on film. Side-wise, head-on, from as close as

135

90 feet away—the thrilling moment was preserved to be taken home as incontrovertible proof of the gigantic, ancient artifact he had just found!

When Greene returned to civilization and the priceless film was processed, he found to his delight that he possessed some half dozen clear black and white pictures of the object he had photographed on the remote peak in far-off Turkey. Elated with the possibilities of his discovery, and armed with a convincing portfolio of 8 x 10 enlargements, he tried again and again to interest friends in forming an expedition to return with him to the mountain for further investigation from the ground. With such an array of evidence plus the maps of the area that he had made, it seems incredible that he did not succeed.

At last, perhaps disheartened by repeated failure, indifference, and lack of financial sponsorship to carry out his dream, George Greene tucked his pictures away and left for British Guiana, where he hoped to make a fortune in a placer mining operation there. Here, on December 27, 1962, George Jefferson Greene died, nine years after he had made and photographed his momentous discovery of the Ark. Rumor has it that he was murdered for his gold. Another story states that he fell to his death at a Georgetown hotel.

Greene's untimely death proved to be a double tragedy, for since his departure from the States no trace of his maps and photos of Mount Ararat and the Ark have ever been found. Had he dreamed of finding friends for his project in South America? Had he hoped that his mining operation would provide sufficient funds to finance his own expedition to the Ark? Had he taken the evidence of his discovery along . . . ?

Nobody knows.

Or, before he left on the ill-fated trip from which he was never to return, did Greene secrete the photos among the many belongings he had left behind? Did he, perchance, place them in the safe deposit vault of some unknown bank?

To date, nobody seems to know the answer to these baffling questions, either. Or, if they know, they are not inclined to tell. . . .

But it has been proved, beyond a doubt, that the pictures

did exist. And it is known that the Turkish government did issue a permit for a George Greene to make a flight around Aghri Dagh. It is also known that Greene was a firm believer in the Biblical story of Noah and the Flood.

It is strange, as well as unfortunate, that Greene's discovery and photos were not more widely publicized at the time, or that they at least did not reach more interested eyes and ears. For it was not until after George Greene was dead and his pictures had disappeared, that Clifford L. Burdick, of Tucson, Arizona, accidentally ran into the story.

Burdick, a geologist connected with the Natural Science Foundation of Los Angeles, California, had become interested in fossil tracks, "human or otherwise," as he describes it, "as keys of geologic history and ancient life on earth."

"I spent much time in studying the giant human and dinosaur tracks near Glen Rose, Texas, found in Lower Cretaceous rocks," says Burdick. "Naturally, I was much interested when I ran across a writeup in the *Brewery Gulch Gazette* of Tombstone, Arizona, relating how a Fred Drake had found a fossil human footprint in Cretaceous rocks near Benson, Arizona. I lost little time in contacting Mr. Drake to hear the complete story. Before leaving I chanced to mention another pet scientific project I was interested in, namely, the search for the remains of Noah's Ark on Mount Ararat."

The two men had lunched together, and at the mention of Noah's Ark, recalls Burdick, "you should have seen Drake's face light up."

"Why, I've seen actual photographs of the Ark," he exclaimed. Photos of the Ark? Burdick could hardly believe his ears.

"Well, this is the way it happened," explained Drake. "I was associated with an oil prospecting crew, staying in a motel in Kanab, Utah, about 1954. I became acquainted with an oil engineer by the name of George Greene, who said he had recently returned from Turkey where he had worked for an oil pipeline company. He had a helicopter at his disposal, and during his flights chanced to circle Mount Ararat near the Eastern border of Turkey.

"He was well equipped with cameras to photograph the terrain and pertinent phenomena. As he circled the north

137

and northeast side of the mountain Greene was startled to spot a strange anomaly, an object protruding from rock debris on a mountain ledge, with the striking similitude of the prow of a great ship, parallel wooden side planking and all.

"There were six clear photographs, taken from different angles as they flew around the ship. I am sure Mr. Greene would have given me one of the photos, had I asked for one.

"I will admit that I had never been much of a Bible believer, but these pictures sure made a believer out of me!"

Much to Burdick's disappointment, Drake had lost track of Greene's whereabouts. But it is through the kindness of Fred Drake and his vivid memory of the pictures that had changed his life, that we have the only authentic drawing up until that time, of what the great structure on the side of Mount Ararat is like. Although admittedly crude, it agrees remarkably with other stories describing the laminated sides of the structure, the debris covering one end, the high cliff on one side, a sheer drop-off on the other. Of special interest is Drake's mention of the brush in the area where the Ark is said to rest. It will be recalled that both Schilleroff and Georgensen had also mentioned a swampy, brushy area as they stood on a high cliff and gazed down at one end of a great structure they were told was the remains of the Ark.

A few days after meeting Fred Drake, Burdick received a long distance call from Robert V. Gentry, a scientist connected with the Archaeological Research Foundation in New York. During the course of the conversation, Burdick asked his friend what progress, if any, was being made concerning another possible expedition to Mount Ararat to continue the search for the Ark.

Bob Gentry replied that plans had been about called off due to lack of further information about the Ark. Did Burdick have any new ideas on the subject?

Of course, Burdick did. Some very definite ideas, in fact. And it was only a matter of minutes before the President of the Foundation—George Vandeman himself—was on the line. Fred Drake's story was indeed exciting news—and the search for George Greene was on . . .!

It is almost unbelievable, until one starts to look, how many persons by the name of "Greene" (or "Green"?) are scattered out over the face of this world, and how many of them have gone abroad for one reason or another! And before the right "Greene" was located, the Passport Office in Washington, D.C., had searched through several thousand names in their files to finally come up with the individual whose name and occupation and connection with an oil pipeline company in Turkey had been corroborated.

By this time, months had been consumed, but at last George Greene's son was found, and once more the research came to a grinding, heartbreaking halt. For Greene himself was dead, and neither his family nor any of his old friends seemed to have any idea what had become of his photos of the Ark. But perhaps all was not lost. A special friend was positive the pictures had at one time been left in his care, together with other belongings of George Greene. And both he and his wife were positive that when last seen they had been in a large manila envelope. . . .

And now another and still more intensive hunt was on—this time for a large manila envelope where the all-important photos had last been seen!

Meanwhile, within a few days of Burdick's conversation with Vandeman, he had also called his long-time friend, Eryl Cummings, to tell him of his conversation with Fred Drake. Both Cummings and Burdick had been closely associated in the Ark research since their first meeting in 1945, and this surprising new development stimulated their interest anew.

However, careful study of both Navarra's story and Fred Drake's description and sketches of the Greene photos soon revealed certain discrepancies that called for scientific clarification. Quoting Navarra, who believed that his discovery was "the remains of the flat bottom of the Biblical vessel," Burdick called attention to the fact that "what Greene photographed was the prow of a ship or house boat, with parallel timbers forming the sides of the vessel. The photos probably could not tell if the bottom were intact, as that part was buried in the mud."

Referring to the fact that Greene's discovery was located somewhat lower on the mountain, Burdick suggested the following as a reasonable explanation: "If we may assume that both men (Navarra and Greene) were telling the truth, then evidently what Navarra saw was part of the flat-bottomed boat or scow buried in the ice. What Greene photographed was the upper part of the Ark partly embedded in a mud flow or avalanche. . . . One needs to study the mechanics of ice movement. Contrary to popular belief, ice does not flow en masse as a giant toboggan sled sliding down the mountain. If it went swiftly enough it would, however."

Using as an illustration the geological term "rheid" (a body of rock showing flow structure), Burdick explained that "Ice is a rheid, according to the laws of rheidity. When moving swiftly, like water it would move as one piece, but as a slowly moving object, it has differential movement, or as the structure geologists say, triclinic motion. Also a river flows with triclinic motion. The friction of the bottom and the sides make the bottom and sides of the glacier move more slowly than the center and top. Strong as the Ark was built, it could not withstand such differential motion embedded in the ice. The top would be torn from the bottom and carried farther down the stream in the same length of time. Also the bottom could have been wedged in a depression and stuck there while the rest of the glacier moved on with plastic flow, as hot tar or molten lava flows. This rheidity flow of ice in the glacier could easily explain the discrepancies. . . ."

Because of the fact that the superstructure of the Ark is apparently at a lower elevation, and therefore "more exposed to the weather" so that "it will not last as long," Burdick stressed "the urgency required in locating it. According to Greene or Drake, part of the mud flow had broken away with the melting of the debris and helped to expose the Ark. It might not be long before another such part of the rock slide might carry the rest of the Ark into the chasm. Time is of the essence. *It is later than we think.*"

Burdick's remarks are somehow reminiscent of the Turkish commissioners' report in 1883 that "the angles of the Ark—observe, not the bow or stern—had been a good deal broken in its descent."

In complete agreement with Burdick's conviction that "time" was indeed "of the essence," and that the business of finding the Ark required haste, Cummings, too, began an immediate investigation to try to locate the four persons known by Fred Drake to have also seen the photos of the

Ark. He soon contacted seven, and learned that at one time Greene had shown his pictures in the famous Purple Sage Motel in Kanab, Utah. All of these individuals readily recalled having seen the photos and having heard Greene's account of his discovery, but no one knew anything about the present whereabouts of the missing pipeline engineer.

In 1967, while acting as a field representative for the Archaeological Research Foundation, Eryl Cummings, too, as had George Vandeman before him, visited the southern part of the United States where Greene had made his home, and where members of his family still lived. He hoped, of course, that during the lapse of time some new information about the photos might have turned up.

In Corpus Christi, Texas, he met George Greene's stepson, John, and Greene's good friend, the real estate broker Frank Neff, who still felt sure that at some time he had in his possession the large manila envelope containing the pictures of the Ark.

With renewed interest and enthusiasm, these two men reaffirmed the authenticity of Greene's story, and his dream of some day returning to Ararat with an expedition of his own. Neff's willingness to "move heaven and earth," if necessary in an effort to find the missing pictures was revealed by his toilsome search through long-stored belongings in a number of cities throughout the South. At last only one possible searching-place remained: a garage, explained Neff, that had been ransacked by vandals only about ten days before. One day Neff took Cummings out to view the remains. As he opened the door, Cummings stared in dismay. The contents of the once well-organized shelves had been unceremoniously dumped into a great scattered heap in the middle of the floor!

The two real estate brokers turned away. Some day, perhaps, the luckless owner would be able to sort out the hopeless mess—but not today . . . !

For what had the vandals been searching? Had a certain large—and vitally important—manila envelope been among the items the robbers had carried away? Or was it still buried deep under the pile of debris that would no doubt take weeks of patient work to reorganize and return to the files?

During Eryl Cummings' stay in Corpus Christi, he was

successful in contacting an impressive number of individuals, either by personal interview or long distance calls, who readily recalled seeing Greene's photos of the Ark. It was a chain-reaction type of investigation: one person suggesting a contact with another who he was sure had also seen them, until in all 23 confirmations of the pictures had been made. This was in addition, of course, to the seven persons contacted two years before, bringing the total to some 30 individuals who remembered the photos.

Early in 1970, a California businessman, Juliet Judson, long interested in the discovery of the Ark, took a trip to Georgetown, British Guiana, to visit his son. When he learned of the still-unsolved mystery of the Greene photos, he gladly consented to do some private sleuthing of his own. Before leaving the States, Mr. Judson obtained names and addresses of George Greene's acquaintances and friends in Georgetown who might be able to shed some light on the problem.

Nothing of any great importance was uncovered, however, and an aura of uncertainty still surrounds the case: not uncertainty regarding the existence of the photos, but as to whether George Greene left them in the States, or had them with him in South America at the time of his death.

Certainly the disappearance of the photos constitutes one of the greatest heartbreaks that has yet been encountered in the research on the Ark. But when they reappear, as Frank Neff confidently believes they will one day, modern explorers may look forward to the day when they, too, will be able to follow in the footsteps of Nouri and the investigating party of the Czar and stand, like them, awed and reverent in the overwhelming presence of that gigantic reminder of the ancient world—the Ark.

15

The "Little Bitty Boat"

It was a bright Sunday afternoon in December, 1965, when two men walked into Eryl Cummings' real estate office in Farmington, New Mexico. One was Joe Bosse, a business acquaintance from a nearby town; the other turned out to be his brother-in-law, Walter Hefner, whom Cummings had never seen before.

Cummings had been extremely busy on a project of his own since Joe Bosse had been into his office a few days before; and now he explained, somewhat apologetically, that he had been so preoccupied with a matter of research that had come up unexpectedly over the weekend that he had not been able to get all the details on the promised information for which the men had dropped by.

"Research?" echoed Bosse. "What kind of research do you do?"

"Oh," smiled Cummings, always happy to answer questions on his favorite subject, "I've been doing research on Mount Ararat and Noah's Ark for years."

"Noah's Ark!" interrupted the stranger. "Why, I've seen pictures of Noah's Ark!"

Pictures! Of Noah's Ark! What sudden miracle was this? Somehow, ordinary, run-of-the-mill business seemed very unimportant for a while as the excited questions began exploding into the room. Where? When? Who? and How . . . ?

"I remember them well," said the stranger. "Sister Bertha Davis used to show them to us whenever she told us the story of Noah and the Flood!"

Sister Bertha Davis! What memories that name evoked. Not that we had ever met her personally, but our two small daughters had often gone with their girl friends to visit the elderly bedridden lady in her room at the Paradise Valley Sanitarium near National City, California, many years before. They had loved her dearly, and especially enjoyed the Bible stories she had often told. Could this be the same woman whose name we had so often heard? "Sister Bertha Davis"—this was the same name by which the retired Bible teacher had been affectionately known to her many acquaintances and friends. . . .

"Yes, she was a Bible teacher," said Walter Hefner in response to our eager query. "One summer about twenty-five years ago she held a sort of Bible school for about fifty of us kids in one of the churches (I can't remember now which one) in Holtville, California. . . .

"Yes, the pictures were actual photographs, not just sketches or paintings by some artist. She used to pass them around, and I studied them a lot. Only part of the boat was sticking out. The rest was covered with debris. It didn't look like an ordinary boat, like the pictures of the Ark we see today. It was more like a barge, with a house on top. It looked sort of as if it was made to wallow in the water. You could even see where the timbers joined. . . .

"I used to talk about the pictures a lot when I was young," Walter Hefner grinned. "Even got into a lot of fights over it, until I got my nose broken a couple of times and learned to keep my mouth shut! I hadn't thought about Noah's Ark for years. . . .

"Could I draw a sketch of the way it looked? Sure. Just hand me that piece of paper and a pencil. Now—like I explained, it didn't look like an ordinary boat. The timbers appeared to be hand-hewn, and running horizontally around the ship. . . .

"Where did Sister Davis get the pictures? Well, I have a faint recollection that she told us they had come from some foreign country, but I can't be certain where. . . ."

Walter Hefner busied himself with the sketch. Suddenly he lifted his head. "Say, why don't you call my sister, Maurine—she'll remember about the pictures for sure!"

And sister Maurine did indeed remember very well, even though her brother's question took her completely by surprise. What a shock to realize that we had known her through casual business contacts for a number of years, without even suspecting what a wealth of vital information lay within our grasp just a few miles away! If we had only known. . . .

"The pictures were old, very old," recalled Maurine, excitement creeping into her own voice as childhood memories came flooding back. "They were on heavy cardboard—sort of faded and gray. I've held them in my hands many times."

Maurine, it seemed, had been younger than the other children, and had not attended the Bible story classes at the church with her brother and the older boys and girls. But, since Sister Davis lived close by, she had often gone to visit the Bible teacher in her home, and with other small children of the neighborhood had sat around the table and listened to the fascinating stories she loved to tell.

"The photos," explained Maurine on the other end of the line, "were kept with other pictures in a portfolio about 12 x 14 inches in size that had a pocket in one side. I especially remember that there was a little pencil with a little tassel attached to it. When Sister Davis told us a Bible story she would pass around the special picture that went with it so we could all look at it, then when we had all finished she would put it back in the pocket of the portfolio.

"The picture of the Ark must have been taken from quite a distance away, because it always seemed so small to me," explained Maurine. "In my 8-year-old mind I used to wonder about it. I remember that one time I said, 'But Sister Davis, how could Noah get all those animals in that little bitty boat?' And Sister Davis replied, 'With God, all things are possible.'"

That the pictures were definitely not sketches or paintings both brother and sister agreed, but that they had appeared to be genuine photographs. Maurine agreed, also, that the boat looked more like a house boat—more like a house that had been built on a barge.

"There was another picture, too, that went with the picture of the Ark," went on Maurine. "It was old and faded, too, and was of a stone bench, or maybe it was an altar, with a roof or cover of some kind over it. The roof was partly burned and black.

"Yes, Sister Davis sincerely believed they were pictures of Noah's Ark and the altar he had built."

What excitement to realize how closely these descriptions coincided with several already in the files: the Rosseya story (Chapter 4) which told about the "remains of some burnt wood" and a structure put together of stones "resembling an altar," found on one of the mountaintops near the Ark.

Harold Williams, too (Chapter 12) had mentioned that Haji had told him that "the great door was removed from the Ark and was lying up on rocks forming a sort of roof under which was an ancient altar and smoke from the altar was on the rocks and underside of the great door. . . ."

It was Fred Drake (Chapter 14) who had also noticed horizontal timbers in the photos of George Greene.

It was still more exciting to realize that if this "Sister Davis" of whom we had just learned, was the same "Sister Davis" of whom we had heard so much in former years; and if she just happened to be still alive; and if she still had the pictures in her possession, might we not be on the verge of a major breakthrough? The missing Russian photos, perhaps . . . ?

Or since, according to Maurine, they had appeared to be taken from some distance away, perhaps they had been snapped from the "high cliff" mentioned by the two soldiers, Schilleroff and Georgensen, who had participated in the two-phased Russian expedition of 1917. Or, perhaps, by the commanding officer of the Russian aviator as they circled the ship to get a better view! But how had they been smuggled in? And how had they come into Bertha Davis' hands?

Long distance phone calls flew back and forth between New Mexico and California as further verification of the story was sought. Four other individuals, including Maurine and Walter Hefner's parents, still living in Holtville, remembered the photographs very well. And, miraculously, it seemed, Sister Bertha Davis was still alive—the same Sister Davis who had once been in Holtville before going to the Sanitarium to live.

Then—as had happened so many times before—disappointment stuck its ugly face around the door. For it was discovered that the now aged Bible teacher had practically no memory of her earlier life—and no memory at all, apparently, that she had ever possessed any pictures of the

Ark! And yet—one of her closest old friends and associates who had been recruited to assist in a renewed investigation in 1970, gave a perhaps significant report. She had asked Bertha Davis about her pictures of the Ark during one of her more lucid intervals several years before. At that time the old Bible teacher had readily recalled them, and believed they were still packed away somewhere in her belongings.

But the pictures were not in her room. It had already been learned, away back in 1965, that when she had been moved to another floor, the aged woman had directed that many of the possessions she knew she would never use again should be destroyed. Had the priceless pictures of the Ark been among these things?

For years it had been increasingly obvious that some power beyond human ken must be at work to counteract or completely destroy every shred of concrete proof for the existence of the Ark: the Bolshevik uprising just at the time the Czar's ground expeditions had dispatched documentary, scientific evidence that the White Russian aviator's story had been true; the Harold Williams' fire that had destroyed both the Haji Yearam story and the former atheist's deathbed confession that he had seen the Ark; the old newspaper files that had gone up in smoke; the untimely death of George Greene and the disappearance of his photos and maps. Thus, although bitterly disappointing, the outcome of the search for Bertha Davis' pictures, even though hopes had been so high, did not come as a total surprise. There had been other disappointments before. Even the unwitting destruction of the long-sought *Stars and Stripes* in 1959 would fit into the same frustrating category as these otherwise unexplainable events!

As the intrigued script writer for a major Hollywood producer was to put it in 1967: "This is the most fantastic story I have ever heard! You almost get your hands on the evidence and then—poof!—it disappears . . . !"

But the Bertha Davis story was not to end in utter defeat. Early in 1970 Phyllis Randall arranged with hospital authorities to make a thorough search of their aged patient's long-unopened boxes and trunks in a last-ditch attempt to find the missing pictures. All day long she searched, assisted by a member of the hospital staff. But not a trace of the faded old photos were found—not even the ancient portfolio Maurine Bosse remembered so well.

But this renewed investigation did finally turn up a clue. Among the individuals who had known Bertha Davis in her earlier days was an elderly housekeeper who recalled an incident that had taken place around 1941 when Bertha Davis had just arrived. There had been considerable excitement in the building, she said, over some very unusual pictures the new patient had in her room. Although the busy housekeeper had not taken time to go in and look at them herself, she remembered seeing little knots of people gathred in the halls discussing what they had seen. Among her memories of the incident was a vague impression that the exciting pictures had not actually belonged to Miss Davis at all, and were being returned. Were they the pictures of the Ark? What else could have caused so much excitement and discussion in the halls! Had she been wrapping them to mail? Had the old and faded photographs that Walter and Maurine remembered so clearly only been "on loan" during the Holtville days, only a short time before Bertha Davis had moved to the hospital to make her home? To whom had they belonged? And who are the people who saw them? Nurses, doctors, maids? Other patients or friends, now long since scattered and gone?

Pictures of Maurine's "little bitty boat," anybody . . . ?

16

The Mountain
Strikes Back

The greatly accelerated rumors and reports of sightings of Noah's Ark in the 20th century have naturally stimulated an active desire in many individuals to organize an expeditionary party to Ararat in an attempt to verify these stories for themselves.

One of these men was John Libi, who, as early as 1954, launched the first of his seven unsuccessful trips to the great mountain he was sure contained the secret of Noah's Ark. This was the year, you may recall, between the second and third expeditions of Fernand Navarra, of France.

To John Libi, the capricious moods of Aghri Dagh would prove that she had not been named "the painful mountain" without just cause. Repeatedly, her more terrifying aspects would force the determined explorer to abandon his attempts; but, refusing to acknowledge defeat, Libi would reorganize and try again.

It might almost be said that John Libi was born a mountaineer, since his birthplace was on the slopes of one of the highest mountains of his native Bulgaria, and his mountaineer father had climbed all the highest peaks in Central Europe, including some of the Swiss Alps.

John Libi himself came to the United States at the age of 17, the year the First World War began. During his next 50 years in California, he was to follow in his father's footsteps by climbing many of the highest peaks in his adopted State. Not content with these minor victories, he set his sights on faraway and as yet unconquered Mt. Everest in the Himalayan range. But all attempts to organize an expedition to scale the famous peak failed, and Libi was at last forced to abandon the project.

But it would seem that Libi, with his background and extensive experience in mountain climbing, and his command of seven languages (including Turkish, which he had learned to speak fluently in his native home) was especially well-equipped for the colossal task of searching for the Ark.

An amateur archaeologist who had also been interested in the story of Noah and the Flood since his boyhood days, Libi, too, had read everything he could find about the Ark in history books and in the Biblical accounts in different tongues. He became convinced that the Ark was on top of Mount Ararat, and that finding it "would be a great discovery for Christians all over the world."

However, each of Libi's attempts to wrest its secret from Aghri Dagh were plagued by some kind of misfortune and even downright disaster.

On his first trip, in 1954, Libi made two ascents to the top of the mountain, believing, as many other explorers still believed at that time, that the Ark would be found on the summit.

His first setback came in the form of two bears (were they the same that had threatened Navarra two years before . . . ?) who chased the terrified explorer until he broke out in a profuse sweat, which was followed by chills and a severe fever. This unfortunate experience incapacitated Libi for more than a month during the best climbing season of the summer.

After Libi had recovered from his bout with the fever, he, with his party of six civilians, a Turkish Army officer and guards, made a second attempt during the first week of September. This trip proved disappointing, too, since the bad weather of autumn had already set in. On this first expedition he also narrowly escaped death in a big rock slide "with big rocks smashing past like dive bombers," as he described it later to news reporters.

Libi, who described himself as "chief elevator operator at a San Francisco bank," with "other interests in restaurants, cocktail lounges and candy stores," paid his own way, and estimated that his initial try had cost him "several thousand dollars."

But Libi was not completely disheartened by his summer's disappointing experiences: he had sighted what appeared to be a "promising 500-foot-long mound . . . a thousand feet below" the peak of Mount Ararat.

The following year Libi and his same group were back, ready to investigate the exciting possibilities he had noticed the year before. But 1955 was a year of great international tension, and permission to explore the mountain was denied because Mount Ararat was within a militarized zone and the Russians, just across the Araxes River, were once again crying "Spy!" and denouncing the American expedition as being merely a camouflage for espionage activities.

Three years later, Libi was ready to try again. In 1958 he succeeded in organizing a large expedition consisting of 40 persons, with the same Turkish officer leading the ten men of the military contingent in the party. The remainder of the group were civilians, including a number of newspaper correspondents, who, like Edwin Greenwald of the Smith expedition in 1949, were also doomed to disappointment.

This time, only two days after the climb began, on July 20, Libi fell from a high cliff on the mountain for a distance of 30-40 feet, and sustained such severe bruises that he was forced to return to Dougabayazit for hospitalization. This unfortunate accident very effectively ended the expedition for that year.

In 1960, the indestructible Libi, with a much smaller group of fifteen, led by the same loyal Turkish lieutenant as in previous years, made still another attempt. This time he nearly lost his life from pneumonia, and the expedition ended when its leading and most enthusiastic spirit had to be hospitalized in Ankara.

Had Libi given up? Definitely—No! "As long as breath remains . . . I will continue the search for Noah's Ark," the Turkish newspapers quoted the intrepid American explorer upon his return.

True to his word, 1962 saw Libi on his way to Aghri Dagh once more. But this time he did not get any farther than the sunny land of Italy, where pickpockets relieved him of his wallet and all his traveller's checks. . . .

Three years later, however, Libi, described by newspapers as still "strong and spry despite his 69 years," was ready to try again.

It was with high hopes that the party of ten, including the still faithful Turkish Army officer of all the previous expeditions, established high camp on July 16, 1965, for the weather appeared to be unusually promising.

But alas! their bright hopes were soon dampened, for on the very next morning a very wet drizzle set in, which by noon had turned into a veritable cloudburst. The downpour continued all afternoon, then turned into snow. At sundown the capricious moisture turned back into rain, and the soggy explorers were forced to endure the rumble and crash of thunderstorms the rest of the night.

But far worse than the drenching was the anxiety the party endured. For at 5:00 a.m. of the day before—the day that had started out to be so promising and bright—the Turkish officer had set off on a training hike to the summit with two civilian members of the group. When the three men did not return, Libi became greatly concerned, but tried to assuage his worry by telling himself that they must have been able to come back down the mountain as far as some local shepherd's camp to spend the night. But this had not been the case. For thirty-three terrifying hours the three men had been hopelessly lost on the treacherous Aghri Dagh. All of this time had been spent searching vainly for the camp, trapped by the storm, yet never daring to give up. At last they "made their way down a perilous precipice and around the foot of the mountain" before they were finally able to locate and return to camp.

To add to the problems, three other members of the party had also started out on the first day of the storm, with the intention of trying to find the body of an Austrian doctor who had been killed a few days before on a separate expedition. Fortunately, this group had only gone a short distance from camp when the cloudburst struck at noon, and were able to make their way back. The body of the Austrian doctor, so far as is known, has never been recovered.

When the three lost climbers finally returned, at 6:00 p.m. on the third day, they were so utterly exhausted that the disheartened leader disbanded the expedition.

According to newspaper reports, Libi believed that "the ark is inside one of three stone corrals about 500 feet from the top of the mountain." He was "convinced the corrals are manmade—put there to mark the spot the ark landed after the flood." It was a great disappointment not to be able to investigate this spot due to the severity of the weather that year.

"It was a terrible experience," said Libi when interviewed by the press. "The weather was so bad—I have never seen such terrible wind and rain. Sahap (the Turkish Army officer) and his two friends went out to find the place where there were walls. I waited for two days and one night. They did not return. I was crying like a child when I feared they might be dead in the storm. At last they returned after three days. Their feet were swollen. Only a strong climber like Sahap could have escaped the elements. I embraced him and I cried. All of our food and equipment have been washed down by the flood. We could stay no longer, so turned back. No one could realize that there could be such a storm in July."

1967 saw what appeared to be the last of John Libi's determined attempts to unravel the mystery of Noah's Ark. On August 16, his party of nine, which included a business man from Ankara, a professional mountaineer, and a newspaper reporter, set out from Dougabayazit for the mountain. The other six members of the party consisted of Kurdish mountaineers.

To complicate the situation, the expedition had been joined in Dougabayazit by a group of four Belgians who were also searching for the Ark. Libi and his group had returned to Dougabayazit, after four disheartening days on Aghri Dagh, to wait for more favorable conditions. "The weather (was) so inclement and snowy, cold with a fall of snow" (the weather was of cyclone nature, reported Libi later on). "It was so bad that we were unable to do any searching after the snow was falling on the ground. We had the additional complication of having an earthquake on Mt. Ararat. There had been six prior camps to find the Ark and on the seventh attempt the weather was the worst of any attempt."

But in spite of the hazardous conditions, the Belgians, experienced in climbing European peaks, set out alone on August 24. Three days later one of the climbers was back to report the news that one of his companions had fallen more than 300 feet to his death. By the time the young climber's body had been recovered and sent back home, Libi was ready to call it quits.

"I know the Ark is on Mt. Ararat," he insisted. "I have been prevented from reaching it by the weather. I could wrestle with the mountain, but I could not wrestle with God."

When Libi, who said that he had "made so many trips to Ararat that I am acquainted with it like I am with San Francisco," reached the United States once more, he stated his conviction that God did not intend for him to find the Ark. "After 14 years of search," he declared, "I find that God forbids me from digging the Ark out of the mountain. So, I am through forever looking for the Ark."

But—hope dies hard in the human heart. And the man who, not so many years before had vowed that "as long as breath remains" he would continue to search for the Ark, still found it difficult to give up his dream. In 1969 Eryl Cummings met John Libi again in the hotel in Dougabaya-zit. Perhaps, drawn by the same irresistible impulse that had led the famous Ark explorer to the mountain so many times before, it was a farewell gesture to the Ararat he so loved and feared, since no public report of his final expedition has ever appeared.

17

Science Pursues
the Quest

Although the initial attempt of the Archaeological Research Foundation of New York had proved a great disappointment when the aerial photos of what they had hoped would be the Ark (see Chapter 13) had turned out to be nothing more than a "freak of nature," their efforts and determination to find the true remains of Noah's great ship had only just begun.

The Foundation membership, composed of men and women wholeheartedly dedicated to the vindication of God's Word, to which they believed the rediscovery of Noah's Ark would make a notable contribution, sponsored three separate expeditions to Mount Ararat between the years 1961-1966, as well as two small expeditions or "private probes" in the late summers of 1967 and 1968.

A brief history of the Foundation's work, although not successful in its major objective, should rightfully be included in any story of research on the Ark, since many invaluable contributions to the general knowledge and topography of Mount Ararat have been made. Many earnest and dedicated individuals have sacrificed in countless unsung ways—not only in time and means, but in tedious hours of research required on an obscure project of this kind. To the families of those who have dared, year after hopeful year, to risk life and limb in an effort to wrest its secret from that truly "painful mountain," Aghri Dagh, must also go a salute for the courage "above and beyond the call of duty" with which they have sent their men forth to do battle for the Truth.

Avante garde for the group in the summer of 1961 were Dr. Lawrence B. Hewitt, physician and botanist from Huntsville, Alabama; and Wilbur Bishop, a businessman and member of the Foundation board, from Cleveland, Tennessee. To these men can be credited two major accomplishments for the year. Official permits for the exploration of Mount Ararat were secured by special Turkish ministerial action, thus forming a solid basis for all subsequent expeditions for the group. They also secured excellent aerial moving pictures and still photographs of the icecap of Aghri Dagh, the surrounding slopes, and the Ahora Gorge.

To obtain a closer view of the gorge, Dr. Hewitt and Bishop, accompanied by a military escort and a native guide, set off toward the east side of the great chasm by horseback. They then ascended as far as the 12,300-foot level by foot, from which point they made the grueling descent to the depths of the canyon below. They crossed the incredibly difficult terrain of the canyon floor, then clambered up the steep and treacherous slopes on the other side. Their destination was Lake Kop, on the northwest face.

However, hampered by lack of vitally needed supplies and willing carriers, as well as by a badly sprained ankle sustained by Wilbur Bishop during the climb, the two explorers were forced as had Libi before them, to abandon their project for that year.

By August of 1962 a group of nine men, including Gordon Mansell, famed Mount Everest climber from England, and the late Harry (Bud) Crawford, an Army-trained alpinist from Denver, Colorado, were ready to attack the mountain for the purpose of trying to relocate the area of previously reported sightings of the Ark. Base camp was set up at 12,000 feet, but, on the massive mountain they were viewing for the first time, they admittedly "lost their bearings," and after three weeks of unsuccessful search they were ready to go back down the mountain and start home.

Here, however, they chanced to meet the Turkish Army officer who had been with Libi on two of his previous expeditions. It will be recalled that at that early date in the modern explorations it was still believed by most explorers that the Ark was buried deep under the ice cap at the summit of Aghri Dagh, at an elevation of nearly 17,000 feet. It

156

would be some time before the significance of the Haji Yearam story would be realized: of a great ship-like structure protruding from a glacier in a small bowl or valley perhaps two-thirds or three-quarters of the way up the mountainside; and the George Greene story had not yet come to light. The eternal ice-cap never melts, of course, and the glacial fingers that hold the mountain in their relentless grasp do not begin their descent until a mile below the peak.

Nevertheless, the Army officer assured the climbers that they were not looking high enough, and encouraged them to try again. With renewed hope, the explorers made their way back up the mountain, established a camp much higher than before, and this time Harry Crawford and Mansell succeeded in scaling the peak.

To Crawford must go the distinction of being the fifth American ever to reach the summit of Aghri Dagh, a feat which he repeated seven times in subsequent years. At the top, between the low peaks of the summit, the two men found a frozen lake, in the eternal ice-cap some 500 feet thick. As they gazed upon it their pulses bounded with excitement, even in tht intense cold and bitter, biting winds. Was a dark shadow visible under the ice? Was it possible that they were looking down upon the remains of the Ark . . . ? It was impossible to tell for sure. It would be necessary to return with scientific equipment at a later time.

Two years later, in June of 1964, the impressive list of nineteen expedition participants testifies to the fact that at last, for the first time, perhaps, since the Czar's two-phased investigation in 1917, a full-scale exploration was underway. Raymond Moore, Ph.D., of the Department of Higher Education, U.S. Office of Education, in Washington, D.C., was the Chief Scientist in charge. Assisting him in this department were William S. Dougal, from Santiago, Chile; William Cromie, geologist, World Book Encyclopedia Science Service, Inc., Houston, Texas; Sevket Kurtis, the photogrammetrist of the "phenomenon" fame, Columbus, Ohio; and George Silberberg, physicist and Photo-Instrumentationist, U.S. Naval Ordnance, Test Station, China Lake, California. Nicholas Van Arkle, a 30-year-old mathematics professor from Leiden, Holland, also later joined the group on the mountain to work on his doctorate in glaciology.

The medical staff was in charge of Dr. Lawrence Hewitt, who had helped lay the groundwork in 1961. He was assisted by Drs. Norman Kendall and John Lunt, surgeons from Denver, Colorado. Photographers Mike Anguitti, of Mobil Oil Company, New York; and Roger Brown, of Summit Films, Vail, Colorado, were on hand to make movies and stills in the event discovery was made. Scheduled to assist and guide the scientists were Chief Mountaineer, Gordon Mansell; Harry Crawford and Richard F. E. Pownall, of Denver; and William Reed, Ankara, Turkey.

V. L. Nabors, from Ross Aviation, Fork Rucker, Alabama, served as pilot for the plane. Dennis R. Moore, son of Dr. Raymond Moore, and a student from Southwestern Junior College, Keene, Texas, acted as Telemetry operator; Sidney Phillips, Air Reduction Corp., Huntsville, Alabama, was Project Director, and George Jernigan, a student from Ankara, Turkey, was in charge of camp logistics. Wilbur Bishop accompanied the group as Purser.

However, although no major disaster struck any individual member of the group, the 1964 expedition was plagued from its beginning by a series of unfortunate occurrences that delayed and hampered the investigation that had been so carefully planned. The international situation, including tensions between the United States and Turkey over Cyprus; strained relations between Russia and Turkey, and the fact that Ararat was in a restricted military zone just across the Araxes River from Russia, with the entire nation on a military alert—these all added up to tremendously complex problems, both civil and military.

In spite of the problems, the only one of the five other major expeditions that had been planned by various groups in 1964 that succeeded in obtaining the necessary permissions from the Turkish officials was the Archaeological Research Foundation, which was also invited to return in 1965.

Because of the weeks of seemingly unavoidable and exasperating delays, it was not until August 12 that work was finally begun in the scientific aspects of the expedition. These, of course, included studies in geology, glaciology, astro-physics, and meterology. Dr. Hewitt's medical clinics for the natives who inhabited the area did much to break down prejudice and establish good public relations with the suspicous and sometimes marauding Kurds. But then, just as it was felt that at last real progress was being made, the cold weather began to close in. As early as August 28 water sources were already freezing, and the personnel was short of cold weather gear. It was reluctantly decided to break camp and return to the States.

Considering the time available, the adverse conditions, and the unavoidable delays, the 1964 expedition nevertheless accomplished a great deal. Even though no "artifacts of significance" were found, it was felt that a solid foundation had been established on which to base future expeditions along the lines of geological and glaciological studies. And a most important scientific discovery had been made. "The fact that the mountain is an ice pack, rather than a shifting ice formation (glacier), tolerates the possibility of the containment of an ancient artifact there, provided the mountain is not totally volcanic," reported Raymond Moore, leader of the expedition, after his return.

During the next two years a gradual shift of opinion took place among Foundation leaders and members regarding the location of the Ark. In 1965 both George Vandeman and Harry Crawford made trips to visit Eryl Cummings in New Mexico to review with him the material in his files regarding the various reports of those who had claimed discovery of the ship. "Why have we not succeeded in finding the Ark?" was the question uppermost in their minds.

"Because none of the discoverers have ever reported that they found it near or at the summit," Cummings replied. "All reports indicate that it is buried in the fringe of the ice cap, and possibly at an elevation of between 13-14,000 feet." Where, then, should a renewed investigation begin?

Since Ararat is no ordinary mountain, since it encompasses an area from its low base of some 500 square miles, since its summit is capped by icebeds sometimes 600 feet deep with glacial fingers gripping the canyon-riddled upper slopes like the tentacles of an octopus, since its northeastern flank is pierced to its very heart by the mysterious, mist-shrouded, almost inaccessible Ahora Gorge—just where would a man or an expedition begin the search . . . ?

There were hundreds, perhaps even thousands of treacherous fissures, of unexpected, yawning crevasses, any one of which might hold the remains of the Ark in its frozen grasp.

It was at this critical juncture that the value of the long years of research was at last recognized. For when the various stories of discoveries had been once more compared and the stories coordinated, a certain pattern of similarity began to emerge. And there were clues that had been too long overlooked or almost ignored. It was recalled that the villagers, climbing the mountain to see Reshit's "weird" discovery in 1948, had gone up the northern side. Navarra had ascended the west face, then taken a course due east around the ice cap until he reached the northwestern edge of the Ahora Gorge. The Turkish commissioners of 1883, and Haji Yearam, too, had related the extreme hazards and difficulties experienced in reaching the resting place of the Ark. The Russian expeditions of 1917 had also experienced great hardships before they finally arrived at the object apparently sighted on this side of the mountain by one of their own pilots from the air.

The conclusions were obvious. If the stories of all these previous discoveries were reliable, the search for the rediscovery of the Ark would have to concentrate on the rugged, forbidding northeastern side.

Thus, in 1966, hopes again soared high. For one thing, the weather around Aghri Dagh seemed unusually propitious from the very start. A preliminary survey by Harry Crawford in early spring revealed the fact that in March the snowline had receded high on the mountainsides, where in ordinary years there were many feet of snow still burying the base. According to the memory of the oldest inhabitants it was the warmest season in fifty years. Since the Ark had reportedly been seen many times at the close of an "unusually hot summer"—might not this be *the year . . . ?*

Eager optimism marked the preparations for another expedition to this remote frontier land. By June the party was ready to start. Headed by Dr. Lawrence B. Hewitt, of Huntsville, Alabama, and Harry (Bud) Crawford, the now-veteran climber from Colorado, this smaller and much more mobile group consisted of Alva Appel, of Washington, D.C.; William S. Dougall, now a Pan-

American climber from Seattle, Washington; Nicholas Van Arkle, who had returned to complete requirements for his doctorate in glaciology by his summer's work; veteran creation geologist and scientific writer from Tucson, Arizona, Clifford L. Burdick, who had also completed work for his doctorate in geology; and his long-time friend and hiking companion on many a lesser mountain, Eryl A. Cummings, of Farmington, New Mexico, who had longed for so many years to set his feet on Ararat's rugged slopes.

The 1966 expedition was under government contracts, to study and bring back scientific data on the botany, the geology, and the glaciology, of the mountain. These commitments must first be fulfilled, then the all-important archaeological objective could be carried out.

As regards the government contracts, the expedition proved a great success. Regarding the hoped-for discovery of the Ark, once more disappointment was to be their lot.

The summer's work, however, had not been lost. In many ways much progress had been made, and the expedition proved to be the most fruitful and rewarding of any of the previous attempts. For example, Van Arkle's glacial team was able to pinpoint what was probably the original peak of Ararat before a volcanic up-push of unknown centuries ago. Also, the geologist Burdick, and his assistant, Eryl Cummings, established beyond question the important fact that Aghri Dagh is *not* "totally volcanic"; and that much of its northeastern face is "original" mountain of granitic rock, exposed in ancient times by a great explosion into the very heart of the great peak. Hundreds of feet of movie film had recorded both the beauties and treacheries of this ancient mountain of sacred lore; and Cummings had captured for later study other hundreds of vividly fascinating and colorful three-dimensional pictures of Ararat and the interesting people who have lived for centuries at its feet.

But as with A. J. Smith, Libi, and the previous Foundation expedition before them, the 1966 group also found many frustrations and insurmountable problems with which to cope. An excellent interpreter is lost, by army transfer. Weeks pass before he can be replaced—slow, maddening weeks, when little progress can be seen. Then an aged, but wealthy and influential Kurd, friendly and cooperative because of Dr. Hewitt's kindly ministrations a couple of years before, who says he knows the location of the Ark and is willing to act as guide—becomes very ill before final arrangements can be made to accept his offer, and is never able to go.

And always—the unproductive search for Reshit who, if he still lives and can be found, might be persuaded to retrace his steps to the boat-shaped object he had reported discovering high on the mountain almost twenty years before . . . !

Then, on the ice cap, there was that sudden, almost fatal plunge into an icy grave when Nicholas Van Arkle broke through an innocent-appearing but deceptive crust of snow to plummet some 30 feet into a deep crevasse. Only quick action on the part of the expert Swiss glacial team to which he was roped checked his fall and hauled him safely out, winded but unharmed, to return eventually to his wife and unborn child.

There were deadly puff adders to avoid on the lower slopes, and mosquitoes and flies; and at night the defiant scream of the panther and the ferocious baying of the fierce Kurdish dogs who guarded the camps and the flocks.

There was the rich, creamy sheep's milk many travellers must learn to savor and enjoy—as well as the native yogurt that imparts so much strength for the climbs. There were the delightfully friendly urchins from the neighboring camps—whose pilfering ways made life one constant round of watchful care. There were angry moods to be fended off when the foreigners' public relations did not strike their parents just right, and they retaliated with trampled water supplies and black looks. There was *cameraderie* and love for common dangers shared—and precious memories to be treasured long.

The great mountain, too, was a creature of moods. One moment serene and gracious, majestic against a background of azure blue; the next hurling fiery thunderbolts amid torrential rain, or pelting icy balls of hail on the luckless heads of the climbers scrambling to find hasty shelter under the nearest rock; there were rolling billows of fog, blinding blizzards and smothering snow; the ever-hurtling boulders, the sudden avalanches from melting snow on the

162

ice cap that dumped hundreds of thousands of tons of whiteness on the very spot where a pair of venturesome explorers had stood but the day before.

And always the challenge, the burning hope, that the next canyon, the next crevasse, the next high, hidden mountain valley, might yield that most precious of all ancient artifacts since the time of the Flood—the Ark whose blueprint had been designed by God Himself, the ship whose handtooled timbers had been fashioned by strong antediluvian hands for the preservation of the human race . . .

But once more summer—and searching time—was running out. The autumn storms could be expected at any time. A deadline had been set. There was nothing to do but pack up the gear and call it a day. Reluctantly, the mighty mountain was left behind. Much had been accomplished. Much, much more remained to be done, but it must wait for another year.

18
After Many Days

The members of the Archaeological Research Expedition did not leave the vicinity of the mountain as a group. One by one, two by two, they made their way back to Erzerum, to hot baths, good food, clean clothes, and from thence back to civilization and home.

At last only two of the men remained in the beautiful, modern, Ornak Hotel in this ancient Turkish University town, also headquarters for the U.S. Army on the Eastern frontier.

It was Friday afternoon, the 19th of August, 1966.

As Clifford Burdick and Bud Crawford hurried to tie up the loose ends and pack equipment for storage until the hoped-for next attempt, catastrophe almost overtook them.

Burdick, on his way to the officers' dining room on an upper floor of the hotel, was suddenly startled to find himself swaying back and forth in a most alarming fashion. Could he be experiencing a heart attack, after his strenuous summer on the mountain . . . ?

Then the truth dawned, as the doors above him burst open and an avalanche of uniformed, wildly hurrying men surged toward him down the winding stairs, nearly bowling him over in their frantic haste. Somehow, the tall, spare figure managed to put himself into reverse and join the mad exodus from the many-storied building that still rocked and reeled behind them as they reached the comparative safety of the street.

In his room Bud Crawford, too, was startled as the neatly arranged boxes began flying over his head from the stacks along the walls. It was not his first encounter with a

Turkish earthquake, and he, too, made a hasty exit and joined his companions in the milling street.

Many lives were lost that fateful Friday afternoon in the older sections of Erzerum and during the subsequent shocks that rocked the area during the next few days. The native houses with their rock-covered roofs became tombs for hundreds, perhaps thousands, of the luckless dwellers who chanced to be inside when the tremor struck. The devastation was not confined to this one locality alone, but spread death and destruction over considerable areas of this Eastern section of Turkey.

It was an anguished weekend for the families and friends of the expedition group as radio, television, and newspapers carried harrowing accounts of the disaster to the Western world, until word of their safety finally came through.

Meanwhile, in Ankara, Eryl Cummings, who had preceded by a day the last two members of the party, thus escaping the earthquake, had one more important item of business he hoped to finish up before leaving Turkey for home.

In 1946, when Carveth Wells had publicly endorsed the Sacred History Research Expedition over the KFI Broadcasting Company in Los Angeles, the news of the proposed investigation of Mount Ararat to search for the Ark somehow reached the Turkish press.

This story, in turn, was noticed by five Turkish soldiers, veterans of the First World War, who claimed that on their way home from Baghdad they had climbed Mount Ararat and discovered and measured the Ark. Upon learning that an American group had been organized for the same purpose, the soldiers made their way to the United States Embassy and offered their services as guides.

Since the Attache in charge had not received any official notice of such a group, and did not know the names of any of its members, the soldiers were requested to put their offer in writing and leave it in the Embassy in case an expedition ever did appear.

Years passed. The expedition, of course, had never materialized. The Attache kept the undelivered letter in his file. When he left the service of the government for a teaching position in Roberts College in Istanbul, for some unexplained reason he took the letter along. More time passed.

The letter grew yellowed and old. Rumors had circulated for some time about its existence, but no one who had hopefully visited the now retired college professor had been able to persuade him to produce it. There always seemed to be a good excuse.

But, thought Eryl Cummings, with a surge of that hope that is said to spring eternal in the human breast, it was worth at least a try, and he could not bring himself to leave Turkey without making the attempt.

An interview was arranged with Dr. Moore, and over the proverbial tea and cakes the following afternoon, the story of the summer's expedition was told. The aged man, now past 90 years of age, listened with deep interest. When the conversation veered to the beginnings of the research in 1945, he suddenly arose, excused himself, and went into another room. When he returned a short time later, he was carrying an envelope in his hand.

"Here is something in which you might be interested," he remarked, smilingly handing the envelope to his guest.

The letter! It was a dream come true! Inside these yellowed pages might be spelled out the difference between the failure or the ultimate success of the search for the Ark. True, it had been sighted and reported many times in the recent past.

But, as if some diabolical influence had been at work to keep the facts from coming to light, disaster or disappearance of the evidence had always occurred at just the critical time. And because of this fact, there had been nothing more tangible to work on than clues as to the actual location of the site, so that the difficulties of the search had been multiplied a thousandfold in this almost inaccessible area so crisscrossed by wild canyons and ravines, so hazardous because of rock slides and treacherous crevasses, by avalanches and falling rocks.

And now—to be holding a letter from men, who only twenty years before, had claimed discovery of the Ark; and, better still, men who at one time had expressed willingness, even eagerness, to guide a party to the spot! Would these men still be alive? Was their story true? Had their interest waned? Or had the letter been delivered twenty years too late . . . ?

The letter was immediately translated, of course, and

proved to be both brief and to the point: "When returning from World War 1, I and five or six of my friends passed by the Ararat. We saw Noah's Ark leaning against the mountain. I measured the length of the boat. It was 150 paces long. It had three stories. I read in the papers that an American group is looking for this boat. I wish to inform you that I shall personally show this boat and I request your intervention so that I may show the boat." The name and address of the writer followed; but would he still be alive?

A letter was dispatched at once. Now there was nothing to do but return to the States and await results. By the first week of September, surprisingly, the answer came. But the news it contained produced mixed emotions. For all of the soldiers were now dead, and although the writer, Duran Ayranci, was the same scribe who had written the letter for his friends so many years before, he himself had never seen the Ark. His knowledge, he explained, consisted only in what his friend Sakir had told him. But his letter sounded sincere, and he seemed willing to help, and his memory still seemed keen as to the details Sakir had described.

Near the top of Aghri Dagh, he wrote, was a decayed boat, put together with wooden nails, and resting on a rock. The ship extended from north to south, and this was all, he said, that he was able to tell. This was the beginning of a somewhat frustrating correspondence with the elderly Turk, who gave his age as 70; insisting, however, that he was still hale and hearty and willing and able to climb the mountain and guide a party to the Ark. The greatest frustration, however, was in the area of translation; but gradually, over a period of several months, the following sometimes puzzling information was gleaned:

The five Turkish soldiers had "by chance" climbed onto a mountain called "cudi," a "hill" very close to the mountain of Ararat. In the Koran, "the Moslem's holy book," it was mentioned that Noah's Ark should be "on the mountain of Cudi." And according to Sakir, our correspondent's late friend, "The Ark is on that hill, facing north-south, and the body is on the west side of the hill."

Cudi . . . ! Could this be another name for Al-Judi? You will no doubt remember that according to James Bryce, Al-Judi was supposed to be located many miles to the southwest of Ararat or Aghri Dagh. Still, our Turkish friend had mentioned "Aghri," and that "Cudi" was "very close." The party had also climbed *"the* Ararat" when they found the Ark. But no matter how they were juggled, the pieces of this new puzzle just did not seem to fit!

Then came another letter with still more puzzling detail. "I asked from all my friends. The ones who came with Sakir, all are gone. He had told only to these friends. He told me in broad sense. If I go I will recognize as if I have seen it. In our holy book it tells that it is on Mount Cudi. I asked from a friend who is from around that place. He told me that he has seen the Mosque of Arc (we call Nuh). Cudi Mountain is not as high as Mount Aghri and it is attached to Mount Aghri. They are both the same mountain. As Sakir told me, the boat is very large. One of the wood measures about 4 metres. This is what the Koran writes. The northeast side is leaning on a big rock and it has decayed a bit. He said it is all ice. That is why it will not decay. . . . Sakir is one of the five soldiers . . . he is dead . . . the position of the boat is close to the top of the mountain. One can climb from the west of the mountain."

At this point the Turkish exchange student who had been helping with translations and letters volunteered a helpful clue.

"The Aghri Mountain area is very mountainous," she wrote. "The local people give different names to each small part of the mountain. Cudi is mentioned in the religious stories I heard as a child. It might be one of the names given to Aghri in these stories. I could not find it on the map."

This certainly agreed with the words of Dr. Lawrence Hewitt as he once tried to describe the vastness of the great mountain of the Ark. It consists of "mountains upon a mountain," he had said. Sir Robert Kerr Porter had written, too, that Ararat appears as if "all the hugest mountains in the world had been piled on each other." Now our translator, Miss Habiba Mir, had told us essentially the same thing, that each of these smaller mountains has a name of its own, and that the name "Cudi" had figured in the "religious stories" she had heard as a child. Religious stories about what . . . ? Noah and the Ark?

The mystery deepened with each letter from our Turkish

friend: Cudi, Judi, Gudi—Ararat and Aghri Dagh! "They are the same mountain," our correspondent had tried to explain. But, at that point in the research, there seemed little likelihood that the Biblical account and the Moslem's Koran could possibly agree on the location of the resting place of the Ark, even though the story of Noah and the Flood had been interwoven through each. It was confusing, frustrating, and at last it began to appear that the letter written so long ago and read with such anticipation and joy, had been nothing more than a cruel hoax—perhaps even a scheme to extract American money from an unsuspecting and possibly lucrative source. Even though Sakir's description fitted so remarkably with other stories in the file, there seemed no way to reconcile Al-Judi and Aghri Dagh!

Thus it happened that the letters—so puzzling and apparently so contradictory—were tucked away and almost forgotten. For certainly there was nothing sufficiently conclusive in them to merit a chapter in a book! And yet—it was difficult to dismiss Sakir's provocative and apparently sincere story completely from the mind. . . .

Then suddenly, late in the summer of 1968, the missing pieces of the puzzle began to fall into place.

It had been surprising to discover, in the earlier days of the research, that even such illustrious scholars as James Bryce and Sir Henry Rawlinson had such nebulous ideas about the location of the mountain called Al-Judi. Bryce, too, had studied long and carefully to ascertain the facts, and, as you will recall, considered himself to "hold a brief" on the subject of the Ark. His studies, of course, had led him to the conclusion that the Ararat of the Araxes basin was the true "mountain of the Ark." However, it seems apparent that he was by no means certain of the location of the Al-Judi mentioned in the Koran.

In quoting the Jewish historian, Josephus, concerning a legend which placed the Ararat of the Bible much farther to the south in the valley of the Tigris and the Zab, Bryce stated (rather uncertainly, it would seem): "That legend *appears* also to be received in the Koran, where the Ark is said to have rested upon a mountain called Gudi" (emphasis supplied).

Bryce admitted also, in his address before the Royal Geographical Society in London in 1878, that he spoke "under the correction of Arabic scholars," but he *believed* Gudi to be the name given in the Koran, and that he *thought* "that the Gudi of the Koran is commonly identified by Arabic geographers with the mountains lying in southern Kurdistan upon the borders of what we now call Assyria" (emphasis supplied).

It was something of a shock to discover that his illustrious opponent, Sir Henry Rawlinson, the English soldier and Orientalist who had distinguished himself by deciphering the Behistun inscription of Darius I (the Great) of Persia in 1846, which vindicated the Bible at a time when the historicity of the Old Testament was under fire, leaned more heavily toward the recently discovered "Gilgamesh Epic" than toward the Biblical account of the Flood. In his discussion with Bryce following the latter's lecture on his ascent of Ararat in 1878, Rawlinson referred to the Babylonian "Epic" where "the Ark was made to rest upon Mount Nizer, which was explained to be another name for the range of Judi." And, of course, maps of the ancient Babylonian and Assyrian empires place Mount Nizer far to the southeast of Ararat. . . .

It will be recalled that Rawlinson had taken a strong position against Bryce's assertion that the Ararat of Armenia is the Biblical "mountain of the Ark." Sir Henry, who admitted that he had only a "more or less" connection with Armenia during his forty or forty-five years as Turkish-Arabian Consul-General in Baghdad, and who only knew "something of the mountain (Ararat)" from an unsuccessful attempt to climb it in 1834, scoffed at the idea that "the mountain in question" had anything at all to do with "the biblical Ararat." Rawlinson left no doubt in the minds of his listeners that he believed as strongly in the authenticity of Mount Nizer (which was supposed to be another name for the "range of Judi") as Bryce believed in Ararat!

But was there any way of proving which of these eminent gentlemen was right . . . ?

So, it was with keen awareness and the somewhat doubtful hope of solving an ancient problem, that Bryce's address and the journals of Major Robert Stuart's party were carefully reviewed once more. The results were more than

171

gratifying. For it was during this re-evaluation and study that a previously overlooked fact emerged.

Bryce's sympathies and interest, of course, had been primarily with the Armenian race, and his emphasis had more or less centered around their traditions and folklore concerning the Ark. Stuart, on the other hand, wrote with great perception and understanding about the Kurds.

It was astonishing to realize, in view of Sakir's story, that the traditions of the Moslem Kurds also centered around Ararat, or, as they call it, Aghri Dagh—that to them, as well as to the Armenians, it has also been considered a "holy mountain," and "forbidden to mortal man" from earliest times.

Why, then, the confusion about Al-Judi and Aghri Dagh? Why did so many so-called authorities place them so many miles apart . . . ?

It was during this reassessment of the research that another previously unrecognized detail came to light. Although to this point the terms "Ararat" and "Aghri Dagh" had been somewhat loosely interchanged, it now began to appear that perhaps they might not mean *exactly* the same thing. The discovery of this fact suddenly lent new interest and importance to Sakir's reluctantly abandoned story, and seemed to indicate that the name "Ararat" referred to the mountain as a whole, while perhaps "Aghri Dagh" meant only the ice-capped peak.

For, you will remember, the five Moslem soldiers had climbed "*the* Ararat." They had seen the Ark on a smaller mountain (the as-yet-not-positively-identified "Cudi"), which is "not as high as Mount Aghri," but "attached to it," and that "they are both the same mountain"!

The glimmer of light was brightening, but there were still obscure corners it had not reached. . . .

Stuart also, writing of his impressions of the mountain as a whole, nevertheless differentiated between it and the "*sacred heights* of Aghri Dagh." He mentions that "after three hours of stiff work, we arrived at the foot of the cone . . . we stood in the immediate presence of the vast *cone-shaped mountain 6000 feet high,* covered with eternal snow *to its very base*" (emphasis supplied). This would seem to indicate that Stuart, too, in 1856, recognized the ice-cap as a mountain in its own right, since certainly the "eternal snows" can refer only to the summit heights, which do not extend to the "very base" of Ararat mountain as a whole. And of course, it was at the base of this great "cone" (ice-cap) that he first experienced the strange, superstitious reluctance of his Kurdish guides.

However, even though at this point the finer distinctions between Ararat and Aghri Dagh seemed fairly well established, there was still the unsolved problem of Sakir's purported discovery, and the relationship, if any, between Cudi, Judi, Al-Judi, or Al-Djoudi (as it is sometimes spelled). Could it be that the various translators of the Koran had taken liberties with the spelling of the word, and that they all actually referred to the same mountain? And was that mountain connected in some mysterious way with Ararat and Aghri Dagh . . . ?

Endless trips to the library and much poring over books and maps over a period of many months, revealed the following significant facts regarding the relationship between the Koran, the Hebrew Scriptures, Al-Judi, Ararat, and Aghri Dagh:

It was G. Margoliouth, M.A., who, in his introduction to Rodwell's translation of the Koran, started a productive train of thought: "The relative value of any given system of religious thought must depend on the amount of truth it embodies as well as the ethical standards which its adherents are bidden to follow. Another important test is the degree of originality that is to be assigned to it. . . . On the question of originality there can hardly be two opinions now that the Koran has been thoroughly compared with the Christian and Jewish traditions of the time; and it is, beside some original Arabian legends, to these only that the book stands in any close relationship. The matter is for the most part borrowed, but its manner is all the prophet's own."

The *Standard American Encyclopedia* (Vol. IV, 1903) corroborates Margoliouth's statement in the following words: ". . . Mohammed is said to have drawn up the Koran with the assistance of a Persian Jew, Rabbi Warada Ibn Nawsal, and a Nestorian monk, the abbot of the convent of Addol Kaise, at Bosra, in Syria . . . it appears beyond a doubt . . . that he was acquainted with the religions of the Jews and Christians. . . ."

173

Thus a definite historical and literary connection was established between the Moslem's sacred book and the Scriptures of the Hebrew and the Christian worlds. Could as definite a connection be proven between Al-Judi and Aghri Dagh?

A footnote in Lamsa's translation of "The Short Koran" revealed the author's opinion that "the Mountain Al-Judi was probably Mount Kardo, in the chain of mountains north of Iraq. . . ."

A relief map of Iraq disclosed that the only significant mountain range north of Iraq appeared to be the one from which rose, in solitary and dominating splendor, the great snow-crowned peak of Aghri Dagh! It revealed also that Baghdad was due south of Ararat, and that the route taken by the five soldiers on their way home to Turkey after the First World War might very well have led past Ararat at the time they claimed to have climbed the mountain and discovered the Ark.

It was one of George Washington Carver's favorite sayings that "Anything will give up its secrets, if you love it enough." Had the "secret" of Aghri Dagh and Ararat and Al-Judi begun to yield? Did the Mount Kardo of Lamsa's "Short Koran" actually refer to Ararat and Aghri Dagh . . . ?

Then one day, while searching for a tantalizing, only half-remembered quotation long hidden in the file, an unexpected and astonishing discovery relating to the mystery suddenly leaped, full-blown, from the page. Buried in the heart of an ancient and yellowed clipping entitled "Ararat," taken from an encyclopedia with the penciled dates of 1830-31 in the margin, and on loan from Col. Alexander A. Koor, the following words finally closed the gap between conjecture and fact:

"Ararat, a mountain of Asia, in Armenia, on which the Ark of Noah rested after the cessation of the deluge. Concerning the etymology of the name Dr. Bryant observes, that it is a compound of Ar-Ararat, and signifies 'the mountain of descent' . . . *it is called by the Arabs Al-Judi,* and also Thaminin . . ." (emphasis supplied).

"Ararat—called by the Arabs Al-Judi . . ." How natural for Mohammed, the author of the Koran who had borrowed his Old Testament stories from Hebrew scholars of his day, but himself a son of the Arabian desert, to give the great mountain an Arabian name! What a simple solution to a problem that had seemed so complex! Ararat, the "mountain of descent"; the "monarch of the Armenian plains"; the most widely-accepted focal point for Moslem and Christian traditions of Noah and the Ark—had been Al-Judi all the time!

Strange that it had taken so long to discover such an obvious fact, for there is no doubt that the article had been read, uncomprehendingly, many times before. Strange, also, that such men as Bryce and Rawlinson had not discovered it in their day. It almost seemed as if God, Who sometimes "moves in mysterious ways His wonders to perform," had "seen fit to conceal this thrilling and momentous revelation until the time was fully ripe.

Almost immediately, as if to add the final touch of authenticity to this strange sequence of events, a long impatiently-awaited letter arrived in the mail. This letter came in answer to an inquiry concerning those other puzzling names: Cudi, Judi, and Gudi, and was signed by Ismael Akbay, a top Turkish missile scientist in Huntsville, Alabama, who had taken time out from his crowded schedule to answer an urgent request. Enclosed were copies of pages from still another English translation of the Koran.

According to Mr. Akbay, this translation had been made by Yosuf Ali, "the authority in (the) Moslem religion and in (the) English language." It agreed with the previously researched translations of Rodwell, Lamsa, and Sale, that the Ark had indeed rested on Mount Judi after the Flood. Additional explanatory footnotes followed:

"Let us get a little idea of the geography of the place. The letters J, B, and Kudi are philologically interchangeable, and Judi, Gudi, and Kudi are sounds that can pass into each other. There is no doubt that the name is connected with the name 'Kurd,' in which the letter r is a later interpolation, for the oldest Sumerian records name a people called Kuti or Gutu as holding the middle Tigris region not later than 2000 B.C. . . . That region comprises the modern Turkish district of Bohtan, in which Jabal Judi is situated (near the frontiers of modern Turkey, modern Iraq, and modern Syria) . . . the region has many local traditions connected with Noah and the Flood. The Biblical legend of

Mount Ararat being the resting place of Noah's Ark is hardly plausible, seeing that the highest peak of Ararat is over 16,000 feet high."

Thus far Yosuf Ali appears to follow the same line of reasoning set forth so emphatically by Sir Henry Rawlinson so many years ago: that the "mountain of the Ark" is located in the Tigris River basin, as opposed to James Bryce's well-researched insistence that the Ararat of the Araxes Basin far to the north is the correct peak.

And then, unexpectedly, this modern Moslem scholar veers to another point of view that dramatically clarifies and confirms Sakir's puzzling reference to a mountain called "Cudi" that is "not as high as Mount Aghri and is attached to Mount Aghri," but that "are both the same mountain."

Said Yosuf Ali: *If it means one of the lower peaks of the Ararat system, it agrees with the Muslim tradition about Mount Judi (or Gudi), and this is in accordance with the oldest and best local traditions.* These traditions are accepted by Josephus, by the Nestorian Christians, and indeed by all the Eastern Christians and Jews, and they are the best in touch with local traditions" (emphasis supplied).

And was it not the Nestorian Archbishop, the Christian Prince Nouri of Malabar, India, who had believed so thoroughly in the existence of the Ark on the northern peak that he made three attempts to find it before he was finally rewarded for his efforts by finding the old Ark there, safely "wedged between two rocks"?

Ararat, Al-Judi, Aghri Dagh! It had taken a long time, but at last all the puzzling details of Sakir's story had fallen into place. There could no longer by any doubt. The soldiers had climbed "the" Ararat. They had seen the Ark on "Cudi Mountain," which was not as high as Aghri Mountain, but was attached to it and was "the same mountain."

As for the prefix "al," a dictionary obligingly explained that it is merely the Arabic definite article "the"—that is, "the" Judi Mountain, and hence the English translation for "the Ararat" which the five soldiers climbed when they found the Ark!

Much, much later, in the spring of 1970, the research librarians at Pacific Union College Library, Angwin, California (where Harold Williams had attended classes so many years before), produced the "Dictionary of Islam," which fully corroborated the ancient article from Col. Koor's file:

"al-Judi. Mount Ararat, upon which the Ark of Noah rested. Mentioned in the Qur'an, Surah xi:46. 'And it (the Ark) settled on al-Judi.' "

Thus the "credibility gap" regarding the apparently conflicting locations of Al-Judi and Mount Ararat was closed. Would this knowledge serve eventually as a catalyst to draw the three great monotheistic religions of the world—the Moslem, the Christian, and the Jew—into a fellowship of a common heritage that had stemmed from the days when Noah and his sons left the old Ark in the Mountains of Ararat to begin a new life in a new and totally different world . . . ? And will not the rediscovery of the Ark affect even the pagan religions in whose traditions, no matter how distorted, the story of a universal deluge as a punishment for the wickedness of the world, still persists?

19

The Search Intensifies

Between 1967 and 1969, several smaller, private probes of Ararat, sponsored by the Archaeological Research Foundation, were carried out. One of these involved the New Zealand archaeologist, Hardwicke Knight, whose story of his discovery of timbers on Ararat is related in Chapter XXV. Other members of the party included George Vandeman, founder and first director of the organization; Dr. Pieter VandenHoven, and Harry (Bud) Crawford, both of the Denver area. On the occasion of Knight's return to the mountain after some 30 years, however, a heavy fall of snow made positive identification of the site impossible, and he was only able to point out the general area where he had found the wood.

Another probe included Fernand Navarra of France, but he, too, was unable to guide his party to the actual location of his 1955 discovery because of an injured foot. He, like Knight, had to content himself with merely pointing out the general area where he had found the wood from a lower position on the mountainside. Happily, the two sites were both on the same side of the mountain, although at different elevations.

In 1969 an organization destined to set tongues of excited inquiry wagging around the world, emerged from the ashes of the then inactive Archaeological Research Foundation. The name itself held connotations of excitement: SEARCH—standing for the words *Scientific Exploration and Archaeological Research;* their objective: to discover, if possible, the remains of the Ark of Noah, and to share

179

this knowledge with the entire world as a sacred legacy of Truth. Ralph E. Crawford, of Washington, D.C., headed this new endeavor. With Fernand Navarra as their guide, they once more returned to the area from which the Frenchman had brought his hand-tooled timber some 19 years before.

Besides Navarra, the party included his older son, "Coco" (Fernand Navarra, Jr.); the now veteran Ararat climber, Bud Crawford, of Denver; Elfred Lee, photographer and illustrator for SEARCH, Washington, D.C.; Hugo Neuberg, physicist and glaciologist of the Arctic Institute of North America; and explorer Ralph Lenton, of the same team. They carried equipment for drilling through the ice, hoping to reach the dark mass believed by Navarra to be a portion of the remains of the Ark.

According to preliminary reports, meager results were obtained, although subsequent newspaper releases stated that a number of pieces of wood identical to Navarra's hand-tooled timber had been recovered from a crevasse at the outer edge of the mass. It appeared that the main body of the dark mass in the center consisted of rock, or perhaps the rocky debris of moraine that had covered the area over the long centuries of time.

It is interesting (as well as enlightening!) to contrast the marked difference in the attitudes of journalists and newspaper reporters in 1969 when this announcement of mere fragments of wood reached the press, with that of the journalists when the Turkish engineers announced their startling discovery and actual entry into an ancient structure on Ararat in 1883 (see Chapter 7).

During the comparatively brief period of 86 years since that time, much corroborating data had filtered through to the press. As a result, the subject of the possible existence of the Ark was no longer treated with the same degree of levity and lightness as before. In fact, the furor over the SEARCH expedition's reported discovery probably created a greater buzz of publicity for the old Ark than at any time since Noah started laying its keel . . .!

In fairness to the 1883 journalists, however, it must be remembered that such an electrifying announcement as the discovery of Noah's Ark came at a time when the Old Testament story of Noah and the Flood had been (more or less!) respectfully laid to rest as a fable and a myth. Its sudden resurrection created an effect almost as startling as a ghost at a garden party, and caught the unsuspecting reporters completely by surprise, uncomfortably astride a theological fence, in most cases not exactly sure which way they ought to jump!

But by 1969 many people had become aware that some kind of a phenomenon resembling an ancient ship had been found on Ararat in Eastern Turkey, and with this new discovery conjectures flew far and wide. Could these pieces of wood actually have come from Noah's Ark . . . ?

Cautiously designated as a "glacial mystery," a "puzzle for faith and science," an "ancient artifact" that, hopefully, would turn out to be Noah's Ark, the announcement of the discovery, as in 1883, nevertheless produced scoffing in certain intellectual circles across the land, notably by "acknowledged experts in archaeology, geology, Semitic languages and Biblical history," according to Philip D. Carter of the *Washington Post,* on February 2, 1970.

In support of this statement Carter quoted Dr. Froelich Rainey, museum director and archaeologist of the University of Pennsylvania. "Absolutely anything is possible in this world," said Rainey. "But if there's anything that's impossible in archaeology, this is it. Radiocarbon dating performed in the university's laboratory has dated a wood sample submitted by Navarra at about A.D. 560, Rainey reported, and a British carbon dating station derived "about the same dates" during an independent analysis. In Rainey's opinion, Noah's flood would have had to occur thousands of years before Christ, and he (Rainey) did not think there was "any possible way you can get around these dates."

Carter also mentioned Dr. William F. Albright, "professor emeritus of Semitic languages at Johns Hopkins University, and an internationally recognized authority on Biblical history," who "compared Navarra's claim with 'a large number of reports by Russians, Turks, and all sorts of Americans.' " Declared Albright: "In the original Hebrew 'the mountains of Ararat' meant the mountains of the Middle Eastern region of Armenia. The mountain called Ararat today did not receive that name until Western travellers

began penetrating Armenia around the 16th century A.D."
(see Chapter I).

However, in spite of the adverse attitudes of the intellectuals, Carter reported that Navarra's lectures and display of a "plexiglass reliquary containing a dark, splintered piece of wood he said he had fished from the diluvial wreckage . . . found an eager audience both among professional explorers from the respected *Arctic Institute of North America* and among fundamentalist Christians hoping to prove that the Bible story of Noah, the Flood, and the Ark is literally true."

And according to R. E. Crawford, president of SEARCH, they were convinced that "something is there, and whatever it is, we intend to expose it and find out as much as possible about it."

Drawing support from a variety of sources, as SEARCH Foundation, Inc., of Washington, D.C., the group proceeded to plan a one million dollar expedition, beginning in the summer of 1970, to explore and de-ice the site of Navarra's discovery to prove, if possible, what actually was there. Said Robert Taylor, director of the *Arctic Institute of North America*, "We need objective appraisal to strengthen the findings. I can't explain how wood of that size and age could get to that height. Whatever is there is going to be of great archaeological interest." It was estimated that some 900,000 cubic meters of ice and moraine would have to be shifted in order to reach the lake and assess the mysterious artifact.

Because the Arctic Institute considered the new "find" of sufficient importance (*Christianity Today*, Sept. 12, 1969), they were prompted to release one of their key men, Ralph Lenton, to the upcoming investigation. In addition they lent expedition equipment without charge. According to the late Bud Crawford, Co-Deputy Director of the project, this included "such sophisticated scientific instruments as radio ice-depth measuring equipment and other complex engineering tools" which would be used to accomplish their publicly announced objectives to "uncover and identify an ancient wooden structure of immense size that may well be the remains of Noah's Ark, as recorded in the Biblical book of Genesis."

Although admittedly not all the group saw eye-to-eye on

the identity of the "artifact," Navarra steadfastly maintained his original conviction that he had found the Ark; and, privately, most of the leaders of the project expressed their own personal belief that the hand-tooled timbers had come from Noah's great ship.

However, it is one thing to plan an expedition, and quite another to carry it out. For months an advance group had been in Turkey working on the all-important permits to enter and work in this highly restricted military zone, but it seemed as if the proper authorities were dragging their feet. Several obscure factors may have been involved: unrest among Moslem university students in Ankara, who actively objected to the Christian connections of the expedition group; and recurrent rumblings from the great Russian bear on the vulnerable Turkish Eastern frontier that the tons of complicated scientific equipment awaiting transportation from Istanbul to Ararat, ostensibly to uncover an "ark," was merely a masquerade for American spies. It was a delicate and difficult situation for a nation whose progressive leadership recognized the lucrative advantages which would follow a rediscovery of the Ark, and the wave of tourism which would surely result.

Nevertheless, according to an official statement by Ralph Lenton and Hugo Neuberg, SEARCH project directors, permission to carry out a 20-day preliminary geological survey expedition on the Northwest side of the mountain, was finally granted by Col. Boram, Commandant of the Dougabayazit military garrison, with reluctant verbal consent from the Provincial Governor of the area.

After final purchases of supplies in Dougabayazit, the advance party proceeded up the mountain with their pack animals and guides. Nine days later, a message from the Provincial Governor directed the party to return to Dougabayazit to await full permissions from Ankara before continuing their work. In compliance with the order, the party proceeded back down the mountain with their supplies. However, in spite of repeated conferences with government officials during the next few weeks, on July 13, the Chief of Security at the Interior Ministry informed the expedition Director that permissions would not be granted. Even though officials appeared cordial to the project, the "internal situation" in Turkey precluded the granting of permissions at that time. No other explanation was forthcoming. There remained no choice for the disappointed explorers but to return home.

But in spite of the unsuccessful efforts of the SEARCH foundation to continue its investigation into the controversial timbers of Navarra's discovery, their attempts cannot be labelled a total loss. The widespread favorable publicity and interest in their project aroused an interest in the Biblical story of the Deluge unparalled in the modern world. It also brought to light the eye-witness account of another member of the Armenian race who claimed that in his early boyhood he had been taken on two different occasions to Mount Ararat to see and worship at the "sacred Ark."

This man, old and ailing, and now living on the Eastern seaboard of the United States, consented to a taped interview with members of the SEARCH group. According to the old man, he had seen the "holy ship" twice—once in 1902 at the age of 10, and again in 1904. Although in places the story was tinged with traces of an excited and awestruck child's innocent exaggeration, since a trip to the Ark was undoubtedly the greatest adventure that could befall an Armenian boy, a number of pertinent details that agreed with other reports of sightings stood out in bold relief. When sorted out and pieced together, the unrehearsed question-and-answer interview added up to a most fascinating account:

It had taken seven days for the young boy and his uncle to reach the foot of Ararat from Azerbaijan, carrying their food supplies on their backs. It seems they had flocks and herds pastured here, and a man briskly preparing cheeses and butter for their winter needs. Their journey had taken them eastward around the mountain, in the general direction of Erivan. Business attended to, the man and the boy took off for their arduous climb.

We can picture the excited curiosity of the 10-year-old lad as he watched his uncle assemble rations and supplies for the trip.

"Uncle, where are we going?" he begged, when a sturdy little mountain eshak (donkey) was finally brought around.

"Georgie, we're going up to see that Holy Ark. . . ."

The reply must have brought shivers of delighted anticipation to the small boy as they set off astride the nimble eshak up the trail.

Since they had come to the mountain from the Persian side facing Erivan, it seems safe to assume that the route taken by the uncle and the boy led up the Ahora Gorge— the same trail Fernand Navarra was to take a half century later, in 1952.

This assumption is strengthened by the fact that at some time during their journey, the uncle announced, "Georgie, you're going to see a holy man." He pointed to a long, low mound ahead. "See this thing here?"

"Uncle, that's a mound," protested the boy.

"That's it," the uncle replied.

Even today, close by Jacob's Well, some five miles up the gorge, can be seen a low mound of stones revered by the inhabitants of the area as the burial place of a legendary monk who once climbed the mountain to visit the site of Noah's Ark.

It was while Navarra and his party were resting at this well in 1952 that the shepherds who had accompanied them regaled them with the legend of this famous monk. This was the spot, it seemed, near which the ancient monastery destroyed in 1840 had stood, and from which the monks had started on their pious pilgrimages to the Ark.

"Which way did they go?" Navarra had asked, his curiosity whetted by the tale.

"That way," replied a young shepherd, pointing to a cleft in the steep cliff ahead. "But *you* can't go there," he warned the would-be discoverers from an alien world. "There's magic there. . . ."

But, to the Armenian uncle and the boy, through whose ancient religion was woven a thousand hallowed traditions relating to the Ark, their journey to worship at the shrine was in the nature of a sacred quest, and they felt no fear. Whatever route they may have taken, they eventually reached the point where their patient beast of burden must be left behind.

Bowing his broad back, the uncle shouldered not only the supplies, but the boy, and started the ascent. Up, up, they climbed, the boy's excitement turning to bewilderment and fear as the familiar world he knew fell far behind.

"Uncle, where are we going?" he quavered, peering

down at the mist-shrouded valley from what he felt sure must be the very top of the world!

But at last they reached their destination, and there stood the old Ark—"just as clear as you can see this car," as the old man was to describe it some 60 years later. To the small boy's awestruck gaze, it appeared to be 1000 feet long and at least 600 feet wide . . . ! (However, if we remember that the length of the Hebrew "sacred cubit" measured some three feet, perhaps this long-cherished impression may not be too far amiss!) The Ark, so he said, was sitting on a large rock, surrounded by snow, on the edge of a cliff so deep and so precipitous that it would have been impossible for any human to reach it from the ground on that side.

There is an exciting tingle of a vicarious thrill as the old man recounts the dramatic details of that unforgettable day. There had been little snow that year, he recalled—which no doubt accounts for the unusual accessibility and visibility of the elusive and oft-times hidden ship. The uncle piled up rocks, bent his 6-foot frame, and hoisted the youngster to the top. The Ark, recalled the old man, was more than 35 feet high.

"Georgie, look in good," came his uncle's voice.

"Uncle, I see a hole in here—I'm scared."

"Don't be scared—the Lord's been here," the uncle called back. Overcome with emotion and awe, Georgie bent over and kissed the Ark (when he recounted his experience to his grandfather after he returned home, the old man fondly predicted, "Georgie, you're going to be a holy man.").

But now, on the mountain, his uncle couldn't resist teasing him a bit. "Georgie, you're about 30 feet high now, huh?"

"Are you going to catch me?" the boy, still frightened, shot back.

"I will—don't jump."

"I won't," promised the boy, and the uncle grabbed him and brought him down. "I'll never forget it as long as I live," declared the old man.

The eager child was popping with questions. Up under the flat, overhanging roof he had spied some openings. What were they for? he wanted to know.

"That is where the air came out," explained the uncle. "No, the animals and humans are not here now—they have all gone away."

The boy gazed from one end of the huge structure to the other with wide, wondering eyes. "Uncle, how in the world did this get here?" he asked.

"Oh, the Lord brought it here—when the Flood came and covered the whole world . . . ."

Another unforgettable detail forever etched on the small boy's mind was watching his uncle brush the snow from the plain, flat roof with his hands. Under the snow, and in spite of it, he recalled, green moss was growing like grass.

The man and the boy stayed on the mountain two, or perhaps three hours. During this brief time the boy's bright eyes took in many details not previously noted or recorded by more adult discoverers of the Ark.

Was the ship square? or round? "No, oh no . . . it was long—and the sides tipped out." The part of the bottom that was visible was, like the roof, "as flat as can be." There was no door on the side they explored—only the window holes in the top under the overhanging roof, about 18 inches high, and perhaps 30 inches long; many of them, perhaps 50—he couldn't count them all—running along the side. For some reason the uncle did not try to walk completely around the Ark—the steep cliff was evidently a most effective deterrent, even to this intrepid mountaineer!

The ship was made from wood—there was "no two ways about it," declared the old man. The grain was plainly visible, but the Ark was "petrified," as hard as rock; he could see no nails, and the sides were so smooth it looked as if it had been molded in one piece. There was no place where one could put his fingers between the cracks, he said. The wood was dark brown, but covered with a soft green mold. His uncle, who evidently had a muzzle-loading musket along, tried unsuccessfully to dent it with a blast of powder. Then he tried to cut off a "good luck piece" with his long steel-bladed knife, but the stone-like material would not yield.

Had the old man seen anything like it since? No, he never had—excepting once, he said. He had seen a tuna fish tanker that reminded him of the Ark. Did it, perhaps, resemble a barge . . . ?

"Exactly!" he exclaimed, relieved that someone had supplied the correct word his limited English vocabulary had lacked. "It looked exactly like a barge." The nose was flat in front, he recalled, with the underneath curve a little more pronounced.

Did he know of anyone else who had ever seen the ship? "Oh yes, many other boys have seen it," was the eager reply. "They used to tell me, 'Georgie, we saw that Ark, too.' " (Where are all these other Armenians now? Did they perish in the bloody massacres that so tragically decimated their ancient race? For in his young manhood George was to be a witness to the horrors of Lake Van when hundreds of his countrymen laid down their lives for the Christian faith.)

The rediscovery of the Ark, the old man agreed, would no doubt start people reading their Bibles again. There are "so many ungodly in this free country now," he said, that "God is going to get angry some day and punish us, and there's no two ways about it!"

"If we keep our minds straight and be true to God," he declared, "we'll be saved. Now people believe in nothing but the dirty dollar, not the Almighty God."

The old man steadfastly refused to surrender his opinion that the pieces of Navarra's wood he saw could not be a part of Noah's Ark. "Almighty God," he insisted, "would never permit the Ark to be cut and broken up."

"When I saw Noah's Ark," he said, "it was absolutely petrified. It was pure stone. It would be impossible to break it piece by piece. I would not believe it if I saw it with my own eyes!" And even though he sometimes had trouble remembering what he had done yesterday, he said, he had no trouble remembering the events of his childhood. To the best of his knowledge what he and his uncle had seen was that "holy thing," the Ark. Its modern discovery would serve "to open people's eyes," he said.

However, in spite of the elderly Armenian's obvious sincerity and keen recollection of the events surrounding his journey to see the Ark, certain apparent discrepancies in his story served to rob it of the attention and study it so richly deserved. For the thoughtful reader will immediately recognize that certain aspects of his descriptions bear a remarkable similarity to other discoveries reported in this book.

For example: the resemblance of the great structure to a barge, which agreed uncannily with Walter Hefner's description of the Bertha Davis' photos he had seen as a boy: that "it was more like a barge, with a house on top. It looked sort of as if it was made to wallow in the water. You could see where the timbers joined" (see Chapter 15).

Its position on a rock at the edge of a cliff was reminiscent of the story told by George Greene to the engineer, Fred Drake, that the ship was sitting on an imbricate fault; also, of the story of the five Turkish soldiers' discovery at the close of World War I, that they had seen and measured the Ark, and that it was sitting on a rock (see Chapters 14 and 18).

The hardness of the wood cannot help but remind the reader of Haji Yearam and his story of the three atheists who tried to destroy the hated object they had discovered by axe and fire; also of Reshit, the Kurdish farmer, who claimed he had discovered "the prow of a ship protruding from a canyon down which tons of melting ice and snow had been rushing for more than two months. The prow was almost entirely revealed." The astonished explorer had "climbed higher to examine it from above," then climbed back down and with his dagger tried to break a piece off the prow. Reshit insisted it was not "a simple rock formation," but a "ship." The prow, he said, was "about the size of a house" (Chapters 9 and 12). This also reminds us of the newspaper report of the Turkish commissioner's discovery in 1883, that "they were surprised to see sticking out of the ice what at first appeared to be the rude facade of an ancient dwelling. On closer examination it was found to be composed of longitudinal layers of gopher wood, supported by immense frames, still in a remarkable state of preservation" (Chapter 7).

Perhaps the most important detail of all not previously mentioned by other reports, is the old Armenian's description of windows near the top of the "sacred" object he had been taken to see. God's direction to Noah had been explicit as to size:

"A window shalt thou make to the ark, and in a cubit shalt thou finish it above" (Genesis 6:16). The fact that

189

the old Armenian remembered the windows as *about* 18 inches high (the generally accepted length of the cubit), adds strength and credibility to his claim that he had actually seen the Ark. And since it is extremely doubtful that he could possibly have knowledge of or access to the related information in this book, surely no charge of collusion can be laid at his door.

After hearing the old man's taped story of the Ark late in November of 1970, Eryl Cummings went east for a personal interview. He was accompanied by Rene Noorbergen, also for many years an avid researcher on the subject of the Ark. Close questioning failed to move the old gentleman's original position or his description of the ship. During subsequent interviews with Elfred Lee, however, over a period of perhaps a year, more and more fascinating details came to light; but never once did he deviate from the story he had told on the recorded interview.

His story, it seems, had first come to the attention of SEARCH through the late Mrs. Mary T. Board, a real estate broker in Maryland, who had tried for years to find someone who would take an active interest in the old Armenian's story of the Ark. She and her husband had known the elderly gentleman for some 20 years. In fact, their first contact had come about as the result of a real estate transaction in which they had sold him the home in which he lived until his death on March 1, 1972.

This first casual acquaintance had ripened into a warm friendship and, as in the case of Haji Yearam on the West coast many years before, he eventually confided in his new friends the thrilling account of his earlier days. Since he had no desire to exploit or commercialize his personal knowledge of the great ship, this vital information lay buried for years. At last, through the SEARCH direct mail program, and at a time when it seemed to answer a specific need, the story came to light.

As the old man gradually unfolded the story of his life, it was learned that he had not only seen the Ark in his early childhood, but many times in his later years as he pastured his own flocks and herds on the slopes of Aghri Dagh. The existence and location of the Ark seemed to be common knowledge in the days when the mountainsides were peopled each summer by members of the Armenian race!

190

The story of the old Armenian's life reads like a modern saga, both believable and true since it fits so closely with the traumatic history of his race. Conscripted into the Turkish army at an early age, he soon gained an enviable reputation in the skill of wrestling—a favorite pastime with the soldiers of that day. And, in his own words, "nobody ever put my back to the floor . . . !" He still bears, on his forearm, the scars from a brand identifying him as a believer in the Christian's Christ!

As a soldier in the crack Turkish troops, the young Armenian eventually found himself on guard duty in the palace of the Sultan himself in Istanbul. As troubles multiplied for his race, he was transferred back to his childhood home at Lake Van, not far from the twin Ararat peaks. Here he was forced to witness the martyrdom of his entire family for the Christian faith.

Terrified, and given 24 hours in which to decide his own fate, the young man managed to escape across the river into Russia during the night. Here, accosted by the Russian border officials, he was again given a choice: to return to Turkey, where he would almost certainly seal his faith with his blood; or deportation to a labor camp in the dread Siberian wastes. Choosing the lesser of the two evils, he spent the next 18 months at hard labor. Upon his release from this enforced servitude, he spent the next seven years eking out a meagre living by selling bread, and hot water for coffee—which sounds almost unbelievably primitive to those of us accustomed to the luxuries of hot water at the touch of a faucet or a plugged-in cord!

Nevertheless, the determined young man eventually managed to escape and secure passage to the land of so many immigrant's dreams—the "holy land" symbolized by the stately Lady of Liberty presiding over New York harbor at the entrance to a fabulous New World! Here, his pockets full of Russian gold, he quickly became disillusioned when a new-found "friend" relieved him of his hard-earned money for its "equivalent" in American money—a lone silver quarter! However, the thrifty young immigrant soon survived the shock, and before long had carved a place for himself in his adopted land.

During these months of interviews and gradually growing friendship with the old man, a dream had been forming in Elfred Lee's mind. Lee, a teacher of art in Washington, D.C., schools, who had been a member of the SEARCH expedition to the Navarra site in 1969, wished above all things to make a drawing of the Ark from the notes taken during his visits with the old man. Carefully, with the interested old gentleman watching and correcting every stroke, a rough draft was soon ready for the drawing board. When the elderly Armenian saw the finished sketch, his reaction was excited indeed: so carefully had Lee reconstructed the entire story that he immediately recognized not only the Ark, but the area surrounding it! There was the ladder dangling some ten feet from the bottom of the ship (whether an original part of the Ark or a later addition by early pilgrims to the Ark he did not know!); there was the continuous ribbon-like "window" under the overhanging roof. There was only one slight mistake: "You didn't get it quite right here—it should have been like this."

Mystified, Lee returned to his notes. Sure enough, he *had* overlooked one important point! The result: the only eyewitness picture of the Ark we have been able to secure to date.

If the widespread publicity over the activities of SEARCH had produced no greater results than the revelation of this hitherto unknown story, it would have been well worth while, for its many matching details serve to add weight to the steadily increasing mass of evidence for the existence of the Ark on our modern Ararat mountain!

However, important as the continued investigation of the Navarra site may be, it must be remembered in this connection that the Frenchman himself only claimed the discovery of the base of the Ark, or its foundation, and that he believed the superstructure of the great ship had been dismantled and carried away long centuries ago. What, then, is the connection between Navarra's discovery and the 3-story structure into which some of its discoverers have claimed they have actually entered and explored?

Since Navarra's wood was recovered from what SEARCH officials describe as a stationary "ice pack," and not a moving glacier; and since the other structure has been variously described as protruding from the end of a melting glacier, does it not seem logical to conclude that Mount Ararat holds *two* fascinating areas of search, rather than one, as has previously been believed by some? Verification of Navarra's timbers is all-important, it is true; but rediscovery of the 3-story structure should also engage the attention and ingenuity of a qualified investigating team as well.

The importance of this rediscovery was pointed out by Carl McIntyre, of the well-known 20th Century Reformation Hour, in the *Christian Beacon*, August 14, 1969. "It is regrettable," he wrote, "that the Associated Press, in sending a world-wide release from Istanbul about the proposed expedition of SEARCH, should have called the Ark 'the fabled vessel' instead of saying that the Bible reports that such an Ark landed on the top of Mount Ararat."

McIntyre, who had been interviewed on the subject as far back as 1945, goes on to say, "It could very well be in God's providence that the remains of Noah's Ark might be located." Speaking of the fact that Sunday School materials of certain major denominations now refer to the first eleven chapters of Genesis as "fables and myths," he states that in the event of a discovery, "This would be God's providential way of rebuking the apostates." Genesis 6-11, Dr. McIntyre points out, "deals with Noah and the Ark. This is almost half of the Genesis 'myth.' God has His evidences now being produced by the archaeologists which have already done much to mock the higher critics" (quoted from *Mount Ararat:* compiled by James Lee).

If this massive structure (referring to Navarra's timbers under the ice) is truly the Ark of the Old Testament, hidden protectively by tons of ice and snow for thousands of years, yet, not completely forgotten, then, perhaps, an ancient prophecy may be fulfilled. This prophecy is found in Apostle Peter's second Epistle, third chapter, verses three to six, which forecasts the attitude of scoffers who in the last days are to be 'wilfully ignorant' of the Flood, so that they deliberately and culpably deny the evident facts set forth in the Bible, and refuse to recognize and acknowledge the clearest evidences proving Scriptural truth including actual knowledge of the existence of the Ark of Noah.

And how much more convincing, we might add, when not only the possible base timbers of Navarra's discovery, but the actual ship discovered by Nouri, the atheists and Haji Yearam, the Turkish commissioners, the Kurdish farmer Reshit, the Russian aviator, George Greene, and others (including the old Armenian whose story has just been told) can be produced as double evidence of the historicity of the Flood!

Perhaps this chapter would not be complete without mention of still more recent corroboration to the story by another elderly Armenian (who also wishes, for reasons of his own, to remain anonymous). This gentleman, now a successful businessman in his adopted land, states that in his youth he lived in Erivan, which as you know, is within easy sighting distance of Aghri Dagh. His firm belief and active interest in the present-day existence of the Ark stems from his very vivid recollection of hearing his fellow-countrymen in that large industrial capital of the Armenian Soviet Republic, discussing the fact that the great ship was not only still on the mountain, but that it had actually been seen.

Unfortunately, the Araxas River and the vigilance of the Russian border guards, are most effective deterrents to anyone who might wish to pursue this additional and intriguing information to its source. But since these two trustworthy and honorable gentlemen have never met, and since their stories so remarkably coincide, there seems no plausible reason to doubt that they are true.

20

The Challenge
of Antiquity

Four Americans and two high ranking Turkish Army officers sat together in the impressively appointed conference room of the military headquarters for the Eastern Frontier in Erzerum. Against a striking background of crimson velvet wall hangings and national flags, they had been discussing plans to penetrate the militarily sensitive zone on Mount Ararat, where the Americans hoped to continue their search for Noah's Ark. One of the two Turkish gentlemen in the room was the chief officer in charge of Army Intelligence; the other was the head of the Third Army, General Baruk.

Another expedition to Ararat! The officers, with customary Turkish courtesy, listened patiently as outlines of the plans were revealed. At last General Baruk spoke:

"You men are here to find Noah's Ark! Our book, the Koran, says it landed on Mount Al-Judi, 250 miles southeast of here. Your book says it landed on Mount Ararat. Which book will win?" Then, with a flash of humor and a twinkle in his dark eyes, the General added: "More power to you! We hope you find it on Mount Ararat . . . !"

It was the summer of 1966. The men, Dr. Lawrence Hewitt, Dr. Clifford Burdick, Alva Appel, and Eryl Cummings left to join their expedition under the auspices of the Archaeological Research Foundation. The story of their summer's work has already been related in Chapter 17. Although the rediscovery did not take place that year, Eryl Cummings' subsequent visit with the aged Dr. Raymond Moore in Ankara on his way home to the States eventually paid off a thousandfold. For, as you will recall, it was through this contact that the surprising relationship between Al-Judi and Ararat came to light.

It was not until the summer of 1969, however, that Eryl Cummings was finally privileged to return to Turkey to continue his long-time quest for the Ark. In the party were two of his friends from the 1966 expedition, Dr. Lawrence Hewitt, the physician-botanist who had been in charge of the group that year, and Clifford Burdick, the geologist whom he had assisted in his survey of the mountain.

This year the small group was "on its own." Dr. Hewitt was anxious to pursue his botanical studies of the "genetic pool" of plant life on Ararat. Burdick hoped to complete his geological survey. Accompanying the small, independent group was Mrs. Opal Hewitt, the doctor's wife.

Their arrival in Turkey had started auspiciously enough. Because of Dr. Hewitt's long-time friendship with the Sunay family, the presidential limousine met the party as they disemplaned in Istanbul, and transported them to the Hilton Hotel where, supposedly, advance reservations had been made. However, through some never-explained circumstance, no rooms were available in the hotel as the travellers presented themselves, weary but hopeful, before the desk. No rooms, that is, except the Presidential suite, at the very modest cost of $100.00 per night!

What to do! The height of the tourist season was on, and inquiry failed to turn up another room in all of Istanbul. It began to look as if it would be the choice between sleeping in the street for the night, or paying the exorbitant price. At that point Dr. Attila Sunay, the president's son, intervened in his friend's behalf, and before long the American party was comfortably ensconced in the palatial suite at the slightly more reasonable cost of $60.00 for the night. Considering the alternative, $15.00 apiece was cheap enough . . . !

Morning brought a delectable bowl of the finest fruits, as well as an enchanting view of the Blue Bosporus across the beautiful formal gardens of the hotel. Fabulous Istanbul! The Byzantium of the ancients, later (for more than 1100 years) known as Constantinople, the capital of the Eastern Roman Empire until it fell to the Ottoman conquerors in 1453; a fascinating blend of East and West, a crossroads of commerce and travel, where great ships ply the waters between its European and Asian shores!

It is a city of historic mosques and soaring minarets, of pre-dawn muezzins calling the faithful to prayer. It is water taxis and a floating pontoon bridge; the home of ultra-modern hotels and the ancient Grand Bazaar, where thousands of inviting shops offer their wares from under the shelter of one vast roof; where antiques from around the world vie with washing machines and typewriters, bobby pins and nylon hose; it is a fleeiting glimpse of a duskily-beautiful dark-haired bride, arrayed in Western bridal attire, as she and her groom dash, laughing, from the open door of a limousine through the entrance to a plush hotel, her billowing veil floating mistily behind! It is a cacophony of cries from drivers of horsedrawn vehicles mingling with the raucous blare of motor horns. Such is modern Istanbul —an indescribable kaleidoscope of color and sound.

But, in spite of the attractions of this teeming metropolis of an ancient land, and the luxuries of its charming hotel, a still more fascinating adventure awaited the small group of travellers from faraway America. Far, far to the East, some 900 air-miles away, majestic Ararat beckoned with irresistible lure. For hidden somewhere on its massive flanks still lay concealed the answer to the question that has haunted modern explorers for so many years: Are reports of the existence of Noah's Ark really true? And would this summer yield additional evidence to corroborate the veracity of the controversial tales . . . ?

Although entirely unsuspected at this stage of the trip, two members of the party were destined to return with a most surprising discovery relating to the archaeological maps of the Ararat area turned over to Eryl Cummings by Col. Alexander A. Koor in 1945 (see Chapter 5). But we are getting ahead of our story again, since this exciting occurrence did not take place until almost deadline time for return to the States.

From Istanbul to Ankara, the beautiful capital of the modern Turkish Republic since 1923, it was a relatively short jaunt by air. Here, the broad avenues, the wide, tree-lined streets, the schools, libraries, theaters, shops and museums rich with relics of Hittite lore, are all a lasting monument to the vision and foresight of the Mustapha Kemal Ataturk, known to his people as "The Father of Turkey," who during the brief 15 years of his presidency modernized the dress, laws, and alphabet of this once-backward land of the Sultans; separated religion from government; provided free education for both children and adults; helped the struggling farm communities; and set the Turkish women free to vote, appear in public, and hold jobs.

Here, in bustling Ankara, necessary last-minute preparations for the rugged trip ahead must be made, and old friendships with Turkish officials and Army officers were happily renewed. Because in Turkey, as elsewhere around the world, the wheels of governmental bureaus "grind exceeding slow," considerable time had been consumed since the party had arrived in Istanbul. But at last they were airborne again, and some four hours later the Turkish Airlines had deposited them on the airstrip at Erzerum, the last outpost before take-off for Ararat, 160 miles away.

Now only two mountain passes intervened between the four sweltering travellers and their goal. At last, from some 60 miles away, the first mystic glimpse of snow-crowned Aghri Dagh appeared against the sky ahead, unbelievably serene and cool in the torrid summer heat as the small mini-bus bounced and rattled along the rough road to Dougabayazit at the foot of the peak.

In Dougabayazit awaited a most happy surprise—the new and modern Hotel Kent, its pleasant rooms, hot and cold running water, and dining room, a far cry from the more primitive accommodations Burdick and Cummings remembered from 1966. Here, in the dining room, the travellers encountered John Libi, the famous 73-year-old Ararat explorer from San Francisco who, with a round dozen of loyal Turkish friends, was preparing for his seventh and last attempt to find the Ark.

Here, too, the new arrivals met the six members of the SEARCH group (see Chapter 19), fresh from their summer's investigation of the Navarra site, who were preparing to leave for a prearranged rendezvous in Ankara. Because of a previous promise not to divulge information prematurely, the entire party—Navarra, his son "Coco," Bud Crawford, Hugo Neuberg, and Elfred Lee—presented a united and noncommittal front. They had nothing worthwhile to report, they said; however, a short time later the

198

news of their claimed discovery of additional hand-tooled wood at the same site as Navarra's discovery in 1955, was released to the press.

The day after the departure of SEARCH, the smaller group began its ascent. First at Ahora, then at 10,500 feet on the slopes above the village, they made their first camps. Through some unlucky fluke, the more commodious tents ordered for the trip had not arrived, and the campers were forced to "make do" with much smaller "pup tents" to which the words "comfort" and "room" could not truthfully be applied!

Dysentery, too, had added its misery to the rigors of the camp, and by the time the necessary acclimatizing period had passed, and it was time to move on up the mountain again, the lone lady in the party was ready to return to a more healthful clime. Accordingly, leaving Burdick and Cummings to negotiate the 10-mule pack train to the new site at 11,500 feet, Dr. and Mrs. Hewitt mounted two of the saddle ponies and started back down the trail. The doctor would return after settling his wife in a safer, more comfortable situation.

And now Ararat began to display some of the more "painful" aspects that had given it the name of "Aghri Dagh." En route to the 11,500-foot camp, Cummings met with a painful accident that could well have cost him his life. Mounted on a saddle-less pony that suddenly took fright, and faced with a split-second decision to save his own neck or the camera in his hand, the luckless rider (when he came to!) found himself on his back on a pile of rocks—the camera survived, but Cummings sustained badly torn ligaments, displaced vertebrae, and a chipped hip bone that would hamper his movements for some time to come. . . .

Somehow, they managed to reach the upper camp and an adequate water supply, and now it was Burdick's turn. Overcome by the dread "mountain sickness" and desperately ill, for days he lay helpless, sometimes actually despairing for his life.

Meanwhile, Cummings had been formulating a plan. A certain remote and inaccessible area on this side of the mountain had intrigued his imagination for some time. To the best of his knowledge, it had never been explored. Four days after his accident, and in spite of his torn and aching back, he engaged two Kurdish carriers and a sturdy boy to carry the gear, and started up the steep and rocky ridge above the camp. Perhaps, he thought, if he could manage to reach the ice-rim, he might be able to find some means of access into the dark, forbidding canyons below, any one of which might turn out to be the "high recess" on the mountain reputed, by the old Armenian tradition, to be the hiding place of the Ark.

Slowly and painfully he climbed, the shifting rocks giving way under almost every step, while the distant valley below assumed fantastic lights and shadows in the late afternoon sun. At an elevation of some 12,500 feet on the treacherous almost razorback ridge, the carriers suddenly stopped and set their loads on the ground. "This is it," they indicated with unmistakable meaning. "We've gone as far as we will go."

A lively argument, mostly in sign language, ensued. The men had already been paid to accompany the climber to the top. For more money, would they proceed? Since "money talks," in Turkey as well as in America, the inducement of the extra payment was irresistible. The additional *liras* changed hands, the packs were shouldered once more and the upward trek began.

At perhaps another 300 feet or so, down came the packs again. This time, as with James Bryce in 1876, no amount of persuasion, or cajoling, or extra *liras* would budge the bearers from their tracks. With emphatic gestures and even bodily force, they tried to turn the equally determined climber around and start him back downward on the ridge. Chattering nervously in their native tongue, they made clear their terrified conviction that he would surely tumble head over heels to his death on the rocks below.

At last, still muttering and mumbling dire predictions as to the fate of the stubborn explorer, the three Kurds shrugged their shoulders in helpless resignation and started the precarious descent of the ridge by themselves. Slowly, actually relieved to be rid of his well-meaning but obstructive friends, Cummings repacked his gear for an overnight stay and resumed the climb.

Within 200 feet of the forbidding rim of the mile-high ice cap, and with darkness closing in, the climber was suddenly deluged with a typical Ararat storm of rain and sleet. With his heavy shoulder pack threatening to topple him backwards down the remaining 70 percent grade between him and his goal, Cummings breathed a prayer for strength to reach the top of the ridge ahead. Almost immediately his strength returned. By using his ice-axe to cut a step ahead of himself as he progressed, he was easily able to finish the climb.

But once on top, to his intense disappointment, there was nothing to be seen except deep, terrifying drop-offs into the canyons he had hoped to explore. No connecting ridges led from his ridge into the cavernous area so devastated and torn by the 1840 upheaval that an entire section of the mountain below this ice-rim had collapsed and dropped into the gorge below. Ahead, and above, a noisy summer waterfall roared over the edge of the ice cap and tumbled precipitously down the sheer cliffs into the abyss below.

It would have been almost certain suicide for a climber to attempt to reach and explore from the edge of the ice cap without a supporting team. More than one adventure-some mountain climber has been swallowed and forever lost in a treacherous crevasse! There was nothing to do but wait out the storm, discover, if possible, a shelter in which to spend the night, and then to return down the mountain to formulate another plan.

To the right, an overhanging ledge promised protection of a sort. Once more the ice-axe was brought into play to hollow out a shallow depression into which the weary explorer could ease his aching back. Another prayer, this time for protection, as well as for relief from a sudden "charley-horse" that threatened to roll him down the mountainside—then sleep, at last, until the first faint rays of light at about 3:30 a.m., when Ararat, with all its flocks and herds, comes alive for another day.

The painful climb, however, had satisfied Cummings mind on one thing—there was no access into the difficult area he had hoped to search—not from this direction, at least. Shouldering his disappointment, as well as his pack, he began the difficult descent to the 11,500-foot camp. Slipping, sliding, with many a *glissade* on his soon-tattered derriere, he arrived safely, and in record time, much to the astonished relief of the Kurds who had left him with such misgivings the afternoon before. The strange American had invaded the "magic zone" and returned alive!

Dr. Hewitt had also returned, and the next day the entire party continued the descent to the foot of the mountain as far as Ahora at an elevation of 5,200 feet. The following day Hewitt and Cummings horsebacked up the opposite ridge of the Ahora Gorge, to a high point overhanging the gloomy, cavernous depths of the abyss below. Their guide had missed the trail, so it was not until late afternoon that the two men reached the spot where they had planned to scrutinize, through binoculars, the labyrinth of canyons into which Eryl Cummings had hoped to find access a few days before.

But here, too, disappointment was to be their lot, for already the thick evening mists, rolling and billowing in magnificent confusion among the crags, obscured all but momentary glimpses of the spectacular view. Nevertheless, in the brief quarter hour they dared to remain (or risk traveling back to camp through snake-infested country in the dark!), both men succeeded in coming away with what are undoubtedly some of the most beautiful pictures of the area ever captured on color film.

Only a week had passed since their arrival at Aghri Dagh—but what a week! Illness, accident, frustration—and yet, all unawares, Dr. Hewitt and Eryl Cummings were about to become involved in one of the most surprising, and possibly the most significant discoveries relating to the history of Mount Ararat ever made; in importance, perhaps, from an archaeological viewpoint, second only to the Karada inscription of the Flood that is described in Chapter 5.

Years before, in 1945, it will be recalled, Col. Alexander Koor had turned over to Eryl Cummings the map of the archaeological sites he had compiled during his tour of duty as a White Russian Army officer in the service of the Czar. He had also explained, as closely as possible, the area where he had discovered the cuneiform and pictorial carvings on the cliff wall that told the story of the Flood.

All previous efforts to relocate the area had failed, however, since with change of domain the ancient Russian names for the Ararat sites had been changed, and no one had been found who seemed to remember what they had once been called. And then, in 1969, and just before deadline time to leave the mountain and return home, an old man was found who remembered the long-sought Russian name.

With only days to spare, a minibus was hastily hired, and the two explorers and their aged friend were transported to the area from which the investigation would begin. The old man and the minibus returned to town. From here on Cummings and Hewitt would be on their own—always bearing in mind, of course, that if they did not make it back to meet the minibus at the appointed time, it would mean an additional 35 mile hike; and, in all likelihood, they would miss their plane reservations back to the States!

We will pass lightly over the adventures (and misadventures!) of the two men as they set out on their quest. But surprisingly, considering the hazards and narrow escapes they had endured in such a short period of time, they had arrived at their destination by noon the next day. Here, in this primitive area, on which they were given to understand no Americans had ever explored, they were astonished to discover what appeared to be a veritable archaeological paradise of which they had not even dreamed!

At the foot of a low hill lay the undeniably ancient ruins of a sizeable stone building, its 30-inch walls basking peacefully in the undisturbed solitude of perhaps milleniums of neglect. Its gaping doorway revealed the crumbling remains of inner walls that had once divided the structure into rooms. Not far away, half-buried in a thick growth of yellowed native grass, the surprised explorers almost stumbled over a long-abandoned grinding wheel five feet in diameter and 16 inches thick, its center perforated by a hole some 16 inches square.

The scattered outlines of a still visible rock dugway led some 700 feet upward to the top of the hill, where a still more astonishing discovery was made. Here, among the ruins of several other ancient buildings, rose the curving walls of an extraordinary structure, its rounded exterior beautifully fashioned from handhewn rock. In height it was perhaps 20 to 25 feet on the lower side; its diameter was probably 16 to 18 feet. The northern face of this remarkable building had miraculously withstood the ravages of uncounted centuries of Ararat's rigorous clime. As in the building at the foot of the hill, no roof was visible, but where the wall on the southern exposure had collapsed, the outlines of an oblong room could be seen beneath the rubble.

The two men made their way around the brow of the hill to the base of the structure on its lower side. Here they discovered a large rock adorned with eight beautifully carved crosses, guarding the entrance to what appeared to them a tumbled-in subterranean cave. Other inscriptions and crosses could also be distinguished on the other ruins at the site.

Silhouetted against the sky at the crest of a rocky eminence some distance away, the sharply-carved outlines of a nobly-proportioned patriarchal head rose perhaps 8 to 10 feet above the top of the hill. For some reason, the ancient sculptor had faced the bearded, turbaned profile so that its sightless gaze would forever rest on the towering heights of Aghri Dagh . . . !

Even to the untrained eyes of the two amateurs, the remoteness of the area, even its air of undisturbed tranquility, suggested that they had inadvertently stumbled across a major archaeological site while searching for the Karada inscription Col. Koor had told them about.

Eryl Cummings and Col. Koor had often talked and dreamed of the day when they might return for further investigation of the areas mapped out by the former Russian Army officer so many years before. But a quarter of a century had elapsed since their first meeting in 1945, and hope had gradually dwindled for the aging scholar's return. But always, with undiminished enthusiasm, he looked forward to the time when Noah's Ark would be found, and his maps of ancient sites would help to unravel the mystery of Aghri Dagh.

Now, almost unable to believe his eyes, Eryl Cummings gazed with quickening pulse at the crumbling ruins and the crosses and inscriptions he had long hoped to see—remains of an ancient civilization that, when properly understood, would almost certainly increase the knowledge of a bygone age!

Noting that this particular site had not been marked on Col. Koor's map, the two discoverers quickly finished photographing the ruins and made their way back down the rocky hill.

Weeks later, in San Francisco, the story and pictures of the discovery brought an excited reaction from Col. Koor. The photos and descriptions of the circular rock building, he said, harmonized perfectly with the story the natives of Maku (a town near Ararat) had told him many years before: that the tombs of the ancients had been built in this form, usually with a squared-off entrance on the southern end. As for the crosses, explained Col. Koor, who had been acknowledged by Dr. J. O. Kinnaman in 1946 (Chapter 5) as an expert in his field, and "a scholar of high degree of attainment," they were definitely of Sumerian origin.

It had been Dr. Kinnaman, also, who had rated the Karada inscription ("God sowed the seeds of the word into the waters . . . the waters filled the earth . . . his children came to rest on the mountain or peak.") as "a very accurate translation" of the story of the Flood. And now, a quarter of a century later, the old scholar had identified the crosses on Ararat with the oldest civilization of which there is any record at all. . . .

It was Dr. John Wilson (ibid) who had written a letter to Benjamin Franklin Allen in 1945 in which he stated, "For many years there have been persistent and circumstantial reports of some remarkable phenomenon on Mount Ararat. As long as these reports come through intermediaries they remain hearsay rather than evidence. The reports refer also to inscriptions in such a way as to suggest that these inscriptions are of a number and length to justify linguistic analysis. I feel that a scientific expedition supplied with personal scientific abilities and with accurate scientific equipment and under the formal control of the Turkish Service of Antiquities should resolve doubts with regard to the existence of these phenomenons. Objective research in a crucial but little known area will make a contribution to scholarly knowledge."

It was Dr. Wilson, too, who had made the significant and perhaps unwittingly prophetic remark that, "Insofar as antiquity is concerned, all lines of investigation in the future, whether they be American, British, Russian, or others, will eventually converge in the area of Mount Ararat, or a radius of 75 miles from the mountain."

Eight crosses. Eight survivors of the Flood. An ancient tomb at the foot of the Biblical mountain peak. Is it unreasonable to conjecture that there may be some connection between these ruins, the Ark, and Noah and his sons? Did the same hand that recorded the story of the Deluge on the Karada cliff not far away also carve the majestic patriarchal head atop a hill, facing the heights of Aghri Dagh? Did these same hands help fashion this superbly handicrafted ancient tomb?

Had these sturdy structures remained intact until the great blast in 1840 when the mighty mountain was shaken like a reed in the wind? Whose bones might lie crumbling under these tons of debris? What thrilling stories still await discovery in this faraway place? And what of the other as yet-uninvestigated archaeological sites of Col. Koor . . . ?

When we recall the story of Thamanin which, since the remotest ages of antiquity, signified the eight persons who came out of the Ark following the Deluge; and when we consider the eight crosses on Karada hill, our imagination staggers in contemplation of what ancient history may yet be revealed to the modern world!

What a challenge to a competent scientific team to provide answers to such intriguing questions as these! Who will be privileged to unravel the mystery of what George Vandeman, the founder of the Archaeological Research Foundation in 1960, has so aptly called "the riddle of Ararat"?

A riddle is for solving. And, even as a jigsaw puzzle is composed of hundreds of scattered and apparently unrelated pieces until patiently fitted together into one colorful whole, so the story of the discovery of the ruins of Karada combines to add a thrilling chapter to the saga of Noah's Ark.

21

The Sound
and the Fury

With the discovery of the Karada ruins, of course, a new
dimension was added to the continued investigation of
Mount Ararat. Plans were soon underway for a small,
compact, highly mobile group to return to the mountain
under the name of *International '70*.

Hardwicke Knight, the New Zealand archaeologist and
photographer, was eager to return once more to study and
evaluate the Karada site. A team of young, well-trained
American alpinists looked forward with enthusiasm to
making an all-out search for the superstructure of the Ark.
Dr. John Warwick Montgomery, Chairman of the Division
of Church History and director of their European program
at Trinity Evangelical Divinity School, Deerfield, Illinois,
planned to join the party in early August to gather material
for his regular quarterly column in *Christianity Today*.

Dr. Hewitt, still preoccupied with completing his study
of the "genetic pool" of plant life on Mount Ararat, would
be returning this year "on his own." Dr. Burdick's age and
health discouraged another visit to the mountain where he
had been so desperately ill the year before. The members
of the SEARCH organization had dedicated their summer's efforts to continuing the highly scientific pursuit of
the Navarra site. Eryl Cummings headed the new group.

With the experience born of two previous trips, all necessary documents for each member of the party were in
hand well in advance of the deadline for Turkish permits.
All was in good order—or so it was believed. When the
permits failed to arrive it was discovered—too late!—that

the busy individual to whom the all important information had been entrusted for forwarding to the proper authorities, had failed, through some oversight, to get them in the mail.

Reluctant to abandon the project entirely, Eryl Cummings, largely at his own expense, set out for Turkey hoping to secure a simple tourist permit that would enable him to proceed to Ararat as originally planned. He was joined in New York by Mark Albrecht, fiery-haired young Christian journalism major fresh from the Berkeley campus of the University of California, and a grandson of a prominent Lutheran clergyman.

Once in Turkey it was soon learned that even had their original plans materialized, expeditions to Ararat, as such, had run into unexpected and apparently insurmountable difficulties. However, their personal permits to the mountain were readily obtained, and the two redheaded explorers set out. For the youthful Mark, it was a long-anticipated thrill; for Cummings, just turned 65, the continued pursuit of a 25-year dream.

At the Kent Hotel in Dougabayazit, the extent of the SEARCH dilemma became known. Here they found Ralph Lenton and Hugo Neuberg, disheartened by the early termination of their 20-day temporary local permits, as well as their total failure to obtain the necessary government permits to continue their work (Chapter 23), packing their equipment and preparing to leave.

It is difficult for the non-Turkish mind, of course, to comprehend the connection between a search for Noah's Ark, to which the Moslem's own holy book, the Koran, also attests, and the "internal security" of a nation to which such a discovery would bring only the most salubrious results. Nevertheless, the identical situation arose again in 1971, when Eryl Cummings returned to Turkey in a joint effort with Dr. Lawrence B. Hewitt to continue both Dr. Hewitt's botanical research and Cummings' search for the Ark. However, it must be recognized that the geographical position of Mount Ararat, and its highly sensitive military location on the very borders of its powerful and atheistic Soviet neighbor to the north, has no doubt been one of the most potent and increasingly frustrating deterrents to every organized attempt to rediscover the Ark in recent years.

But in 1970, Cummings and Albrecht, with the hope that their smaller, more mobile group, with none of the elaborate scientific equipment that might arouse the wholly unwarranted suspicion that they were spies, set out with light hearts at 4:00 a.m. on the day after their encounter with the men of the larger expedition group. Thankful that their own 3-week permits and military clearance were safely in hand, no foreboding of disappointment clouded their joy.

After proceeding by truck to the frontier outpost of Ortelu, they would transfer their gear to *esheks* (donkeys), for which they had previously arranged, en route to Lake Kop where their base camp would be set up. They were accompanied by Yucel Domnez, an expert Turkish alpinist, university student and journalist; the other member of the party was a native guide.

However, the *esheks,* usually so annoyingly prompt at the crack of dawn, were not there when the truck arrived. To save precious time, the party breakfasted on the deliciously crusty French-type bread fresh-baked in Dougabayazit the day before.

At last! A mere hour and a half late, the donkeys arrived. Carefully rearranging and reloading their supplies, the men mounted their ponies and the small procession set off up the sketchy trail. All day long they climbed, winding their way up the lower slopes of the towering mountain that dwarfed the human beings so eager to test their puny strength against its massive heights. Colorful Kurdish camps enlivened the scene; a note of comedy was introduced when a frightened young Kurdish lass, riding a saddleless pony, passed them on a dead run up the steep rocky trail. Perhaps she (or her mount!) had never seen two red-headed humans before. . . .

By late afternoon they had arrived at the lush high mountain valley on the plain of Kip Ghioll, only a short distance below Lake Kop. Here, on the grassy, level floor of the plain, with a sparkling spring of pure water nearby, the party set up camp. Sleep would be doubly welcome that night, after the long hard day. . . .

But alas! capricious Ararat let loose a sudden barrage of rain, hail, sleet, and snow that quickly inundated the area with some four inches of frigid water. Shivering, freezing (for Ararat at 11,300 feet can be bitterly cold even in early August), the men managed, between breaks in the storm, to drag their supplies and tents to a rocky prominence where the drainage was greatly improved. Then, still shivering and cold, they crawled into their downy sleeping bags and snuggled down for the night.

At dawn the rattle of Cummings' cooking gear aroused a sleepy and reluctant camp. But another long hard day lay just ahead; it was important to get a head start.

While Cummings, by now an old hand at camp cookery, deftly whipped up a meal, the younger men rearranged the packs and prepared for the anticipated two weeks of exploration ahead. The native guide would remain at the camp to keep an eye on things against their return. From here on out, it would be legwork for the three explorers, for no loaded pack animal could keep its footing on the steep, rocky slopes above Lake Kop.

It is amazing what a nourishing hot breakfast will do to restore aching muscles and sagging morale, and it was an eager, cheerful trio who shouldered their packs a short time later and started up the hill.

A few hundred feet above their camp, the hikers passed Lake Kop—a shimmering azure gem set ruggedly in a bed of craggy volcanic rock, and fed by a slowly-melting glacial finger that had escaped from the eternal ice fields above. Since it is the only lake on the mountain, its placid summer beauty is often ruffled by the milling of the hundreds of sheep and shaggy-haired goats whose owners bring them to quench their thirst at its brink.

It was in this high mountain lake that Navarra had thought in 1952 that he might find the remains of the Ark. It was here, too, that he and his son Raphael had paused for refreshments before starting the more strenuous stages of their climb in 1955.

Now, skirting its northerly side, Cummings and Mark and Yucel proceeded easterly for some two miles over the moraines, then, turning sharply back to the southwest, they started toward the ridge that would lead to the west side of the Parrot glacier.

Here, about half-way up the ridge as the climbers paused for a bite of lunch at noon, they saw a rare sight. Poised gracefully against the horizon perhaps a mile away, a flock of tawny wild mountain goats could be seen leaping gracefully from crag to crag until they disappeared from sight. The reason for their haste and agitation was soon discovered: a nimble-footed hunter soon appeared, following swiftly in pursuit of the elusive game!

By 4:00 p.m. the three climbers had reached an elevation of some 14,000 feet. Here, at the entrance to a shallow, sloping cave under an overhanging rock, Cummings called a halt. This is where he would wait, he announced, while Mark and Yucel returned to base camp for the rest of the gear and additional supplies.

Yucel was aghast. Stay here alone? All night? at 14,000 feet? *NO* . . . ! But Cummings was firm. He was not about to make that strenuous climb twice in three days—not at his age! What was there to fear? He had already survived one memorable night at the same elevation farther around the mountain in 1969. And this time he had a cave. . . .

Yucel was not convinced. "Listen, Yucel," said Cummings, in an effort to allay his fears, for the young alpinist was genuinely concerned. "You know Allah?"

The follower of the Prophet nodded his head. "Well," explained Cummings, carefully choosing his words, "me and Allah—we stay here. You and Mark—you go back down. There's two of you, there will be two of us—Allah and me. You understand, Yucel?"

Slowly a comprehending grin spread over Yucel's face. Once again he nodded, this time in agreement. Surely, if Allah was on their side, there was nothing to fear. With a gesture of cheerful resignation, he turned and led the way down the steep mountainside.

Cummings watched until the blue and the maroon parkas had disappeared from sight. Then he turned, and with his ice-axe began levelling a body-sized depression from the sloping space under the big rock.

But the makeshift cave did not turn out to be exactly a bed of ease. At the first suggestion of dawn, he crawled stiffly from his freezing shelter to straighten his aching back. There, in the freshly fallen snow, he discovered the huge paw prints of a mountain lion that had paused, sometime during his fitful spells of dozing, to sniff curiously at his very door. He had often heard their defiant screams in 1966, as he lay awake outside his tent under the Anatolian skies listening to the fierce baying of the Kurdish dogs as they guarded their master's flocks and herds. But thus far, he had only glimpsed the wild goats on the dizzying heights above, and the deadly vipers on the plain below. This was the nearest he had come to a personal encounter with any of the predatory beasts of Aghri Dagh. Surely, "Allah" had protected him during the night. . . .

Restless, needing relief from his cramped quarters, Cummings carefully and slowly zigzagged his way in the eerie light through the maze of ice-covered, freshly-frosted boulders above the cave; clinging for support to such rocky ledges as afforded a precarious hand-hold as he climbed, his trusty ice-axe saving him many a nasty fall on the slippery 70 percent grade.

At last, on a level with the lower edge of the ice cap, and perhaps 400 feet away, he found what he had been hoping to see—a large bare rock protruding from the deep snow, its flat surface a mute invitation to stretch his weary bones and rest. Feeling exceedingly small and insignificant, and very much alone, Cummings eased himself onto the rock and gazed around. Where, amid all this overwhelming grandeur of ice and snow, rock and treacherous crevasses, did the Ark still lie concealed? When—and through what agency—would God again reveal this matchless and certainly one of the oldest weapons in His arsenal of Truth?

Some 17 years before, George Greene had photographed it on the edge of an imbricate fault. But George Greene was dead—his pictures had disappeared. As yet no one had been discovered with the knowledge necessary to guide a party to the spot. Had some shifting of the mountain since 1952 changed the position of the old ship? Would this be the year when some sharp-eyed explorer would stumble across it again—out of sight in that deep canyon, or hidden behind that next ridge? Hoary and weathered from exposure to the wild elements of Aghri Dagh since the protective glacial deep-freeze had begun to recede, would it not be increasingly difficult to spot? And even though comparisons of the various discoveries of years gone by had pinpointed it on this northeasterly side, the rugged area still presented almost unbelievable obstacles to the search. Or, perhaps, God had dropped a veil of secrecy over the great ship once more, until a still greater spiritual crisis confronted the children of men. . . .

How would announcement of the next discovery be received? The atheists in 1856, when faced with the unwelcome fact of the existence of the Ark, reacted with malevolence and lies. Like the men of the Apostle Paul's scathing denunciation in Romans 1, they "did not like to retain God in their knowledge," and so, unmindful of their Creator's warning, they had deliberately and with "malice aforethought," "changed the truth . . . into a lie . . ."—with what baleful effects on the world of their day only the last Great Judgment will reveal.

In sharp contrast Nouri, whose dedication to Truth had led him three times to Ararat in search of the Ark, had viewed the old ship with delighted but reverential awe, and had gone forth to herald his discovery to the world. Had the facts already been nulified in the 30-odd years since the atheists had falsified their report? For Nouri's story made astonishingly minute ripples upon the thinking of even the religious leaders of his time!

Through the years of research, while the various reports of discoveries slowly grew into a colorful, beautifully coordinated pattern of facts confirming the modern-day existence of the Ark, it became frustratingly obvious that an opposing power was persistently dogging the trail. Like a murky shadow, a sinister, supernatural influence seemed constantly to hamper or destroy every shred of documented evidence that came to light concerning the Ark. Surely it was more than mere coincidence that well-attested evidence such as the aviator's story in the Army's *Stars and Stripes* had been innocently destroyed only days before its long-sought documentation might have been of untold assistance in the search. Did it, perhaps, contain an important clue as to the location of the Ark . . . ?

Then there was the mystery of Bertha Davis' faded old pictures, and the photos made from the helicopter by George Greene. Who could doubt the collective veracity of the many trustworthy individuals who not only had heard the stories, but had actually seen the pictorial proofs? Who can explain why they had simply vanished into thin air?

Why had Harold Williams almost lost his life in the same fire that had destroyed the only copy of Haji Yearam's important and incriminating story—and the newspaper report of the deathbed confession corroborating the facts? Why had the godless Bolshevik revolution reputed at the very moment when the luckless courier, with all his detailed and documented reports of the scientific investigation of the Ark, had left the mountain en route to take them to the Czar? Why . . . ?

And yet, in spite of (or even, perhaps, because of) the many adversities and disappointments that had dogged the path of research, Cummings had become more than ever convinced that the ever-widening trail would lead to a triumphant conclusion at last. The deepening conviction that where there were so many utterly fascinating little wisps of smoke, there must also be a slow-burning, smoldering fire, had woven itself like a crimson thread through the very fabric of his life. And, in spite of the harassments of this unseen foe, the encouraging presence of a still greater Power had been present through the long years.

Now, as Eryl Cummings reviewed the Providences that had brought him for the third time to this lonely mountainside, he felt more than ever the worthiness of his cause. The words of Harold Lindsell, of *Christianity Today*, might well have been the echo of his own thoughts:

"Any simpleton knows that we live in a day of revolution. But the great question is, what is the meaning of the revolution? I think there is a message in the wind. Culture and civilization are saying something. As I read the Scriptures, the first message I get is this: The center of the real struggle is not here on earth. The center of the real struggle is God versus Satan. It is light versus darkness. The battle is being fought in the cosmos as well as on the earth. It is an unseen as well as a seen work. What we see is not the totality of reality. Beyond sight and sense and sound and smell, there is the greater reality of the struggle between the unseen forces of God and of Satan.

"The second message I get from the wind is this: This present world is doomed. The scent of death is upon it. It is committing suicide and nothing can save it. It must die before ever it can live again. The judgment of God has already been pronounced upon it." ("Theistic Suicide," in *Action Magazine*, Spring, 1970.)

The ever-present reality of this warfare had been graphically described by the Apostle Paul as he wrote to the Ephesians many centuries before: "For we wrestle not against flesh and blood, but against principalities, against powers, against the rulers of the darkness of this world, against spiritual wickedness in high places . . ." (Ephesians 6:12).

To the militant apostle, as to many a reformer after him, this battle for the "pulling down of (the) strongholds" of Satan (2 Corinthians 10:4) had often resulted in hand-to-hand, life and death combat with the foe, as evidenced by the amazing list of afflictions he had somehow survived (2 Corinthians 11:23-27). When at last his head rolled under the executioner's axe in the courtyard of a Roman dungeon, he died content. It had been "a good fight." He was ready to lay down the cross. He had earned his crown.

The fury of the struggle had not slackened with the years. As the hour approached for the climactic battle between the forces of right and wrong, between Truth and specious lies, the mighty tug-of-war between the opposing forces markedly increased. The grip of false theories concerning the origin of man and the beginnings of our world that began as a mere trickle in 1839, would soon swell into an irresistible torrent destined to sweep countless millions from the moorings of their ancient faith. The new "higher criticism" of the Bible would soon gain an unbelievably "strong hold" over the only-too-susceptible minds of men.

It was at this moment that the first reported modern sightings of Noah's Ark began to reach a confused and vacillating world. It was as if God, in His pity for the souls of benighted men, had introduced into the battle a "secret weapon" of His own, reserved, as the hail and snow of Job's ancient prophecy, "against the time of trouble, against the day of battle and war" (Job 38:22-23). Could the old Ark, preserved as it had been under centuries of ice and snow, have been one of the "treasures" God had "reserved" for this very time? To quote again from *Assault of the Unknown* (Sullivan: McGraw-Hill, 1961), "even great cataclysms are filed away in ice for future reference."

And now, these modern-day "references" to the Ark, with its dramatic reminder of the "great cataclysm" of the ancient world in punishment for their sins, was like a "voice crying in the wilderness, Prepare ye the way of the

215

Lord . . ." (Matthew 3:3)—the mighty Creator of the heavens and the earth. . . .

Had the struggle against these unseen forces been worth all the long years of sacrifice and strain? Cummings emerged slowly from his reverie, suddenly conscious of the intense cold. Surely, the long struggle had not been in vain. Some benefit must eventually accrue. What would this summer's investigation bring to light? Would it narrow the area of rediscovery still more . . . ? Snatches of Dr. John Wilson's long-familiar words drifted into his mind as he reviewed the events in his life since 1945:

"For many years there have been persistent and circumstantial reports of some remarkable phenomenon on Mount Ararat . . . the reports refer also to inscriptions . . . objective research will make a contribution to scholarly knowledge . . . insofar as antiquity is concerned, all lines of investigation in the future . . . will eventually converge in the area of Mount Ararat. . . ."

Then the still more forceful statement of Dr. Gilbert Grosvenor seemed to hang suspended in the still air: "The discovery of the Ark of Noah would be the greatest archaeological discovery of all time."

Inscriptions. Karada. The reports of a great wooden structure bearing all the earmarks of the Biblical Ark. Yes, the struggle, and the research, and the toil had been well worth the price.

Cummings thought of Navarra, whose discovery lay embedded in an ice pack only a short distance below. Would scientific investigation prove what the French explorer so sincerely believed—that he had actually found the base of the Ark? Would still more intensive search reveal the superstructure of the upper stories not very far away? A scant half mile to the east lay the snow field where Hardwicke Knight had once stumbled over great timbers of soggy wood. Was there any relationship between this and the Navarra find? What would this summer's search bring to light?

Their plans had been well and carefully laid. Skirting the ice cap in an easterly direction, he and Mark and Yucel would leave the Parrot glacier to the west, and the site where Navarra had discovered wood. They would proceed around the mountain to the point above the Ahora Gorge, below which Cummings had slept in 1969, and close to the ice field of Hardwicke Knight. They would investigate, if possible, the Cehennem Dere which feeds the Black Glacier on the far depths of the canyon floor.

Then, if humanly feasible, they would descend from the towering ice rim of the vast *cirque* that so abruptly terminates the lower reaches of the Abich I glacier, onto the rocky benches below. Here, they fondly hoped, they would have bird's-eye access to that great network of forbidding crevasses and canyons among the wild crags below. If the results were negative, they still would have accomplished a great deal by narrowing the area of search still more.

But Cummings' most pressing need at the moment was a little more much needed rest. Yucel and Mark were not expected back for another day. Stretching himself full-length on the rock in his well-padded high-altitude hiking clothes, the weary climber dropped immediately into a deep and relaxing sleep.

The storm of the night before had passed. While Cummings slept, the dawn rapidly brightened into sunrise, the sunrise blossomed into a beautiful day, calm and tranquil under a deep indigo sky. The temperature warmed to freezing; the rock upon which the climber slept basked in the creeping rays of the morning sun.

Suddenly the silence was broken by a crunching sound in the crusty snow. Dazed by slumber, Cummings sat up and peered around. Had the mountain lion returned? Or perhaps it was an inquisitive bear. Both Navarra and Libi, he recalled, had experienced terrifying encounters with these great grizzly beasts, and he, too, was unarmed. . . .

And then he saw the familiar blue parka of Yucel, searching for him among the rocks. The young alpinist was alone. What did it mean? Why had he returned so soon? He had not been expected for another day. Had some accident befallen Mark . . . ?

In a moment the wiry Turk stood beside him, seemingly not at all winded by his hasty climb. The news was bad. Two *gendarmes* (the native police) had come to the camp, he said, with a government request that all American explorers should leave Ararat—at once!

Leave Ararat? At once . . . ? "But our permits" . . . ? protested Cummings, dumbfounded by this turn of events.

What a calamity, just as they were about to begin their summer's search! There must be some mistake!

Unhappily, Yucel explained. According to the gendarmes, he said, the orders restraining the SEARCH group from further explorations that year had been expanded to include *all* American climbers—even those who had been able to secure formal clearances for their work! (Much later, the reason for the summary termination of Cummings' and Albrecht's permits came to light. It is hoped and believed, however, that the unfortunate rescinding of the permits did not come about through any deliberately malicious personal intent, but rather through a combination of circumstances understandable and no doubt unavoidable at the time.)

A descent is always more difficult than a climb, especially when one's hopes have just collapsed like a pricked balloon. But at last, in record time, Cummings and Yucel arrived at the camp below Lake Kop to find everything astir. The *gendarmes* had brought *esheks* and ponies for the return trip. It was all in a day's work for these affable, courteous gentlemen of the law. To Cummings and his crestfallen young friend Mark, it was the summary cancellation of months of planning, hard work, and dreams.

Disappointments always seem to ride a bit harder on youth than upon those who have become more inured to the vicissitudes of life. The young journalist had staked so much on this trip! But it had not been a total loss—he had seen the great "alabaster peak" of which he had dreamed; he had even climbed its rocky slopes. Even with the disappointment, it had been an experience to treasure long. He would still be able to return home with a great tale to tell. . . .

Sadly, the little group broke camp and set off down the slopes they had climbed with such anticipation only two days before. For one does not argue with the military in a foreign land—one merely obeys!

Back at Ortelu, the weary travellers were welcomed and refreshed with true Turkish hospitality before they and their gear were loaded back onto the truck for the return trip to Dougabayazit. Here, the next day, a very apologetic mayor and government officials expressed their sincere regret over the unfortunate circumstances that had forced their recall.

On their way to Turkey a short time before, Cummings and Albrecht had stopped in Paris to make last-minute arrangements to meet John Warwick Montgomery in Dougabayazit in early August. Dr. Montgomery, whose fearless defense of the Bible had earned him the well-deserved title of "Apostle of the Scholars," had become keenly interested in the evidences for the existence of the Ark. He had looked forward with great eagerness to joining the two explorers for a week's extensive search.

However, through some unexplainable change in schedules, Montgomery and his 11-year-old son David did not arrive in Dougabayazit on the pre-arranged date. They reached the city a day after Cummings and Albrecht had abandoned hope for their arrival and had left.

Montgomery, who belongs to that rare breed of men described by Thomas Fuller as "lean of body and visage, as if his eager soul, biting for anger at the clog of his body, desired to fret a passage through it" (Life of the Duke of Alva: 1608-1661), refused to be entirely thwarted by this miscarriage of his plans. Undaunted, he immediately engaged the now footloose Yucel, and he and David set out to scale Ararat from its southern side. Undoubtedly David, albeit with many assists, is the first known American youngster to ever make it to within 600 metres of the summit of one of the most celebrated mountains in the world!

It had been part of Cummings' plan to revisit the Karada ruins before returning to the States. With a more plentiful supply of film than in 1969, he had hoped to return with a complete pictorial record of the ancient site. However, because of the uncertain status of American explorers in the vicinity of Ararat at the moment, he and Albrecht reluctantly abandoned their plans and returned home.

Disheartened by the summer's turn of events, Cummings at first shunned all thought of returning to Turkey in 1971. But the lure of the quest is strong: like Fernand Navarra before him, the haunting memory of Ararat filled his days and nights as he sought to quell his disappointments in the necessary pursuit of everyday affairs. Would he ever see Aghri Dagh again—that "painful mountain" that seemed to mock so many years of hope . . . ? Not, decided Cummings, unless indications of Providence, through no efforts of his own, should clearly point out the way.

Less than a month had passed before a phone call from an associate in California brought the surprising information that a philanthropist who had heard of the years of research through some unknown source, wished to know more about the work with the thought of sponsoring another expedition in 1971. By the time the Easter season had rolled around, two lengthy interviews had taken place, the evidences from the just-completed manuscript for this volume had been read, and the decision to finance the summer's work had taken place.

About the same time, assurances of bonafide Turkish permits through another unexpected source convinced Eryl Cummings that, from all indications, Providence had opened the way for his return. This time his party consisted of the two alpine climbers, Earl and Eric Furman, who had looked forward to this experience since the previous year. After picking up a VW Minibus in Germany, the three men crossed Europe into Turkey, where they were joined by the third member of their crew, Dr. Robert Sibley, of the American Hospital in Paris, France. Their small group, in turn, soon joined forces with Dr. Lawrence B. Hewitt, the Alabama botanist determined to complete, if possible, his work on the Ararat "genetic pool," and his associate, Dr. Donald Brown, from the Loma Linda University in California. The two groups, although with differing objectives, would be working in adjacent areas, and it was felt they would strengthen each other's efforts. Dr. John Warwick Montgomery planned to join the party on August 9.

But again, as on previous trips to Turkey, it was soon learned that the "bonafide" permits which, hopefully, should have allowed the explorers to proceed to Ararat with no further delays, had not cleared *all* departments of State—a procedure necessary, it seems, before local officials will allow any work to begin.

Meanwhile, believing the way to be officially cleared, Cummings and his party had proceeded to Erzerum to await the arrival of the other group. Instead, a long-distance call to Ankara brought the disappointing news that they must return to the capital for more negotiations before they would be allowed to begin. Reluctantly, the nose of the Minibus was turned in the opposite direction from the goal, and the rugged 900-mile journey back to Ankara was begun.

Weeks passed. Tedious weeks, filled with alternating hope and despair. Weeks filled with haunting memories of the anguished waiting of A. J. Smith in 1949; the various attempts of the Archaeological Research Foundation during the frustrating '60's; the seemingly insurmountable obstacles that had also plagued the SEARCH organization in more recent years. Would this summer's attempt to rediscover the Ark once more end in defeat . . . ?

At last, one happy day, all the parties concerned were advised to proceed immediately to Dougabayazit, at the foot of Aghri Dagh, to await issuance of the final permits so they could begin their season's exploration. Joyfully, the Minibus set out to retrace the 900 long hot miles to the distant Eastern frontier. The scorching midsummer heat, the tightly-crammed car—what did these minor discomforts matter to the four occupants who now so hopefully anticipated the fruition of their plans? At last—at long last—their search could begin!

Meanwhile, however, as the Minibus and its crowded occupants bounced merrily along, all unaware, over the rough, dusty roads, a chilling atmosphere regarding the fate of the American expedition had settled down over one important governmental department in Ankara. Only one department—in all that complex network of officialdom that, from the top down, had approved the project of searching for Noah's Ark—refused to sign the necessary permits! The directive to proceed to Dougabayazit to await final confirmation appeared to have been premature . . . ! Once more, in spite of every effort to comply with governmental regulations and requests, an expedition to search for the Ark had come to a grinding halt. There appeared to the disappointed travellers no solution except to bow to circumstances beyond their control and pray that with the passing of time the apparently hopeless stalemate might change.

As Dr. Montgomery put it in his quarterly column under *Current Religious Thought* in *Christianity Today* (January 7, 1972): ". . . because of continuing tension within the Turkish bureaucracy between those who favored our cause and those who did not, Mr. Cummings allowed discretion to serve as the better part of valor and personally forewent exploration; he wisely saw that to press the permissions too far might have created grave problems for the future."

In the concluding paragraph of his article (aptly titled "Arkaeology 1971"), Montgomery neatly wraps up the feelings of all die-hard "Ark-aeologists" in these words: "Further work now awaits another August and the grace of the Turkish authorities . . . we couldn't stand the strain of Ararat if the winds of unbelief in the authority of God's Holy Word didn't impel us to do all that is possible to confirm its trustworthiness."

Meanwhile, as the would-be explorers in Turkey fretted away their valuable searching-time in a futile wait, another frustrating experience was taking place in California, many thousands of miles away.

Because verification of the *Stars and Stripes* story mentioned in Chapter 8 (More Aerial Discoveries) still seemed of major importance, a renewed search for the original article was taken up once more. For this story, although so strangely elusive, had the ring of truth; and surely, if only for the sake of those who doubted its veracity, no stone should be left unturned in one final effort to discover the facts.

Every possible source of information was tapped—from University libraries and Army archieves, to officers who had served in Tunisia during that period of time. Of course other capable teams of researchers, led by such men as Alva Appel of Washington, D.C., and Dr. John Warwick Montgomery, had also spent untold efforts in trying to run this story down. But the attempts to ferret out one small item seen in an Army newspaper some thirty years before had always proved to be a monumental and disappointing task. There had been so many "theaters of war," so many confusing editions of the *Stars and Stripes* in which to look. And, understandably, no one could possibly recall the masthead of the particular issue in which the story had been seen; nor, of course, the exact date! It began to appear as if the research had once more led to a dead-end street. . . .

Then, just as the gloomy clouds of defeat began to close in, a tiny glimmer of a silver lining gave new hope. Clues began to come to light from still another source—clues, if they could only be substantiated that might yet provide the long-sought verification of the aerial stories of Chapter 8. These new clues concerned a Russian wire-photo that, reportedly, had appeared in a Seattle (Washington) newspaper sometime, presumably, between the years of 1940-1950, or thereabouts. Three individuals of sound mind and excellent memory distinctly recalled seeing, and commenting on the story when it had appeared. To add still more excitement and incentive to this new angle of search, two Seattle University research librarians also remembered seeing the wire-photos at about this same time. And everyone agreed that the photo had come from a Russian source during World War II!

Once more an intensive search was on. Once more hopes soared high. Soon microfilms—dizzying dozens of them—began parading their nostalgic news of an earlier, war-torn decade through the hand-operated machine, while eyes blurred and nerves grew taut. But still the mysterious picture eluded all efforts to pin it down. Must this search, too, be written off as a "lost cause" . . . ? Had another "dead-end street" been reached? Surely, so many sane and honest persons could not have made such a blundering mistake. The picture *had* been seen. It had made sufficient impression at the time to be readily recalled some 30 years later when the subject arose. Why, then, had it proved so difficult and baffling to find . . . ?

Then, early in 1972, just as this book was about to go into print, when the final galley proofs had been corrected and were ready to be returned, another long-distance call brought the electrifying news that yet another reliable individual had seen Russian aerial photos of the Ark—not merely badly reproduced wire-photos in the Seattle *Times,* but the actual pictures from which no doubt the newspaper picture had been made!

The individual in this case is a Jewish scientist, Donald M. Liedmann, M.D., Ph.D. He was apparently first contacted by James M. Lee, formerly of SEARCH Foundation, in 1969 in Chicago. His story was so interesting and significant that it was later recorded in the form of an actual interview with Mr. Lee. We reproduce the following interview:

INTERVIEW WITH JAMES M. LEE:
November 15, 1970

LEE: Doctor Liedmann, we first met at the Hilton Hotel in Chicago at the International Convention of the Full Gospel Business Men's Fellowship International. Demos Shakarian, the International President, had asked me to attend the convention and show the pieces of wood found on Mount Ararat in 1969 by the SEARCH Foundation Team, and the movie film of that expedition. You will recall that I was standing at a table showing interested persons the print of an original painting of the mountain, when you walked up to the table, pointed to the picture and said, "The Ark is there!" You seemed to be so positive in your remark that we entered into a discussion of the subject and then learned that you had a very remarkable experience which you partially revealed to those standing there. Doctor Liedmann, will you please tell us about some of the background of your family, your experiences in Sweden, and how it is that you are so confident in your own mind that Noah's Ark still remains high up on the upper slopes of Mount Ararat?

LIEDMANN: Yes, I will be happy to do so, Mr. Lee. I was born in Sweden of Orthodox Jewish parents who had migrated from the Russian Ukraine. From them I learned the Russian language. As a Jew I also learned the Hebrew and Aramaic languages. I have been interested in many different archeological discoveries around the world—especially those connected with Old Testament history. My experience concerning Mount Ararat was a remarkable experience in itself, as you will see, and I still marvel at it myself. I have never related this story of my experience to anyone since it happened in 1947 and 1948. I received my medical degree in Upsala, Sweden, where I also studied and received my specialty in neurosurgery. I should mention here that I had been studying medicine for approximately five years when I quit my studies and volunteered for the RAF for a six month tour of active duty. I fought against the Germans, and was shot down twice by them and was injured in my back. After my recovery I went back to medical school again and began studying hematology at Heidelberg. It was on one of my trips down there that I became acquainted with a Russian Air-Force major. This was in Hamburg. As everyone knows, the Russians, the English, and the Americans were all fighting together as the common enemies of Germany. This Air-Force major and I found that we had many things in common: we were both squadron leaders during the last portion of World War II; we had both been flying since early manhood; we both spoke the same Russian dialect; and he was born in the Ukraine and my ancestors came from there. Thus we had many common interests to discuss socially. On several occasions when we met by appointment I would invite him for dinner and social entertainment. It was on these occasions that he described to me different happenings, which, naturally, no one in his position should have mentioned to anyone in the Western world.

LEE: What was the nature of the happenings which he revealed to you?

LIEDMANN: This Air-Force major had been a squadron leader in the Russian Air Force and was in command of a group of three planes which had taken in a number of special missions over Mount Ararat. To my understanding, they were going there at very specific times each year, because, as this major explained to me, there are only 30 to 38 days during the year that the glaciers in that area are melted enough to make it favorable for taking pictures. Which day of the month it was I cannot recall, but nevertheless, the first time I met him in 1947 he showed me at that time three distinct pictures taken on Mount Ararat. They were marked at the 13-14,000 foot elevation, or 4,500 meters approximately. These pictures also showed a Russian aircraft with their insignia on the wings. Each of these pictures showed a boat-like structure which he pointed out to me to be what is mentioned in the Bible as Noah's Ark. I asked him a number of times why they were so interested in taking those pictures. He just laughed with a little grin and didn't answer my question. One of those pictures showed the ship protruding out of the ice approximately 80 to 90 feet and it was tilted slightly downwards. In the bottom of that area was a little melted pond or lake. The glacier was shown with the mountain summit in the upper right of that picture and the other pictures were taken at a similar angle. To me it appeared that they were taken on the north side. He wouldn't give too many of his own explanations of this, because, as he pointed out time and again, those photographs were the property of the USSR.

LEE: Were any photographs taken other than in 1938?

LIEDMANN: Yes. I met the same man a year later in 1948, also in Hamburg, Germany. At that time he showed me another set of pictures. Let me mention this. Those first pictures which I mentioned before were taken in 1938 at approximately the 14,000 foot elevation. Those other pictures which were shown me in 1948 were taken more recently. Just how recently I don't know. He only mentioned that "these have been taken since I saw you." How this happened I can't explain. To me it had no significance at the time for the simple reason that I was not a Christian, but a Jew. I did not pay too much attention, other than that I believed absolutely that Noah's Ark was there. I know the Old Testament very well, and so knew the Ark must still be there.

LEE: How much of the Ark was exposed to view?

LIEDMANN: This is what can be explained about those pictures that were taken the last time. On this occasion he showed me almost a dozen pictures. The ark was covered up much more than the first time with maybe only 12 or 15 feet of the vessel showing. Only a tip of it was showing. Some sections could be seen through the glassy clear ice. These were the pictures that were shown me on those two different occasions. The first one was shown to me in 1947, and the second one in 1948. All of these photographs were concerning Noah's Ark on Mt. Ararat, and there always appeared a Russian aircraft in the picture. I asked him for a copy of these pictures, but he said, "These are the property of the Russian government and I cannot give them out, nor give any more information regarding these pictures." Regarding the mountain—he described it as a high, rocky, volcanic mountain and that since it belonged to Turkey they could not do any research on it. This I could understand.

LEE: Did you meet this Air-Force major other than on these two occasions?

LIEDMANN: The third time I met that same major he was with a number of his companions and when I asked him about his expedition he wouldn't talk or mention anything about them. He completely ignored the subject. In fact, he told me, "I don't know what you are talking about." That was on the third occasion that I met this same Russian Air-Force major.

LEE: How did you happen to meet him in Hamburg?

LIEDMANN: Why did we meet in Hamburg? As you know, they occupied a portion of Germany. Just about 50 to 60 miles from Hamburg is the city of Lubeck on the border of the Russian occupied area of East Germany. So it was very easy to understand why one or several of the officers were going into the Western world for some private reasons. All of these conversations were made in the Russian language. I am not as good in that language now, but I can still read and understand it.

LEE: How many planes were involved in the flights over Ararat?

LIEDMANN: I should mention that each time they made a mission, or flight, for taking these pictures, there were always three different planes involved.

LEE: Did he tell you anything else of interest?

LIEDMANN: Another interesting point maybe could be that we were talking about ancient times and he said, "Have you seen the mammoth that we found in Siberia in 1901 by some sled-dog party, and the dogs started eating the flesh of that mammoth which had green grass in its mouth. If you would like to see it, come with me to Stalingrad." I went with him and saw in that museum the mammoth which was largely preserved.

Donald N. Liedmann, M.D., Ph.D.

Thus, with this letter and sketch, another strong link in the ever-lengthening chain of circumstantial evidence was forged—a link remarkably reenforcing the conclusions already drawn in Chapter 8! It no longer seemed a question of "if" or "whether" the Ark exists; merely a question of "where" on Ararat's rugged slopes . . . !

For centuries a mysterious mountain has brooded over its surrounding plains. Noah's Ark! Does it really exist on those misty heights? Is it merely fable, or is it fact? The preponderance of evidence indicates that it can be safely considered an established fact!

Today this same mysterious mountain still holds irresistible fascination for those who know the story of the Ark. The inspiring, almost prophetic words of the 19th century traveller and historian Lynch, who visited the area in 1893, still prompt the same deep emotions that so stirred his soul:

"This vast fabric (Ararat) . . . touches chords in the nature of man which sound through all religions . . . Yet how vulgar appear their dogmas . . . in the courts of this great cathedral of the natural world! You feel that this mountain has been the parent of religions, whence they strayed into devious paths. To this parent you would again collect the distracted; in this atmosphere you long to bathe the populations of our great towns. Our morbid dramatists, our nervous novelists, need the inspiration of these surroundings—the promptings of Nature in her loftiest manifestations, from which the life of man can never with impunity be divorced."

And it should never be forgotten that it is on this mountain of Ararat—our modern Aghri Dagh—and not the Jebal Judi range far to the south, that the remains of Noah's Ark have always been found.

The defense rests . . . !

22

Rainbow Over
the Mountain

It was Samuel Taylor Coleridge who said that "Often do the spirits of great events stride on before the events, and in today already walks tomorrow."

And thus it happened on a hot summer's day in the 1930's, that a seemingly unimportant event in the life of Hardwicke Knight foreshadowed a significant detail in the search for Noah's Ark.

Southbound on the old Persian caravan trail near the far-off Eastern Turkish frontier, the youthful traveller paused to gaze, enchanted, at the mighty ice-crowned monarch towering so majestically overhead in the shimmering desert heat. Then, as if drawn by some irresistible spell, he turned his eager footsteps away from the Araxes River and started in the direction of Aghri Dagh.

As the young Britisher trudged along, absorbed in the magnificent sight, his thoughts turned backward to his childhood days, and the fascinating, oft-told tales of Noah and the Flood. In his mind's eye he could still visualize the neat marginal notes in his grandfather's well-worn Bible: "One year and ten days was Noah and all with him in the Ark which this day is deserted by him and all with him in the year 1657 since the earth was formed."

More recently these memories had been revived, as he had listened to the Armenian Katholokos of Echmiazin, the ancient monastery just across the Araxes River in the very shadow of Ararat. In the Ahora Gorge, he had been told, there still existed the ruins of an old cloister, from which the monks had traditionally set forth on their search for relics of Noah's Ark.

His archaeological instincts aroused by these tales, Knight had determined, if possible, to see these ruins for himself. All day long he walked, mile after dusty mile, his heart, like Parrot's in 1829, beating high with anticipation and hope. Since he had no useful maps, he simply bore in the general direction of the peak. But at last the heat of the blistering day began to wane. Clouds had descended upon both Greater Ararat and its lower sister peak. The sky darkened; twilight fell. Suddenly a welcome sight loomed before him in the dusk—a large Kurdish tent where he hoped he might find shelter and nourishment for the night. He had no fear of the hospitable, nomadic Kurds; only a healthy respect for their savage dogs.

As Knight turned eagerly toward the camp, he heard a stealthy sound and was dismayed to discover a band of fiercely armed horsemen closing around him from behind. Who could they be? Surely, their intentions were not friendly—else why were they stalking him in this silent, ominous way? From their attire they did not appear to be strictly military, yet they did not exactly resemble brigands.

The solitary traveller paused uncertainly, and uneasily awaited their approach. All the frightening old tales of robber bands in the vicinity of Bayazit leaped grimly into his mind. But Morier, Tournefort, Porter—their stories had all been written many years before. The Armenian massacres were a thing of the past. The Kurdish tribesmen had resumed their more peaceful pursuits of tending their flocks and herds. Surely there could be nothing to fear—or so he had been given to understand. What, then, could these menacing riders want of him . . . ?

Not long before, Knight had picked up a piece of pottery half buried in the sand. Hopefully, he brandished it in his hand. See, I'm an innocent wayfarer, interested only in the archaeology of your country, he tried to make them understand. But in spite of the friendly overture, a few moments later he had been surrounded and unceremoniously mounted on an extra horse, in the midst of a band of churlish ruffians whose language he did not understand.

Then the party continued on in the general direction of Ararat while the blackness of night settled down. For some miles the party rode on, sometimes grouped together, sometimes in single file. Where could they be taking him, the bewildered captive asked himself as they rode along. Had he fallen into the hands of the notorious Persian "frontier guards"—outlaws who were sometimes issued guns and the semblance of a uniform, and given legal status in an attempt to control their nefarious activities against unfortunate travellers along the trail . . . ?

At last the dim glow of oil lamps announced their arrival among a group of stone buildings. No Kurdish encampment, this—the Kurds did not build such substantial dwellings as these. No fiercely barking Kurdish dogs, either—which was comfort of a sort. Had he been brought thus unceremoniously to some military outpost? Knight never really knew, for there was no semblance of military discipline, no uniformed commanding officer seated behind a desk to whom he could appeal his case.

Instead he was ushered into a loathsome, stuffy, half-underground cellar by one of his surly guards, to endure as best he could the indescribable stench of the filthy room in the company of an unconscious, dying old man. Here, for two interminable days and nights, the prisoner thundered in vain for an interpreter, demanding an explanation for this outrageous detention, and repeatedly shouting the names of all the Russian, Turkish, or Persian officials he could recall. His pleas fell on deaf ears, and brought absolutely no response.

But at last the ordeal ended, and they led the prisoner out. Silently they indicated a hopeless old nag—on which he could not possibly have escaped—and, in company with a few sullen men who still continued to ignore him, the mystified and indignant prisoner was started on his way once more—on a trail that still led roughly northward, still in the direction of Aghri Dagh!

Knight, sore and weak, chose to walk much of the way, using his sorry mount to carry his pack. Too ill from a recurring attack of dysentery during his confinement to take note of his surroundings, he could never afterward be completely sure of the exact route they travelled. At last, however, his taciturn escort abandoned him—on the bare side of the mountain, with no means of transportation, exposed to unknown danger from beasts of prey, without one word of farewell or pity. Knight suddenly found himself alone once more, glad even in his solitude to be rid of his doubtful companions, thankful that his pack still boasted one large chunk of goat cheese and some stale bread.

He was now somewhat south of the great peak of Ararat. His best course to reach his original destination above Ahora would have been to proceed northwards, either between the peaks of the two mountains or around the east side of the lesser peak. This would have brought him directly to his objective at the foot of the Ahora Gorge. However, it would seem that a higher Power was directing the pathway of Hardwicke Knight, and that there must have been a certain divine timetable of events he was carrying out. At any rate, disoriented and confused by his recent experience, and not wishing to find himself back in Persia at the mercy of other "frontier guards," Knight set out in a counter-clockwise direction around the mountain—an exactly opposite direction from what he had originally intended!

His thought had been to maintain a fairly high contour around Greater Ararat, and carry on around the mountain until distant Echmiazin came into view across the plain, then to proceed down the slopes and toward Ahora from that direction. However, as Knight was to reminisce in later years, "making a circuitous journey without a map is nearly always a bit like being twisted around when playing blind man's bluff and then trying to walk straight." Nevertheless, in spite of the handicaps, the determined explorer proceeded—where a lesser spirit might have quailed—into the face of the unknown.

"I continued from ridge to ridge," he recalls, "going down stony slopes on my heels, and laboriously climbing up onto the next ridge. Each ridge as I approached it seemed higher than the one before, and I looked each time for the familiar plain, but there was always another ridge blocking the view."

Knight was still climbing the next day, and ridge was still succeeding ridge, when he crossed one more snow field. He had passed the area above Lake Kop, but there were still two more ice fields to conquer before he could reach the next ridge. The weary climber crossed the first, then skirted below the second. He walked over some soggy timbers at the termination of the second ice field, and climbed half way up the slope of the farther side. Paying scant attention to the presence of timbers at such a height, Knight wondered idly if he had just crossed some ancient trackway as he passed on. Was this, perhaps, the trail to Ahora he had been hoping to find?

Suddenly he paused, then turned back. "Anxious though I was to conserve my strength," says Knight, "I was nonetheless curious, even if my curiosity had been slow to take. I satisfied myself that the soggy mass was indeed timber. It reminded me, when I felt it, of the forest trees said to be prehistoric which are submerged by the sea and appear at low tide at Walberswick on the Suffolk coast of England, or of the timbers of a Spanish galleon that are exposed in a similar way at very low tide on the Welsh coast."

All around was stony rubble that had rolled down the mountainside. Timbers extended in more than one direction; some were parallel and others perpendicular to them. "The timbers could have been massive rectangular beams," he says, "although all I could see was the tops of them exposed level with the surface of the ground and it was not possible to tell how far they extended under the stones. What I saw looked like the frame of a very heavy wagon."

At first thought, Knight considered the possibility that he might have stumbled on the remains of a gun carriage from some medieval military campaign. The timbers did not look in the least like fallen logs or trees, he assures us, or he would have ignored them. "Not only were they rectangular in themselves," he explains, "but they formed a framework which was also rectangular."

It was impossible to say if the timbers were hand-hewn, since there was no texture left upon the surface, which the discoverer described as "soggy and dark," perhaps nine inches to a foot in width, and only a few feet of them were exposed by the melting of the ice field at its lower end. Quickly breaking off a piece of the waterlogged wood, Knight resumed his climb.

Had Hardwicke Knight inadvertently stumbled across pieces of wood from the Ark? Is this a possible explanation for his puzzling detention a few days before, and of his unscheduled detour to the opposite side of the mountain? He had not planned to climb the high ridges, nor reach the area of the snows. And if his mysterious captors had taken him directly to Ararat and released him as much as 48 hours before, would these soggy timbers have been exposed, would the snows of the ice field have been melted back . . . ? These are questions for the student to ponder well, although at the time even Hardwicke Knight did not seem to attach any particular significance to his discovery. As he says, "The ground was too cold and my strength inadequate to allow me discover more."

During the few moments that Knight had stopped to retrace his steps to examine the wood, he had become blanketed with the intense cold, and a severe pain in his chest robbed him of that "composure which is necessary for a proper evaluation of an artifact," as he puts it; so, as the discovery of the wood seemed of minor importance to him at the time, and as night was rapidly coming on, he set off for the next ridge. The icy wind lashed his eyes into tears as he climbed the steep slope, and he was obliged to sit down and wipe them when he reached to top. We will let Knight describe the scene that next met his startled gaze:

"In front of me was one of the greatest and ugliest chasms in Mother Earth that I had ever seen. Immediately before me were screes that dropped thousands of feet into a black canyon, the farther side of which was equally steep and dark and remote. This great ravine appeared to be walled by steep screes and in places by precipices in both directions, cutting right across my way, descending to the plain on my left, and cutting deeply into the very heart of the mountain on my right."

The explorer had come face to face with the Ahora Gorge, of course. By his calculations, Ahora was still ahead of him, and he would have to cross the great chasm to reach it. But no matter how he searched, he could find no way to cross to the other side without descending down the perilous screes to the black glacier that looked so forbidding below. Alone, and with so many unknown factors to consider before descending into the abyss, Knight reluctantly abandoned his hopes to visit Ahora and the ruins he had hoped to explore. In the deepening dusk, he turned and set off down the mountain to Igdir, to much needed food and rest.

The soggy sample of wood did not survive. His "evidence" gone, it was many years before Knight mentioned the timbers he had seen so close to the Great Chasm of Aghri Dagh. But the more he reflected, the more he studied and read, the more he came to see that his experience "fitted into a traditional pattern," and the more convinced he became that what he had discovered on the heights of the Biblical peak might have something to do with Noah's Ark. He realized, too, that the same high shoulder of the mountain where he had found the timbers was the same area that all the old traditions had pointed out as the holy site.

"The Biblical description of the Ark is explicit," says Knight. "It was an immense structure made of timbers, and what I had seen was not the whole remains of such a structure, and I have never for a moment thought so. The proportions of the timbers, however, make it seem logical to me to suppose that they are part of a very large and necessarily strong structure. Somewhere in or under the ice higher on the mountain above that place, there might be a larger portion of this structure preserved. Perhaps some day," concluded Knight, "archaeologists will devise some method of searching for and finding these evidences. Such researchers must surely have the blessing of god. But for my own part I am richly blessed to be one of the favored few who have been privileged to see and touch."

One of the still greater "wonders of Ararat" is the rainbow that can frequently be seen in the afternoon "from the north and northeastern slopes arching over the Araxes plain." This rainbow, says Knight, "can scarcely be seen at all from the south and west sides of the mountain; it is seen only as a complete bow from the Great Chasm above Aghura and from the high plateau called Kip Ghioll and the slopes that descend towards Echmiazin. It is precisely this slope of the mountain that all the local traditions point to and acclaim as the very slope down which Noah and his family and herds descended, made their sacrifice to the Lord, and regained the plain."

Knight offers his own scientific explanation for this spectacular sight of a "complete bow" on this particular peak. "This is something peculiar to Ararat," he says. "During the morning the hot air from the great desert mounts the sides of the mountain, and when it reaches the snow it forms clouds, which spring out of a perfectly clear sky.

During the afternoon the sky darkens, and rain, hail, or snow condenses, and the rainbow is seen. At sunset, the hot air from the plain ceases, the cloud around the summit vanishes, and leaves the snowy peak standing out sharp and clear all through the night. The other mountains around the Araxes plain, having no snow upon their summits, remain cloudless and clear throughout the day."

"So if you ask why Ararat?" says Knight. "Why is it that men are drawn to Ararat in quest of the Ark and have practically ignored the lesser mountains which also claim to be the holy mountain of Noah?

"I can only speak for myself and say that when once seen, Ararat was forever the grandest mountain of them all, rising as it does out of the flat plain and not confused among other rival peaks as many higher mountains are—in every day excelling all others. There is left no doubt that it is also the holiest of all High Places."

Should it then be too dificult to believe, as the lovely old Armenian legend tells us, that the Ark does still exist "in one of the highest recesses" of Aghri Dagh—still guarded by angels and secluded from mortal eyes . . . ? Surely, God Himself must have set the stage for the landing place of the Ark where the token of His covenant with Noah could most gloriously be seen above the flooded plain; and gives us one more reason to believe the reports that the great object glimpsed from time to time upon the northern slopes of the majestic mountain must truly be Noah's abandoned old ship!